108. Write-through is a type of side-loaded caching where data is written to both the database and cache. This approach avoids cache misses but is highly intensive on the cache.

109. When choosing a caching strategy, always consider the rate of data change and choose the correct time-to-live (TTL) of the da† ⸺ ⸺ ⸺ ⸺ rate of change of the data.

110. ElastiCache is a managed service that  tores to perform server-side and database cac

111. Memcached is a high-performance, d e supported by ElastiCache. It uses a simple oper: e one or many nested values. All data is servec organization in the platform.

112. Redis is a fully fledged in-memory database supported by ElastiCache. Redis supports complex datasets like tables, lists, hashes, and geospatial data.

113. Redis single node is not replicated, nonscalable, and nonresilient. It can be deployed only in a single availability zone, and it supports backup and restore.

114. Redis multinode cluster mode disabled is a primary read-write instance with up to five read replicas. The read replicas are synchronous and offer resilience and read offloading for scalability. It can be deployed in multiple availability zones.

115. Redis multinode cluster mode enabled is a multinode cluster that adds the ability to reshard the cluster and horizontally add more write capacity for elasticity.

116. Sharding distributes the dataset across multiple primary database engines.

117. RDS service allows up to five read replicas in any availability zone or region.

118. Traditional RDS database read replicas are a very cost-efficient way to provide data for small (terabyte) scale analytics and should be selected as a preferred option when the entire dataset needs to be read offloaded.

119. AWS Aurora service stores all the data on a cluster volume that is replicated to six copies across (at least) three availability zones. Replication is near synchronous, supports up to 15 read replicas per region, and offers seamless scalability.

120. Aurora natively supports MySQL and PostgreSQL databases and costs slightly more than RDS MySQL and RDS PostgreSQL.

121. In the exam, select RDS MySQL or RDS PostgreSQL if there are any cost considerations explicitly stated in the question.

122. High availability is the ability to maintain the application availability in case of failures and errors in the application or infrastructure. It is commonly referred to as one nine (90 percent), two nines (99 percent), three nines (99.9 percent), and so on. Five nines is considered to be available "all the time."

123. A service-layer agreement (SLA) defines the uptime that your application will theoretically be able to deliver.

124. To calculate the combined uptime of a replicated application, use 100 percent minus the multiple of the failure rates.

125. Availability zones are fault-isolation environments within AWS regions.

126. AWS managed services typically are deployed across at least three availability zones for full resilience.

127. To make your application highly available, maintain two or more replicas in the same availability zone, across availability zones, or across AWS regions.

128. Cross-region replication allows an AWS service to survive a regional outage and can be used to mitigate any disaster situation.

129. The Virtual Private Cloud (VPC) is the place where applications are deployed and maintained; it enables you to define both public and private network environments with complete control over routing and granular security.

130. The network address is defined as the number of static bits at the beginning of the address.

131. The host address is defined as the remaining bits not in use by the network.

132. Five addresses are reserved by AWS for subnet basic functionality: the network address, broadcast address, router at the first usable host address, the IPAM service (DHCP/DNS) on the second usable address, and the third usable address.

133. VPC and subnet ranges are restructured to sizes between /16 and /28.

134. A private subnet within a VPC has no access to or from the Internet, but it is accessible and can access all other private and public subnets in the VPC.

135. Public IP addresses are attached to an instance at startup and are randomly selected from an AWS-owned pool of public addresses. The address is changed every time the instance is shut down or restarted.

136. Elastic IPs are persistent static IPs assigned to an instance.

137. The Elastic Load Balancer (ELB) service enables you to distribute traffic across multiple instances of an application for high availability.

138. AutoScaling service can automatically scale the number of instances to meet the traffic demands.

139. ELB Classic is the previous-generation load balancer that forwards traffic to one or more availability zones within a region. It is not intended for use with modern, highly available, resilient architectures and will be retired in August 2022.

140. Application Load Balancer (ALB) is the next-generation layer 7 load-balancing solution that can handle HTTP and HTTPS traffic. It automatically deploys a redundant endpoint in each availability zone it serves.

141. Network Load Balancer (NLB) is the next-generation layer 4 load-balancing solution that can handle TCP, UDP, and SSL/TLS traffic.

142. You should avoid the use of SSL in applications because it is not considered secure anymore. Most modern applications support TLS 1.2 and above.

143. Gateway Load Balancer (GLB) is designed to distribute traffic across third-party virtual appliances.

144. Simple routing provides one response of each DNS request.

145. Weighted routing provides responses based on the weight of the values for each record.

146. Fail-over routing provides responses based on the health of two or more DNS targets.

147. Latency-based routing measures the latency from the client to the DNS target and delivers the response with the lowest latency target.

148. Geolocation routing forces users from certain regions or countries into specific AWS regions.

149. Geo-proximity routing routes users from locations nearby to the closest region.

150. Multivalue answer routing returns up to eight responses for each request.

151. Amazon S3 is a highly available (99.999999999 percent) fully managed serverless object storage service accessible via HTTP and HTTPS.

152. S3 supports virtual-hosted-style URLs.
   ▶ {bucket-name}.s3.{region-id}.amazonaws.com}/{optional key prefix}/{key-name}

153. The S3 service previously supported global S3 region virtual-hosted-style URLs where the region parameter was omitted. Buckets created after March 20, 2019, do not support the legacy global endpoint anymore.
   ▶ {bucket-name}.s3.amazonaws.com

154. A path-style URL is currently being deprecated.
   ▶ http{s}://s3.{region-id}.amazonaws.com/{bucket-name}/{optional key prefix}/{key-name}

155. The S3 Standard storage class provides general-purpose online storage with 99.99 percent availability and 11 9s percent durability.

156. S3 Infrequent Access provides the same performance as S3 Standard but up to 40 percent cheaper with 99.9 percent availability SLA and 11 9s durability.

157. S3 Intelligent tiering can automatically determine whether to maintain the object on S3 Standard or S3 Infrequent Access based on the access pattern of the object.

158. S3 One Zone-Infrequent Access is a cheaper data tier in only one availability zone and can deliver an additional 25 percent saving over S3 Infrequent Access. It has the same durability with 99.5 percent availability.

159. S3 Glacier is less than one-fifth of the price of S3, designed for archiving and long-term storage. Restore times are between one minute and seven hours, depending on the type of request.

160. S3 Glacier Deep Archive costs four times less than Glacier and is the cheapest storage solution at about $1 per terabyte per month. This solution is intended for very long-term storage and has the longest restore times of up to 12 hours.

161. S3 Outposts delivers the content from an on-premises AWS Outpost deployment of the S3 service.

EXAM✓CRAM

AWS Certified SysOps Administrator – Associate (SOA-C02) Exam Cram

Marko Sluga
Rick Crisci
William "Bo" Rothwell

Pearson

AWS Certified SysOps Administrator – Associate (SOA-C02) Exam Cram

ISBN-13: 978-0-13-750958-4

ISBN-10: 0-13-750958-8

Library of Congress Cataloging-in-Publication Data: 2022902124

1 2022

Trademarks

All terms mentioned in this book that are known to be trademarks or service marks have been appropriately capitalized. Pearson IT Certification cannot attest to the accuracy of this information. Use of a term in this book should not be regarded as affecting the validity of any trademark or service mark.

Warning and Disclaimer

Every effort has been made to make this book as complete and as accurate as possible, but no warranty or fitness is implied. The information provided is on an "as is" basis. The authors and the publisher shall have neither liability nor responsibility to any person or entity with respect to any loss or damages arising from the information contained in this book.

Special Sales

For information about buying this title in bulk quantities, or for special sales opportunities (which may include electronic versions; custom cover designs; and content particular to your business, training goals, marketing focus, or branding interests), please contact our corporate sales department at corpsales@pearsoned.com or (800) 382-3419.

For government sales inquiries, please contact governmentsales@pearsoned.com.

For questions about sales outside the U.S., please contact intlcs@pearson.com.

Editor-in-Chief
Mark Taub

Director, ITP Product Management
Brett Bartow

Executive Editor
Nancy Davis

Managing Editor
Sandra Schroeder

Development Editor
Christopher A. Cleveland

Project Editor
Mandie Frank

Copy Editor
Chuck Hutchinson

Indexer
Ken Johnson

Proofreader
Donna E. Mulder

Technical Editors
Mark Wilkins
Ryan Dymek

Publishing Coordinator
Cindy Teeters

Designer
Chuti Prasertsith

Compositor
codeMantra

Pearson's Commitment to Diversity, Equity, and Inclusion

Pearson is dedicated to creating bias-free content that reflects the diversity of all learners. We embrace the many dimensions of diversity, including but not limited to race, ethnicity, gender, socioeconomic status, ability, age, sexual orientation, and religious or political beliefs.

Education is a powerful force for equity and change in our world. It has the potential to deliver opportunities that improve lives and enable economic mobility. As we work with authors to create content for every product and service, we acknowledge our responsibility to demonstrate inclusivity and incorporate diverse scholarship so that everyone can achieve their potential through learning. As the world's leading learning company, we have a duty to help drive change and live up to our purpose to help more people create a better life for themselves and to create a better world.

Our ambition is to purposefully contribute to a world where

- Everyone has an equitable and lifelong opportunity to succeed through learning

- Our educational products and services are inclusive and represent the rich diversity of learners

- Our educational content accurately reflects the histories and experiences of the learners we serve

- Our educational content prompts deeper discussions with learners and motivates them to expand their own learning (and worldview)

While we work hard to present unbiased content, we want to hear from you about any concerns or needs with this Pearson product so that we can investigate and address them.

- Please contact us with concerns about any potential bias at https://www.pearson.com/report-bias.html.

Credits

Figures	Credit
Figures 2.1–2.3, 4.2–4.7, 4.10–4.13, 5.1, 5.3, 5.4, 6.1–6.5, 7.1–7.3, 9.1–9.9, 10.1, 11.1–11.9, 11.11, 12.2, 12.3, 12.8–12.17, 13.1–13.7, 14.1–14.8, 15.3–15.5	Amazon Web Services, Inc
Figure 4.1	Medium
Figure 5.2	DeveloperCK
Figures 10.2, 10.3	Google LLC

Contents at a Glance

Table of Contents

About the Authors

Marko Sluga has more than 20 years of experience in IT and has had the benefit of witnessing the rise of cloud computing. Marko has worked on a variety of cloud-related projects, from the early stages of SOC, corporate virtualization, and open-source API offerings to modern, fully automated, intelligent, serverless, and cloud-native solutions. Marko has been working with Amazon Web Services (AWS) since the start of the 2010s and holds three associate, two professional, and three specialty AWS certifications. Marko performs training and advising on cloud technologies and strategies, DevOps, and IT system and process optimization to clients from a wide range of companies, including startups, SMBs, enterprise businesses, and Fortune 500 companies. Marko runs his own cloud training, coaching, and consulting practice under the markocloud.com brand. He is the author of the *AWS Certified Developer - Associate (DVA-C01) Cert Guide*.

Rick Crisci is the founder and principal trainer for Trainertests.com and is an experienced AWS and VMware instructor. Original content by Rick can be found on a variety of platforms including Pearson, LinkedIn Learning, and Udemy, with more than 30 courses, over 250,000 students, and exceptionally high course review scores. Rick also teaches live hands-on AWS courses regularly for Pearson on O'Reilly.

Prior to becoming an instructor, Rick had over 15 years of real-world experience. Some career highlights include designing high-speed Internet networks in the early 2000s and managing virtualization and networking teams for a financial institution.

In 2017, VMware recognized Rick as the first runner-up for Instructor of the Year for the Americas. This honor was largely due to the glowing feedback from his students. Rick seeks to help students learn by taking complex concepts and providing clear and simple explanations, diagrams, and analogies.

At the impressionable age of 14, **William "Bo" Rothwell** crossed paths with a TRS-80 Micro Computer System (affectionately known as a "Trash 80"). Soon after, the adults responsible for Bo made the mistake of leaving him alone with the TRS-80. He immediately dismantled it and held his first computer class, showing his friends what made this "computer thing" work. Since that experience, Bo's passion for understanding how computers work and sharing this knowledge with others has resulted in a rewarding career in IT training. His experience includes Cloud, Linux, UNIX, IT security, DevOps, and programming languages such as Perl, Python, Tcl, and BASH. He is the founder and lead instructor of One Course Source, an IT training organization.

Dedication

I would like to dedicate this book to my wife and children for their continued support of projects like this book.
—Marko Sluga

I would like to dedicate this book to my wife, Jessica, whose constant dedication to helping her students is always an inspiration, and to my children, who give me a purpose to work for. Also, to my mother for giving me confidence to pursue big goals, and to my father who showed me the value of hard work, dedication, and always putting his family before himself.
—Rick Crisci

Normally, I use this space to thank my wife, daughter, and parents. While they continue to be my biggest supporters, I feel compelled to dedicate this book to those who embrace lifelong learning. Thank you all for making this book a small part of your learning goals.

"There is no end to education. It is not that you read a book, pass an examination, and finish with education. The whole of life, from the moment you are born to the moment you die, is a process of learning."
—Jiddu Krishnamurti

—William "Bo" Rothwell

Acknowledgments

I need to thank Rick and Bo for helping make this book a reality. I would also like to thank Nancy Davis and Chris Cleveland for their generous support during the creation of this title.

—Marko Sluga

Thanks to Marko for giving me the opportunity to help with this book, and to Nancy Davis for keeping this thing going. I'm appreciative of the opportunity to work with such wonderful people.

—Rick Crisci

Thanks to the entire Pearson team for all of the gentle pushes, patience, and dedication to making this book a success.

—William "Bo" Rothwell

About the Technical Reviewers

Mark Wilkins is an electronic engineering technologist with a wealth of experience in designing, deploying, and supporting software and hardware technology in the corporate and small business world. Since 2013, Mark has focused on supporting and designing cloud service solutions with Amazon Web Services, Microsoft Azure, and the IBM Cloud. He is certified in Amazon Web Services (Architecture and SysOps). Mark is also a Microsoft Certified Trainer (MCT) and holds certifications in MCTS, MCSA, Server Virtualization with Windows Server Hyper-V, and Azure Cloud Services. Mark currently develops AWS curriculum on technical aspects of AWS architecture for O'Reilly Media, Pluralsight, and LinkedIn Learning. His published books include *Learning Amazon Web Services*, *AWS Certified Solutions Architect - Associate (SAA-C02) Cert Guide*, *Windows 2003 Registry for Dummies*, and *Administering SMS 3.0*, *Administering Active Directory*.

As a consultant, **Ryan Dymek** has been building, designing, and improving cloud solutions for some of the largest companies in the world for more than 10 years. Ryan began working with AWS cloud solutions in 2009 and in 2016 added GCP to his portfolio. Ryan transforms teams and organizations using DevOps principles and solid architectural approaches through a model of culture and "people first" philosophies. Ryan has trained more than 10,000 people over the past 6 years on topics such as DevOps engineering, security, cost optimization, performance tuning, and operational excellence.

We Want to Hear from You!

As the reader of this book, *you* are our most important critic and commentator. We value your opinion and want to know what we're doing right, what we could do better, what areas you'd like to see us publish in, and any other words of wisdom you're willing to pass our way.

We welcome your comments. You can email or write to let us know what you did or didn't like about this book—as well as what we can do to make our books better.

Please note that we cannot help you with technical problems related to the topic of this book.

When you write, please be sure to include this book's title and author as well as your name and email address. We will carefully review your comments and share them with the author and editors who worked on the book.

Email: community@informit.com

Reader Services

Register your copy of *AWS Certified SysOps Administrator – Associate (SOA-C02) Exam Cram* at www.pearsonitcertification.com for convenient access to downloads, updates, and corrections as they become available. To start the registration process, go to www.pearsonitcertification.com/register and log in or create an account*. Enter the product ISBN **9780137509584** and click **Submit**. When the process is complete, you will find any available bonus content under Registered Products.

*Be sure to check the box that you would like to hear from us to receive exclusive discounts on future editions of this product.

Introduction

Welcome to *AWS Certified SysOps Administrator – Associate (SOA-C02) Exam Cram*. This book will help you get ready to take and pass the AWS Certified SysOps Administrator – Associate (SOA-C02) exam.

This book is designed to remind you of everything you need to know to pass the SOA-C02 certification exam. Each chapter includes a number of practice questions that should give you a reasonably accurate assessment of your knowledge, and, yes, we've provided the answers and their explanations for these questions. Read this book, understand the material, and you'll stand a very good chance of passing the real test.

Exam Cram books help you understand and appreciate the subjects and materials you need to know to pass AWS certification exams. *Exam Cram* books are aimed strictly at test preparation and review. They do not teach you everything you need to know about a subject. Instead, the authors streamline and highlight the pertinent information by presenting and dissecting the questions and problems they've discovered that you're likely to encounter on an AWS certification exam.

Let's begin by looking at preparation for the exam.

How to Prepare for the Exam

This text follows the official exam objectives closely to help ensure your success. The AWS Certified SysOps Administrator – Associate exam covers 6 domains and 14 objectives, and this book is aligned with those domains and objectives. These official objectives from AWS can be found here:

> https://d1.awsstatic.com/training-and-certification/docs-sysops-associate/
> AWS-Certified-SysOps-Administrator-Associate_Exam-Guide.pdf

As you examine the numerous exam topics now covered in the exam, resist the urge to panic! This book will provide you with the knowledge (and confidence) that you need to succeed. You just need to make sure you read it and follow the guidance it provides throughout your SysOps Administrator – Associate journey.

Practice Tests

This book is filled with practice exam questions to get you ready!

▶ **CramSaver questions at the beginning of each major topic in each chapter:** These difficult, open-ended questions ensure you really know the material. Some readers use these questions to "test out" of a particular topic.

▶ **CramQuizzes at the end of each chapter:** These quizzes provide another chance to demonstrate your knowledge after completing a chapter.

In addition, the book comes with two full practice tests in the Pearson Test Prep software available to you either online or as an offline Windows application. To access the practice exams, please see the instructions in the card inserted in the sleeve in the back of the book. This card includes a unique access code that enables you to activate your exams in the Pearson Test Prep software.

If you are interested in more practice exams than are provided with this book, Pearson IT Certification publishes a Premium Edition eBook and Practice Test product. In addition to providing you with three eBook files (EPUB, PDF, and Kindle), this product provides you with two additional exams' worth of questions. The Premium Edition version also offers you a link to the specific section in the book that presents an overview of the topic covered in the question, allowing you to easily refresh your knowledge. The insert card in the back of the book includes a special offer for an 80 percent discount off this Premium Edition eBook and Practice Test product, which is an incredible deal.

Taking a Certification Exam

After you prepare for your exam, you need to register with a testing center. At the time of this writing, the cost to take the AWS Certified SysOps Administrator – Associate exam is $150 USD for individuals. The test is administered by Pearson VUE testing centers with locations globally or as an online proctored exam.

You will have 180 minutes to complete the exam. The exam consists of a maximum of 65 questions. If you have prepared, you should find that this is plenty of time to properly pace yourself and review the exam before submission.

Arriving at the Exam Location

As with any examination, arrive at the testing center early (at least 15 minutes). Be prepared! You need to bring two forms of identification (one with a picture). The testing center staff requires proof that you are who you say you are and that someone else is not taking the test for you. Arrive early, because if you are late, you will be barred from entry and will not receive a refund for the cost of the exam.

> **ExamAlert**
>
> You'll be spending a lot of time in the exam room. Plan on using the full 180 minutes allotted for your exam and surveys. Policies differ from location to location regarding bathroom breaks. Check with the testing center before beginning the exam.

In the Testing Center

You will not be allowed to take into the examination room study materials or anything else that could raise suspicion that you're cheating. This includes practice test material, books, exam prep guides, or other test aids. The Testing Center will provide you with scratch paper and a pen or pencil. These days, this often comes in the form of an erasable whiteboard.

Examination results are available after the exam. After submitting the exam, you will be notified whether you have passed or failed. The test administrator will also provide you with a printout of your results.

About This Book

The ideal reader for an *Exam Cram* book is someone seeking certification. However, it should be noted that an *Exam Cram* book is a very easily readable, rapid presentation of facts. Therefore, an *Exam Cram* book is also extremely useful as a quick reference manual.

The book can be read cover to cover, or you may jump across chapters as needed. Because the book chapters align with the exam objectives, some chapters may have slight overlap on topics. Where required, references to the other chapters are provided for you. If you need to brush up on a topic, you can use the index, table of contents, or Table I.1 to find the topics and go to the questions that you need to study. Beyond helping you prepare for the test, we think you'll find this book useful as a tightly focused reference on some of the most important aspects of the AWS Certified SysOps Administrator – Associate (SOA-C02) certification.

This book includes other helpful elements in addition to the actual logical, step-by-step learning progression of the chapters themselves. *Exam Cram* books use elements such as ExamAlerts, tips, notes, and practice questions to make information easier to read and absorb. This text also includes a very helpful glossary to assist you.

> **Note**
>
> Reading this book from start to finish is not necessary; this book is set up so that you can quickly jump back and forth to find sections you need to study.

Use the *CramSheet* to remember last-minute facts immediately before the exam. Use the practice questions to test your knowledge. You can always brush up on specific topics in detail by referring to the table of contents and the index. Even after you achieve certification, you can use this book as a rapid-access reference manual.

Exam Objectives

Table I.1 lists the skills the AWS Certified SysOps Administrator – Associate (SOA-C02) exam measures and the chapter in which the objective is discussed.

TABLE I.1

Exam Domain	Objective	Chapter in Book That Covers It
1.0 Monitoring, Logging, and Remediation	1.1 Implement metrics, alarms, and filters by using AWS monitoring and logging services	Chapters 1, 2, 3
1.0 Monitoring, Logging, and Remediation	1.2 Remediate issues based on monitoring and availability metrics	Chapters 1, 2, 3
2.0 Reliability and Business Continuity	2.1 Implement scalability and elasticity	Chapters 1, 4, 5, 6
2.0 Reliability and Business Continuity	2.2 Implement high availability and resilient environments	Chapters 1, 4, 5, 6
2.0 Reliability and Business Continuity	2.3 Implement backup and restore strategies	Chapters 1, 4, 5, 6
3.0 Deployment, Provisioning, and Automation	3.1 Provision and maintain cloud resources	Chapters 1, 4, 7, 8
3.0 Deployment, Provisioning, and Automation	3.2 Automate manual or repeatable processes	Chapters 1, 4

Exam Domain	Objective	Chapter in Book That Covers It
4.0 Security and Compliance	4.1 Implement and manage security and compliance policies	Chapters 1, 2, 3, 6, 9
4.0 Security and Compliance	4.2 Implement data and infrastructure protection strategies	Chapters 1, 2, 3, 6, 10
5.0 Networking and Content Delivery	5.1 Implement networking features and connectivity	Chapters 1, 4, 5, 11
5.0 Networking and Content Delivery	5.2 Configure domains, DNS services, and content delivery	Chapters 1, 4, 5, 12
5.0 Networking and Content Delivery	5.3 Troubleshoot network connectivity issues	Chapters 1, 4, 5, 13
6.0 Cost and Performance Optimization	6.1 Implement cost optimization strategies	Chapters 1, 14
6.0 Cost and Performance Optimization	6.2 Implement performance optimization strategies	Chapter 15

The Chapter Elements

Each *Exam Cram* book has chapters that follow a predefined structure. This structure makes *Exam Cram* books easy to read and provides a familiar format for all *Exam Cram* books. The following elements typically are used:

▶ Chapter topics

▶ CramSavers

▶ CramQuizzes

▶ ExamAlerts

▶ Notes

▶ Available exam preparation software practice questions and answers

> **Note**
>
> Bulleted lists, numbered lists, tables, and graphics are also used where appropriate. A picture can paint a thousand words sometimes, and tables can help to associate different elements with each other visually.

Now let's look at each of the elements in detail.

▶ **Chapter topics**—Each chapter contains details of all subject matter listed in the table of contents for that particular chapter. The objective of an

Exam Cram book is to cover all the important facts without giving too much detail; it is an exam cram.

▶ **CramSavers**—Each chapter kicks off with a short-answer quiz to help you assess your knowledge of the chapter topic. This chapter element is designed to help you determine whether you need to read the whole chapter in detail or merely skim the material and skip ahead to the CramQuiz at the end of the chapter.

▶ **CramQuizzes**—Each chapter concludes with a multiple-choice quiz to help ensure that you have gained familiarity with the chapter content.

▶ **ExamAlerts**—ExamAlerts address exam-specific, exam-related information. An ExamAlert addresses content that is particularly important, tricky, or likely to appear on the exam. An ExamAlert looks like this:

ExamAlert

Make sure you remember the different ways in which you can access a router remotely. Know which methods are secure and which are not.

▶ **Notes**—Notes typically contain useful information that is not directly related to the current topic under consideration. To avoid breaking up the flow of the text, they are set off from the regular text.

Note

This is a note. You have already seen several notes.

Other Book Elements

Most of this *Exam Cram* book on SysOps Administrator - Associate follows the consistent chapter structure already described. However, various important elements are not part of the standard chapter format. These elements apply to the book as a whole.

▶ **Glossary**—The glossary contains a listing of important terms used in this book with explanations.

▶ **CramSheet**—The CramSheet is a quick-reference, tear-out cardboard sheet of important facts useful for last-minute preparation. CramSheets often include a simple summary of the facts that are most difficult to remember.

▶ **Companion website**—The companion website for your book allows you to access several digital assets that come with your book, including

   ▶ Pearson Test Prep software (both online and Windows desktop versions)

   ▶ Key Terms Flash Cards application

   ▶ A PDF version of the CramSheet

To access the book's companion website, simply follow these steps:

1. Register your book by going to: PearsonITCertification.com/ register and entering the ISBN: **9780137509584**.

2. Respond to the challenge questions.

3. Go to your account page and select the **Registered Products** tab.

4. Click the **Access Bonus Content** link under the product listing.

Pearson Test Prep Practice Test Software

As noted previously, this book comes complete with the Pearson Test Prep practice test software containing two full exams. These practice tests are available to you either online or as an offline Windows application. To access the practice exams that were developed with this book, please see the instructions in the card inserted in the sleeve in the back of the book. This card includes a unique access code that enables you to activate your exams in the Pearson Test Prep software.

Accessing the Pearson Test Prep Software Online

The online version of this software can be used on any device with a browser and connectivity to the Internet, including desktop machines, tablets, and smartphones. To start using your practice exams online, simply follow these steps:

1. Go to http://www.PearsonTestPrep.com.

2. Select **Pearson IT Certification** as your product group.

3. Enter your email/password for your account. If you don't have an account on PearsonITCertification.com or CiscoPress.com, you will need to establish one by going to PearsonITCertification.com/join.

4. In the **My Products** tab, click the **Activate New Product** button.

5. Enter the access code printed on the insert card in the back of your book to activate your product.

6. The product will now be listed in your My Products page. Click the **Exams** button to launch the exam settings screen and start your exam.

Accessing the Pearson Test Prep Software Offline

If you wish to study offline, you can download and install the Windows version of the Pearson Test Prep software. There is a download link for this software on the book's companion website, or you can just enter this link in your browser:

http://www.pearsonitcertification.com/content/downloads/pcpt/engine.zip

To access the book's companion website and the software, simply follow these steps:

1. Register your book by going to PearsonITCertification.com/register and entering the ISBN: **9780137509584**.

2. Respond to the challenge questions.

3. Go to your account page and select the **Registered Products** tab.

4. Click the **Access Bonus Content** link under the product listing.

5. Click the **Install Pearson Test Prep Desktop Version** link under the Practice Exams section of the page to download the software.

6. After the software finishes downloading, unzip all the files on your computer.

7. Double-click the application file to start the installation, and follow the on-screen instructions to complete the registration.

8. When the installation is complete, launch the application and select the **Activate Exam** button on the My Products tab.

9. Click the **Activate a Product** button in the Activate Product Wizard.

10. Enter the unique access code found on the card in the sleeve in the back of your book and click the **Activate** button.

11. Click **Next** and then the **Finish** button to download the exam data to your application.

12. You can now start using the practice exams by selecting the product and clicking the **Open Exam** button to open the exam settings screen.

Note that the offline and online versions will synch together, so saved exams and grade results recorded on one version will be available to you on the other as well.

Customizing Your Exams

Once you are in the exam settings screen, you can choose to take exams in one of three modes:

▶ Study Mode

▶ Practice Exam Mode

▶ Flash Card Mode

Study Mode allows you to fully customize your exams and review answers as you are taking the exam. This is typically the mode you would use first to assess your knowledge and identify information gaps. Practice Exam Mode locks certain customization options because it is presenting a realistic exam experience. Use this mode when you are preparing to test your exam readiness. Flash Card Mode strips out the answers and presents you with only the question stem. This mode is great for late stage preparation when you really want to challenge yourself to provide answers without the benefit of seeing multiple-choice options. This mode will not provide the detailed score reports that the other two modes will, so it should not be used if you are trying to identify knowledge gaps.

In addition to these three modes, you will be able to select the source of your questions. You can choose to take exams that cover all of the chapters, or you can narrow your selection to just a single chapter or the chapters that make up specific parts in the book. All chapters are selected by default. If you want to narrow your focus to individual chapters, simply deselect all the chapters and then select only those on which you wish to focus in the Objectives area.

You can also select the exam banks on which to focus.

There are several other customizations you can make to your exam from the exam settings screen, such as the time of the exam, the number of questions served up, whether to randomize questions and answers, whether to show the number of correct answers for multiple-choice questions, or whether to serve up only specific types of questions. You can also create custom test banks by selecting only questions that you have marked or questions on which you have added notes.

Updating Your Exams

If you are using the online version of the Pearson Test Prep software, you should always have access to the latest version of the software as well as the exam data. If you are using the Windows desktop version, every time you launch the software, it will check to see if there are any updates to your exam data and automatically download any changes that were made since the last time you used the software. This requires that you are connected to the Internet at the time you launch the software.

Sometimes, due to many factors, the exam data may not fully download when you activate your exam. If you find that figures or exhibits are missing, you may need to manually update your exams.

To update a particular exam you have already activated and downloaded, simply select the **Tools** tab and select the **Update Products** button. Again, this is an issue only with the desktop Windows application.

If you wish to check for updates to the Pearson Test Prep exam engine software, Windows desktop version, simply select the **Tools** tab and select the **Update Application** button. This will ensure you are running the latest version of the software engine.

Contacting the Authors

Hopefully, this book provides you with the tools you need to pass the AWS SysOps Administrator - Associate exam. Feedback is appreciated. You can follow and contact the authors on LinkedIn:

Marko Sluga:

https://www.linkedin.com/in/markosluga/

Rick Crisci:

https://www.linkedin.com/in/rickcrisci/

William "Bo" Rothwell:

https://www.linkedin.com/in/bo-rothwell/

CHAPTER 1

Introduction to AWS

This chapter covers the following official AWS Certified SysOps Administrator - Associate (SOA-C02) exam domains:

- ▶ Domain 1: Monitoring, Logging, and Remediation
- ▶ Domain 2: Reliability and Business Continuity
- ▶ Domain 3: Deployment, Provisioning, and Automation
- ▶ Domain 4: Security and Compliance
- ▶ Domain 5: Networking and Content Delivery
- ▶ Domain 6: Cost and Performance Optimization

(For more information on the official AWS Certified SysOps Administrator - Associate [SOA-C02] exam topics, see the Introduction.)

Before we dive into the inner workings of Amazon Web Services (AWS), we need to cover the basics of cloud computing and the AWS platform itself. This approach allows you to build your knowledge of the AWS cloud from the ground up. A good understanding of the cloud and AWS core concepts will make it much easier to grasp complex service-level concepts and design decisions that AWS has opted for when providing a certain service or feature.

We recommend you take the time to cover the basics even if you feel that you are familiar with general cloud computing concepts already because the definitions and acronyms explained in this first chapter will be used in future chapters without additional explanation.

What Is Cloud Computing?

This section covers the following official AWS Certified SysOps Administrator - Associate (SOA-C02) exam domains:

▶ Domain 2: Reliability and Business Continuity

▶ Domain 3: Deployment, Provisioning, and Automation

▶ Domain 4: Security and Compliance

CramSaver

If you can correctly answer these questions before going through this section, save time by completing the Cram Quiz at the end of the section.

1. Which characteristic of cloud computing as defined by NIST describes the ability of the cloud resources to be expanded or contracted at a moment's notice?

2. List the three delivery models defined by NIST.

3. Which cloud deployment model requires the most consideration from a security point of view?

Answers

1. Answer: Rapid elasticity. The cloud provider needs to ensure there is ample capacity for all users to expand and contract the resources their applications consume in real time as required.

2. Answer: IaaS, PaaS, and SaaS. The three delivery models defined by NIST define how a service is consumed and determine the level of interaction the user has with the underlying compute services.

3. Answer: Hybrid cloud. Due to the fact that a hybrid deployment is connected across a private and public cloud solution, there are typically additional security considerations that you need to address when considering such a deployment.

In recent times cloud adoption has accelerated at an unprecedented rate. Finding an enterprise that does not utilize the cloud to some extent is now virtually impossible. Although cloud adoption has been in progress for well over a decade, the recent requirement to overcome economic and health hardships of 2020 has put additional emphasis on utilizing the cloud. The rapid move to virtual workforces and the need for instant access have provided a decisive push for enterprises that have so far been keeping the cloud option on the sidelines.

All of these rapid moves, however, mean that you start using services without covering the basics. And as everyone knows, a house is only as good as the foundation it is built on. This is the way we would like to start building your knowledge of the AWS cloud.

Luckily for us, the good people at the National Institute of Standards and Technology (NIST) have come up with a clear definition of the standards and features a cloud computing environment must have. These can be broken down into three categories:

▶ Cloud deployment models

▶ Standard features of the cloud

▶ Service delivery models

Cloud deployments come in four types:

▶ **Public cloud:** Any publicly available cloud service such as AWS. Most public cloud providers deliver cloud services in several geographically distinct locations that are independent of each other and (in the case of AWS and others) distributed globally. Using multiple locations with an all-in public cloud deployment can be considered more reliable than a deployment on-premises and can help you deliver content to global audiences in the most efficient manner. Most public cloud providers have services that allow for the replication and backup of services and data across multiple locations in a transparent manner.

▶ **Private cloud:** A cloud environment deployed within an organization available only on the private network. These are typically found in enterprises that are required to adhere to certain regulation or laws, or environments where a massive investment into IT systems has already been taken in the past. Having your own cloud can also be a good option when the application requires local computing at the lowest latency possible.

▶ **Hybrid cloud:** A connected cloud deployment across a private and public solution. Hybrid is becoming a more popular option for many enterprises seeking to expand their capacities into the public cloud. One consideration of hybrid cloud is that there are additional security concerns due to the fact that the private and public resources are connected. You need to consider both how you secure the connection itself and how to grant access to resources from one cloud platform to another. However, the hybrid cloud is a great option when mission-critical systems are required to switch from private to public cloud and vice versa in case of disruptions or resource constraints and for backup and disaster recovery.

▶ **Community cloud:** A hybrid deployment where members of a community share their resources to all members of the community. Community cloud deployments are mostly found in academic circles and open-source projects.

The standard features of cloud computing are

▶ **On-demand self-service:** The ability for the customer or an application that the customer operates to provision resources at any time through a self-service portal or API.

▶ **Broad network access:** The ability for the customer or an application that the customer operates to access the resources and services available in the cloud from a broad network. With public cloud solutions, this means the Internet, whereas with private cloud solutions, this is limited to the corporate or private network.

▶ **Resource pooling:** The characteristic of the cloud resources to be pooled into logical groups and isolated from other tenants or customers of the cloud at the account and network level.

▶ **Rapid elasticity:** The ability of the cloud resources to be expanded or contracted at a moment's notice. The cloud provided needs to ensure enough capacity so that all customers can expand their application resource usage to any (reasonable) size at any moment. The cloud provider also needs to give customers the ability to shrink the resources in use by their application when not in use.

▶ **Measured service:** The characteristic of the cloud service that measures resource consumption and infrastructure performance and provides the data collected to the cloud provider and the customer.

Finally, there are three service delivery models:

▶ **IaaS:** Infrastructure as a Service delivers raw compute, storage, and network capacity to the cloud customer. The customer is required to understand, configure, maintain, and secure the environment that they have created. Although IaaS requires the customer to be well versed in many different technologies, using IaaS as the deployment model, however, provides the most flexibility.

▶ **PaaS:** Platform as a Service delivers more refined and more specific services such as databases, application front and back ends, and message queues. These are deployed via a simple API call, which enables developers to easily deploy solutions with one simple call even from within code. PaaS is also deployed, configured, managed, and secured by the provider, thus releasing the customer from these tasks. PaaS usually delivers a good mix of features and flexibility and helps reduce management overhead; however, due to the nature of the delivery model, it is not suitable for all cases like IaaS.

▶ **SaaS:** Software as a Service focuses on delivering services in an end-user consumable fashion. SaaS deliveries are working, fully functional applications that should be relatively easy for any user to consume from a client application or simply through the browser. The functionality is limited to the software in question, and these kinds of solutions are useful when little or no customization is required.

The different deployment models also influence the level of responsibility of the provider and customer. Because the ownership of the infrastructure, the platforms, and the application layer is divided between the provider and the customer, each of them must ensure their portion of the application is configured correctly, patched, and secured. This is commonly referred to as shared responsibility and should be considered a key factor in choosing the deployment model.

Figure 1.1 demonstrates the level of responsibility of the customer and the provider.

Responsibility	IaaS	PaaS	SaaS
User identity, accounts, and access	Customer		
Data			
Application			
Platform components (DB, Web servers...)			
Network access (routing, firewalls, ports...)			
Encryption			
Operating System			
Virtualization/Containerization			
Hardware (Storage, Network Compute)			
Datacenters, dark fiber, uplinks	Provider		

FIGURE 1.1 The shared responsibility model in IaaS, PaaS, and SaaS

All this talk about the cloud can make you feel as though the era of datacenters is over, but that is not the case. The datacenter market has grown quite significantly since the rise of cloud computing; however, most of the data-center activity now surrounds the underlying platforms that run the cloud services.

By taking a look at Figure 1.2, you can easily see how the datacenters, the hardware, and the NIST definitions are all tied together to provide cloud services.

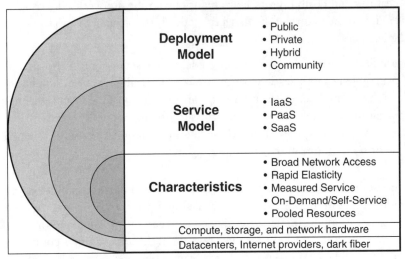

FIGURE 1.2   Visual model of cloud computing as defined by NIST

Cram Quiz

Answer these questions. The answers follow the last question. If you cannot answer these questions correctly, consider reading this section again until you can.

1. Which feature of cloud computing enables customer isolation at the account or network level?

   ○ **A.** Rapid elasticity

   ○ **B.** Resource pooling

   ○ **C.** Monitoring

   ○ **D.** Firewalls

2. Which of the following service delivery models allows you to deploy a database with a single API call?

   ○ **A.** DBaaS

   ○ **B.** IaaS

   ○ **C.** SaaS

   ○ **D.** PaaS

3. Which of the following cloud deployment models are suitable for backup and disaster recovery? (Choose all that apply.)

   ○ **A.** Public cloud

   ○ **B.** Private cloud

   ○ **C.** Hybrid cloud

   ○ **D.** Community cloud

Cram Quiz Answers

1. **Answer:** B is correct. Resource pooling enables cloud resource isolation from other tenants or cloud customers at the account and network level.

2. **Answer:** D is correct. Platform as a Service allows for functional services like databases to be delivered via a simple API call.

3. **Answer:** A and C are correct. Both public and hybrid clouds can be used for backup and disaster recovery.

The AWS Cloud

This section covers the following official AWS Certified SysOps Administrator -
Associate (SOA-C02) exam domains:

▶ Domain 3: Deployment, Provisioning, and Automation

CramSaver

If you can correctly answer these questions before going through this section,
save time by skimming the Exam Alerts in this section and then completing the
Cram Quiz at the end of the section.

1. What are some of the important factors to consider when choosing an
   AWS region?

2. How can you accelerate the delivery of content across the globe if your
   application is deployed in a single AWS region?

3. What are the most common tools that allow you to interact with AWS
   services?

Answers

1. Answer: When you are choosing a region, usually the most important consideration would be the data residency or sovereignty, which determines if
   the data can even reside in the selected region. Another factor to consider
   would be proximity to the users. A region that is closer to the users will
   allow for a much better experience due to lower latency for each request.
   You should also consider if the services you are intending to use are available in the region. Finally, consider the region with the lowest price for the
   service. Regions are located in different areas where costs of operation
   might differ, which eventually leads to different prices for services.

2. Answer: AWS operates a content delivery network (CDN) that operates
   in all edge locations. The CDN can help you deliver the content to users
   across the globe with the lowest latency possible.

3. Answer: The management console, a graphical user interface that is accessible from anywhere using a browser, the AWS command-line interface
   (CLI), and the AWS software development kits (SDKs).

Amazon Web Services (AWS) was launched in 2006 by Amazon and is widely
recognized as the first true public cloud computing platform. The company was
spun out of the knowledge that the IT specialists in the company have gained
while running the amazon.com platform. The services that have been created
over time allow you to deploy applications with extremely high availability,
unlimited performance, and unbeatable reliability at any scale with the most

modern features. Lots of effort has gone in to providing capabilities and features that make management, operations, and automation of the environment a breeze.

AWS Global Architecture

The AWS global architecture has four components:

▶ Datacenters

▶ Availability zones

▶ Regions

▶ Edge locations and regional edge caches

Datacenters

The smallest piece of the AWS infrastructure is a datacenter. AWS builds its own datacenters as well as operates in third-party facilities. Customers have no visibility at the level of datacenters and their locations. The lowest level of AWS resource abstraction is an availability zone. A typical AWS datacenter has the following characteristics:

▶ Between 50,000 and 80,000 compute units per datacenter in approximately 500–100 racks

▶ Approximately 11 petabytes storage capacity per rack

▶ Up to 100 terabits per second of connectivity on a proprietary redundant network layer and network security stack

Availability Zones

Datacenters are grouped together into an availability zone. An availability zone is designated as a fault isolation environment where a failure might affect all datacenters in the group. Multiple availability zones are independent of each other and are connected with low-latency private links to create a region. Many services are distributed across availability zones to provide high availability; however, if a service deploys an instance into one availability zone, you are able to deploy another copy to another availability zone to make it highly available. For example, one EC2 server instance can be deployed on only one hypervisor in one datacenter; this means it can reside in only one availability zone. To make an application highly available, you need to deploy two identical EC2 instances, each in its own availability zone.

Regions

A number of AWS regions are distributed across the globe. When you deploy your application, you also choose a region that will enable you to reach your intended audience with the lowest latency possible. When choosing a region, you should always consider the following factors:

▶ **Data sovereignty:** Are there laws that you need to conform to in a certain region, or can you store the data anywhere?

▶ **User proximity:** How far from the users can you host the services?

▶ **Regional resilience:** Regions can go down too. Do you need to withstand a region outage?

▶ **Service availability:** Is the service you are using available in the region? Not all services are available in all regions.

▶ **Regional pricing:** Pricing in regions is different because AWS charges what it costs to run services in a certain region.

On top of an availability zone's high availability within a region, you can also create applications that are replicated across regions; however, when designing cross-region deployments, make sure to consider the following factors:

▶ Synchronous replication across multiple regions is probably not possible due to higher-than-single-digit millisecond latency between the locations.

▶ Replication traffic counts against outgoing data transfer costs.

▶ Several managed services are designed to provide built-in replication support across multiple regions. Consider using those.

▶ Ensure that a plan is in place to recover and resynchronize after a region outage.

▶ Client latency can be increased in case of failover to a distant region, which can negatively influence user experience and still breach the conditions of the application's service-layer agreement (SLA).

Edge Locations

Edge locations are globally distributed locations that provide an additional latency reduction when delivering applications from AWS. Most of the capacity in an edge location is dedicated to CloudFront, a content delivery network that can help deliver static content with fast response times, usually in the double-digit millisecond range. You can also terminate connections and even return dynamic responses to users using the Lambda@Edge processing functions at edge locations. These allow you to implement authentication, verification, and other features such as detection of user agents and browser types.

To provide the lowest latency for the DNS service, all of the Route 53 servers are deployed in all edge locations across the globe. This vast distribution allows the Route 53 service to be highly resilient and allows AWS to promise a 100 percent SLA on the Route 53 service. The API Gateway can be integrated at the edge location to provide lower latencies for API calls, which can have a tremendous impact on the performance of a global application. Security services like AWS Shield and WAF being deployed at the edge location can also greatly increase the resilience of applications.

Accessing AWS

All management calls to all services in AWS are API calls. This allows both humans and machines to seamlessly access AWS services. AWS also provides access tools that simplify how you access the environment. The simplest way to access AWS is via the AWS Management Console, and most of the exam also focuses on practical examples in the console. However, if you would like to perform some custom calls and automate some interaction with AWS, you can always choose to use the AWS command-line interface. The CLI enables you to run command-line calls and scripts (including Bash, PowerShell, and batch) from Windows, Linux, and Mac. The CLI is built on the AWS boto3 SDK (the Python SDK); however, other AWS software development kits (SDKs) are available for multiple other programming languages. The SDKs enable developers to interact with AWS services directly from the source code.

Cram Quiz

Answer these questions. The answers follow the last question. If you cannot answer these questions correctly, consider reading this section again until you can.

1. A Linux administrator well versed in Bash scripting asks you to help select the right tool for AWS automation deployment. Which of the following tools would you recommend to automate an AWS infrastructure deployment from within a Linux operating system? Select the simplest solution.

   ○ **A.** AWS CLI

   ○ **B.** AWS SDK

   ○ **C.** CloudFormation

   ○ **D.** API calls to the management console

2. Which steps would you need to take to make an application deployed on EC2 highly available within a region? (Choose all that apply.)

   ○ **A.** Deploy two instances in one availability zone.

   ○ **B.** Deploy two instances in two different availability zones.

   ○ **C.** Ensure the application data and state are synchronized between the instances.

   ○ **D.** None of these answers are correct. EC2 is inherently highly available in a region.

Cram Quiz Answers

1. Answer: A. The simplest solution for automating deployments from an existing Linux environment would be the AWS CLI. Anyone familiar with Bash scripting would be quick to pick up the syntax and able to automate an AWS deployment with ease.

2. Answer: B and C. To enable a service like EC2 to run a highly available application in AWS, you need to deploy two instances in two different availability zones. Additionally, you need to set up the application layer in a way that will ensure the application data and state are synchronized between the two instances. Deploying two instances in one availability zone ensures that high availability of the instance cannot guarantee resilience at the availability zone level.

Six Benefits of the AWS Cloud

This section covers the following official AWS Certified SysOps Administrator - Associate (SOA-C02) exam domains:

▶ Domain 1: Monitoring, Logging, and Remediation

▶ Domain 2: Reliability and Business Continuity

▶ Domain 3: Deployment, Provisioning, and Automation

▶ Domain 6: Cost and Performance Optimization

CramSaver

If you can correctly answer these questions before going through this section, save time by skimming the Exam Alerts in this section and then completing the Cram Quiz at the end of the section.

1. Which aspect of the AWS cloud can make a large financial impact when comparing the AWS cloud to an on-premises deployment?

2. When operating an application in AWS, what would be the most common way of determining the required resources that an application will consume during the next day, week, month, or year?

Answers

1. Answer: Having the ability to consume services in a pay-as-you go approach can make a measurable impact on the cost of running an application.

2. Answer: In AWS you are not required to make projections and guesses. You depend on monitoring and logging to provide the insight into the load of the application and respond accordingly by dynamically increasing and decreasing the resources provisioned for the application.

An application can be deployed in many different ways. Generally, we look at either deploying the application on-premises or deploying to AWS. When considering where to deploy your application, you need to look at the six benefits of the AWS cloud:

▶ **Trade capital expenses (CapEx) for operating expenses (OpEx):** By consuming services through a pay-as-you-go model, you can run a complete IT stack from operating expenses. Invest CapEx into your core business, not your IT.

▶ **Stop guessing about capacity:** By using the flexibility and on-demand approach to deploying services, you can match application resources to the user volume. The more users you have, the more infrastructure you can afford to run.

▶ **Increase speed and agility:** Having the ability to deploy and test the environment in a very short time is crucial for achieving a short time to market for any application. The faster you can reach your audience, the better your chances for adoption.

▶ **Go global in minutes:** Having the ability to deploy your application in multiple locations around the globe in a matter of minutes can be a game changer for certain applications like social networking, chat, and video calling. The lower the latency to the user, the better the experience.

▶ **No more need to run datacenters:** Datacenters are expensive to operate when considering the cost of rent, maintenance, security, and depreciated on installed instruments (AC, power, UPS, racking, cabling etc.).

▶ **Benefit from massive economies of scale:** When AWS purchases equipment, it buys whole production lines. This means cost per unit is massively discounted versus an off-the-shelf unit, and this benefit is directly transferred to the customers. The services AWS provides are thus competitively priced, and as the AWS environment grows, the prices also keep getting lower.

Cram Quiz

Answer these questions. The answers follow the last question. If you cannot answer these questions correctly, consider reading this section again until you can.

1. Which of the following benefits of the AWS cloud allows AWS to provide a relatively low cost per unit of compute, storage, and networking?

    ○ **A.** Massive economies of scale

    ○ **B.** Going global in minutes

    ○ **C.** No more running datacenters

    ○ **D.** Increasing speed and agility

2. Which of the following benefits of the AWS cloud allows you to deliver applications in a reliable and resilient manner from multiple locations?

    ○ **A.** Massive economies of scale

    ○ **B.** Going global in minutes

    ○ **C.** No more running datacenters

    ○ **D.** Increasing speed and agility

Cram Quiz Answers

1. Answer: A. The scale at which AWS acquires compute, storage, and network equipment ranges in the millions of units at once. The low purchase cost per unit is passed on to the cost of the service itself.

2. Answer: C. Because you can go global in minutes, you can also deploy a copy of an application in another region in the same short span of time. Not only can you address a global audience due to this benefit, but you can make your application more resilient and reliable.

AWS Services Overview

This section covers the following official AWS Certified SysOps Administrator - Associate (SOA-C02) exam domains:

▶ Domain 1: Monitoring, Logging, and Remediation

▶ Domain 2: Reliability and Business Continuity

▶ Domain 3: Deployment, Provisioning, and Automation

▶ Domain 4: Security and Compliance

▶ Domain 5: Networking and Content Delivery

▶ Domain 6: Cost and Performance Optimization

CramSaver

If you can correctly answer these questions before going through this section, save time by skimming the Exam Alerts in this section and then completing the Cram Quiz at the end of the section.

1. What AWS service would be able to provide you with a managed, API-addressable DNS service?

2. Which AWS service provides ease of management for encryption keys?

Answers

1. Answer: Amazon Route 53 is a next-generation, API-addressable DNS service from AWS.

2. Answer: Amazon Key Management Service (KMS) provides the ability to manage encryption keys for AWS services and applications at scale.

Many different services are available in the scope of AWS; however, they roughly fall under the two major categories—foundation and platform services. Whereas the platform services completely comply with the PaaS model, the foundation services are an expansion of the basic IaaS with some platform and serverless solutions. Additionally, AWS offers many services for management, deployment, and monitoring of applications.

Foundation Services

AWS foundational services can be functionally divided into the following groups:

▶ Network services

▶ Compute services

▶ Storage services

▶ Security and identity services

▶ End-user applications

Network Services

The network services allow the application's components to interact with each other and also connect the application to the Internet and private networks. Examples of network services include

▶ **Amazon Virtual Private Cloud (VPC):** This service allows you to connect applications with private network ranges, connect those private ranges with the Internet, and assign public IP addresses.

▶ **AWS Direct Connect:** This private optical fiber connection service connects on-premise sites with AWS.

▶ **AWS Site-to-Site VPN gateway (VGW):** This component of the VPC provides the capability for establishing VPN connections with on-premises sites.

▶ **Amazon Route 53:** This is the next-generation, API-addressable DNS service from AWS.

▶ **Amazon CloudFront:** This caching and CDN service is available in the AWS cloud.

▶ **Amazon Elastic Load Balancing (ELB):** This service allows load balancing of traffic across multiple EC2 instances, ECS containers, or other IP addressable targets.

Compute Services

You have a lot of flexibility when it comes to compute services in AWS. The following are examples of compute offerings in AWS:

▶ **Amazon Elastic Cloud Computing (EC2):** Provides the ability to deploy and operate virtual machines running Linux and Windows in the AWS cloud.

▶ **Amazon Elastic Container Service (ECS):** Provides the ability to deploy, orchestrate, and operate containers in the AWS cloud.

▶ **Amazon Elastic Kubernetes Service (EKS):** Provides the ability to deploy, orchestrate, and operate Kubernetes clusters in the AWS cloud.

▶ **Amazon Lambda:** Provides the ability to process simple functions in the AWS cloud.

Storage Services

There are many types of data, and each type requires you to pick the right storage solution. The AWS cloud has several different storage options depending on the types of data that you are storing. Here are a few examples:

▶ **Amazon Elastic Block Storage (EBS):** This solution provides block-accessible, network-attached, persistent storage for volumes that you can connect to EC2 instances and ECS containers.

▶ **Amazon Elastic File System (EFS):** This solution provides a network-attached file system that supports the NFS protocol and allows you to share files among EC2 instances, ECS containers, and other services.

▶ **Amazon Simple Storage Service (S3):** This solution is designed to store unlimited amounts of data; S3 is the ultimate object storage system. All objects in S3 are accessible via standard HTTP requests.

▶ **Amazon Glacier:** This archive storage solution can be automatically integrated with S3.

▶ **AWS Storage Gateway:** This hybrid storage solution exposes AWS as storage services to on-premises servers.

▶ **AWS Snow Family:** These data transfer devices allow for physically moving data from on-premises to the cloud at any scale.

Security and Identity Services

To provide a comprehensive approach to using the AWS environment in a secure manner, AWS provides security services. Examples include the following services:

- ▶ **Amazon Identity and Access Management (IAM):** This service allows for control of access to AWS as well as access to an application in one place.

- ▶ **Amazon Key Management Service (KMS):** This service enables you to define a unified way to manage encryption keys for AWS services and applications.

- ▶ **Amazon Cloud Hardware Security Module (CloudHSM):** This is a cloud-enabled hardware security device.

- ▶ **Amazon Inspector:** This tool provides an assessment of services running in AWS with a prioritized, actionable list for remediation.

- ▶ **Amazon Web Application Firewall (WAF):** This service protects web applications from attacks using exploits and security vulnerabilities.

End-User Applications Services

Within the scope of foundation services, AWS also bundles end-user applications; they include the ability to provide users with everything required to perform their work including but not limited to

- ▶ **Amazon WorkMail:** An enterprise email and calendar service that seamlessly integrates with almost any email client.

- ▶ **Amazon WorkDocs:** A document editor and collaboration service that has its own extensible SDK against which you can develop applications for your workforce or your clients.

- ▶ **Amazon WorkSpaces:** A managed virtual desktop infrastructure (VDI) service where you can create Windows desktops, manage their domain membership, their application configuration, and the distribution of the desktops to the individuals within your organization.

As you can see, some of these services do not fit within the standard IaaS model and the name *foundation services* has a much more fitting ring to this grouping; however, foundation services are designed to provide most of the capabilities that AWS has to offer with platform services and as such are also the basis for some of the platform service solutions.

Platform Services

AWS platform services fall into many categories including but not exclusive to

▶ Database services

▶ Analytics services

▶ Application services

▶ Developer tools

▶ Services for Mobile

▶ AWS IoT

▶ Machine learning services

▶ Gaming services

Next, we take a broad look at some of the AWS platform services.

Database Services

AWS offers the ability to run many different types of managed databases. The following are examples of some database services available in AWS:

▶ **Amazon Relational Database Service (RDS):** A fully managed instance-based relational database service for deployment and managing of Amazon Aurora, PostgreSQL, MySQL, MariaDB, Oracle, and Microsoft SQL Server databases in AWS.

▶ **Amazon ElastiCache:** A fully managed instance-based caching service for deployment of Redis or Memcached in-memory data stores in AWS.

▶ **Amazon DynamoDB:** A fully managed cloud native, serverless nonrelational key-value and document database service in AWS.

▶ **Amazon DocumentDB:** A fully managed instance-based nonrelational document database service in AWS.

▶ **Amazon Keyspaces:** A fully managed serverless Cassandra nonrelational database service in AWS.

▶ **Amazon Neptune:** A fully managed instance-based graphing database service in AWS.

▶ **Amazon QLDB:** A fully managed serverless ledger database service in AWS.

► **Amazon RedShift:** A fully managed instance-based data warehousing service for deployment of petabyte-scale data clusters at very low cost.

Analytics Services

Analytics is an important part of any application, and because of that, AWS offers many services for data analytics. The following are examples of some analytics services available in AWS:

► **AWS Glue:** A serverless ETL and catalog service that provides the ability to manage data at scale and execute data transformation at a very low cost.

► **Amazon Athena:** A serverless interactive query service that gives you the ability to query static data on S3 via SQL.

► **Amazon Kinesis:** A fully managed set of services that offer the ability to capture, process, and store streaming data at any scale.

► **Amazon Elastic Map Reduce (EMR):** A service that provides the ability to run open-source big data workloads in the AWS cloud.

Application Services

Several offerings fit into the application services. They enable you to perform work and provide extensions to your applications that can make them more unified and scalable and can allow you to offload more expensive components running in the cloud. Examples include

► **Amazon API Gateway:** A fully managed API management and deployment service.

► **Amazon Elastic Transcoder:** A cost-effective and scalable fully managed media transcoding service.

Other Examples

AWS also offers services that enable you to address a specific task. The following services allow developers, administrators, scientists, and engineers ease of use of advanced features when developing applications, managing systems, and using machine learning.

► **AWS Pinpoint:** A service that allows developers to easily engage users on their devices with targeted, segmented (ML) marketing using email, SMS, and mobile push.

▶ **AWS Device Farm:** A tool for testing an application on mobile devices in the Amazon cloud at scale before deploying them to production.

▶ **AWS Cognito:** A centralized authentication service for mobile and web users that can easily be federated with external directories through OpenID Connect, OAuth 2.0, and SAML 2.0.

▶ **AWS Internet of Things (IoT) Services:** A set of services designed to provide everything required to run IoT, including the FreeRTOS operating system and components that help manage and work with IoT devices at any scale.

▶ **AWS SageMaker:** Powerful tools that allow developers to design, build, and train machine learning models quickly.

Management and Deployment Services

One of the most important factors in managing applications is the ability to monitor, manage, and automate your applications. AWS offers a wide range of services that can be used to perform these tasks. Most of these have a powerful free tier. Here are some examples:

▶ **Amazon CloudWatch:** The AWS cloud monitoring service, which allows for storing metrics and logs from any device running on AWS or on-premises.

▶ **Amazon CloudTrail:** The API call logging service. Every call in the AWS environment is an API call; thus, CloudTrail enables you to maintain a complete record of actions against your AWS infrastructure.

▶ **AWS Config:** A configuration state recording service that can detect state changes, perform alerting based on rules, and provide resource inventory and relationship mapping.

▶ **AWS CloudFormation:** The standard way to interact with the AWS services through a specification document. CloudFormation provides the ability to implement an Infrastructure as Code (IaC) approach when deploying your applications.

▶ **AWS OpsWorks:** A managed service for running Chef- and Puppet-compatible configuration management services in the AWS cloud.

▶ **AWS Systems Manager:** A managed service for deployment, maintenance, and management of fleets of Linux and Windows servers in the AWS cloud as well as on-premises.

Cram Quiz

Answer these questions. The answers follow the last question. If you cannot answer these questions correctly, consider reading this section again until you can.

1. Which of the following services can be used to make your application more highly available on the network?

   ○ **A.** ELB

   ○ **B.** VPC

   ○ **C.** EC2

   ○ **D.** CloudFormation

2. Which of the following services allows you to gather a record of all AWS API calls for auditing purposes?

   ○ **A.** CloudWatch

   ○ **B.** CloudTrail

   ○ **C.** CloudFormation

   ○ **D.** CloudVault

Cram Quiz Answers

1. Answer: A. Load balancing of traffic across multiple EC2 instances, ECS containers, or other IP addressable targets, thus increasing your application's availability.

2. Answer: B. CloudTrail provides the ability to log all AWS API calls, thus maintaining a complete, auditable record of all requests to the AWS infrastructure.

What Next?

If you want more practice on this chapter's exam objectives before you move on, remember that you can access all of the Cram Quiz questions on the Pearson Test Prep software online. You can also create a custom exam by objective with the Online Practice Test. Note any objective you struggle with and go to that objective's material in this chapter.

CHAPTER 2

Monitoring Services in AWS

This chapter covers the following official AWS Certified SysOps Administrator - Associate (SOA-C02) exam domains:

▶ Domain 1: Monitoring, Logging, and Remediation

▶ Domain 4: Security and Compliance

(For more information on the official AWS Certified SysOps Administrator - Associate [SOA-C02] exam topics, see the Introduction.)

Having a good understanding of what your system is doing in any particular moment is a crucial part of making that system operate in a reliable manner. Traditionally, monitoring meant establishing a system or network operating center (usually abbreviated as SOC and NOC, respectively). That would mean having a room full of screens, the screens being monitored by trained response technicians, who would in turn respond to any anomaly displayed on-screen.

There are two problems with the traditional SOC/NOC design:

1. **Focus primarily on metrics:** Observing metrics of the system being monitored implies that you can usually catch issues only after they impact the system in question.

2. **Human error:** Because the monitoring is being done by humans, the platform is highly prone to human errors, such as misidentifying the issue, misinterpreting data, or simply missing the issue entirely.

Most modern monitoring platforms are designed to be highly programmable in nature and thus can be designed to take care of (most) issues through automation. This approach is sometimes referred to as self-healing.

When designed properly, these systems seldomly ever alert anyone that an action needs to be taken. If a system does get into a condition requiring human intervention (for example, when metrics are out of scope of self-healing), the platform can send out notifications through many different channels, and the response can be very fast.

Modern platforms also provide the capability to track and analyze logs, which enables you to maintain the compliance and security of your system as well as perform remediation preemptively and thus avoid any kind of impact of any issues to the application.

Metering, Monitoring, and Alerting

This section covers the following official AWS Certified SysOps Administrator - Associate (SOA-C02) exam domains:

▶ Domain 1: Monitoring, Logging, and Remediation

▶ Domain 4: Security and Compliance

CramSaver

If you can correctly answer these questions before going through this section, save time by skimming the Exam Alerts in this section and then completing the Cram Quiz at the end of the section.

1. What are some of the characteristics of modern monitoring platforms?

2. Which factors would you consider when assessing a monitoring system's capability to increase security and maintain compliance of your application?

Answers

1. Answer: The capability to meter and collect metrics and logs; the capability to view, graph, and analyze the metrics and log captures; and the capability to trigger alerts, send notifications, trigger actions, and interact with other systems.

2. Answer: Any monitoring platform should have the capability to capture and analyze logs from which you can extract information on login attempts, network access sources and targets, actions being performed within the application, and so on.

We like to tell students, customers, and peers that operating an environment without monitoring is like flying an airplane with sunglasses on, at night, without instrumentation, and no auto pilot. You might be able to estimate what is going on outside and keep flying; however, eventually you are going to crash.

A good understanding of the state of your application is crucial. Not only do you get information on the current performance of the application, but metering, monitoring, and alerting also should be considered essential tools in your troubleshooting, remediation, and security practices. Additionally, you learn how cloud resources are used and thus enable cost optimization as well.

Metering

Metering is a process of extracting information from a platform and storing it for processing. In the scope of this chapter, the information would be operational metrics of the system or platform where the application resides—for example, capturing how many units of CPU, network, and disk capacity are used. On top of the system metrics, you can also meter application-level metrics—for example, the number of active users, connection state information, and numbers of errors. Application metrics usually need to be extracted from the application logs. This implies that any good metering system also needs to be able to collect logs.

Monitoring

What can be done with all the metrics and logs collected by the metering process? You monitor them. Most monitoring systems can connect to a database of metered metrics and logs, which enables you to read, view, graph, and analyze them.

Alerting

Any modern monitoring environment also needs to be able to react to changes in the environment. Any metrics and logs that are out of scope of the typical operating conditions should be able to trigger an alert, and in turn that alert should be able to trigger an action. The simplest actions can be notifications being sent to the users; however, most modern monitoring systems can interact with other systems via APIs and through other remote execution approaches and can be configured to perform automated remediation of issues.

Security and Compliance

Monitoring should also be used as a security and compliance tool. Metrics often can indicate a security issue; for example, a sudden spike in traffic can be an indication of a denial-of-service (DoS) attack. However, metrics alone are not enough to ensure a platform is secure and compliant. Because monitoring platforms can capture logs, you can extract security events and possible issues and send notifications through the alerting feature. Consider capturing information on login attempts, network access sources and targets, actions being performed within an application, and the application infrastructure as crucial factors where security events are captured. Capturing and analyzing these logs can help you maintain compliance and ensure your application is as secure as possible.

Any monitoring platform should also enable you to encrypt the data in transit and at rest.

AWS provides two built-in services that enable you to capture metrics and logs and to perform monitoring and alerting. In this chapter, we cover the following AWS services:

▶ **CloudWatch:** This metrics and log collection service can monitor, analyze, and alert.

▶ **CloudTrail:** This service tracks all requests to the AWS APIs, giving you a complete audit trail of all actions to AWS accounts.

> ### ExamAlert
>
> Some of the exam questions mention the EventBridge service. This service was previously called CloudWatch Events. Chapter 3, "Troubleshooting and Remediation," covers the EventBridge service in more detail.

Cram Quiz

Answer these questions. The answers follow the last question. If you cannot answer these questions correctly, consider reading this section again until you can.

1. You have been put in charge of selecting a monitoring system for your application. You are required to assess several monitoring platforms from a functional point of view. Which of the following factors should you look for in a modern monitoring system?

   ○ **A.** The ability to meter, view, graph, and analyze metrics and logs.

   ○ **B.** The ability to create and trigger alert conditions.

   ○ **C.** The ability to use MongoDB as the underlying database platform.

   ○ **D.** The ability of the platform to interact with external APIs.

2. You have been put in charge of selecting a monitoring system for your application. You are required to assess several monitoring platforms from a security point of view. Which of the following factors should you look for in a monitoring system when considering security and compliance? (Choose all that apply.)

   ○ **A.** The ability to collect, monitor, and analyze logs.

   ○ **B.** The ability to collect, monitor, and graph metrics.

   ○ **C.** The ability to trigger alerts.

   ○ **D.** All of these answers are correct.

Cram Quiz Answers

1. Answer: A, B, and D are correct. Of all the choices, using a specific underlying database is not an important factor when determining the ability of the monitoring platform to be used in a modern application.

2. Answer: D is correct. You should use metrics and logs because they can both help you identify security events and maintain compliance. You also should use alerting to ensure any unusual events can be handled in the most prompt and appropriate manner.

CloudWatch

This section covers the following official AWS Certified SysOps Administrator - Associate (SOA-C02) exam domain:

▶ Domain 1: Monitoring, Logging, and Remediation

CramSaver

If you can correctly answer these questions before going through this section, save time by skimming the Exam Alerts in this section and then completing the Cram Quiz at the end of the section.

1. Name the types of metrics that can be collected by CloudWatch.

2. Which service would you use to analyze the cause of an issue that occurred within your application yesterday?

Answers

1. Answer: CloudWatch can collect standard, detailed, and custom metrics.

2. Answer: CloudWatch Logs Insights enables you to discover causes for past issues.

Amazon CloudWatch is one of the key services that you will need to understand if you want to pass the AWS Certified SysOps Administrator - Associate (SOA-C02) exam. CloudWatch allows you to collect metrics and logs; perform monitoring from within the AWS console or via the API; and create alerts that can send notifications, perform automated actions, and contact other services through their API.

Most AWS services, instances, and objects can output metrics and/or logs into CloudWatch. These are usually referred to as standard metrics, and some services can enable detailed metrics. Standard metrics are usually collected with an interval of five minutes, whereas the services that support detailed metrics enable you to collect the data in one-minute intervals. You can, however, also create custom metrics and logs in CloudWatch, which can help you implement a comprehensive approach to metering, monitoring, and alerting. Standard metrics are not associated with any cost, whereas detailed and custom metrics and logs do incur a small collection and storage charge. Custom metrics can also be easily collected and sent to CloudWatch via the AWS CloudWatch agent, which can be installed in your operating system on EC2 or on-premises.

All of the data you collect in CloudWatch is accessible directly in the AWS console and can also be addressed via the AWS CLI and the CloudWatch API. CloudWatch also has an alarms back end that can track both metrics and logs and perform notifications and interact with other services that can perform automated actions. For example, you can send messages through the Simple Notification Service (SNS) to an alert email and/or to an on-call individual through text messages. You can also trigger actions on other AWS services; for example, you can trigger AutoScaling actions on EC2 instances or trigger Lambda functions that can react to the event.

Data in CloudWatch is stored to a regional repository, meaning all monitoring for a region is completely isolated from any other regions and inherently highly available. For global applications monitoring, configurations can be automated through the CloudFormation service, which we cover in Chapter 7, "Provisioning Resources."

Namespaces and Dimensions

All data in CloudWatch is recorded with a specific namespace format. Default metrics are formatted as *Service:Metric*. For example, the CPU Utilization for the EC2 instances is represented by the following namespace: *EC2:CPUUtilization*.

Dimensions are key:value pairs assigned to metrics to allow for a more granular analysis of those metrics within a specific namespace. CloudWatch allows you to create 10 dimensions for each metric. However, some services have built-in dimensions, and they also count against the limit of 10. For example, the CPU Utilization for a specific EC2 instance with the ID *i-111aaa222bbb333ccc* is represented by the following namespace and dimension: *EC2:CPUUtilization:InstanceId:i-111aaa222bbb333ccc*.

CloudWatch supports custom namespaces that can contain up to 256 alphanumeric characters, periods, hyphens, underscores, forward slashes, hashes, and colons, meaning you can create your own structure for custom metrics. However, it is always a good idea to follow the structure AWS uses for its own services when implementing custom metric namespaces.

CloudWatch namespaces and dimensions can be used to drill down into specific resources metrics and graph them in the management console, as shown in Figure 2.1.

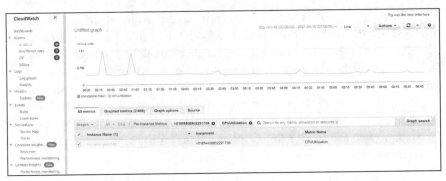

FIGURE 2.1   **CloudWatch Namespaces and Dimensions**

Metrics

A metric represents any data point collected at a certain point in time. A metric has a value and a unit. AWS automatically generates standard metrics with a resolution of five minutes; however, some services support detailed metrics collected on a one-minute interval. Custom metrics are also supported and can be recorded as frequently as one second apart (high-resolution metrics).

CloudWatch metrics are retained for 15 months with the following retention periods:

▶ Custom, subminute metrics are aggregated to minute metrics after 3 hours.

▶ One-minute metrics are aggregated to 5-minute metrics after 15 days.

▶ Five-minute metrics are aggregated to hourly metrics after 63 days.

▶ Hourly metrics aggregates are discarded after 15 months.

If you are required to maintain metrics for a longer period of time, CloudWatch does offer the capability to export metrics to S3.

> **ExamAlert**
>
> While the default metrics retention period is 15 months, the retention of logs in CloudWatch is indefinite. Therefore, you need to specifically delete the logs from CloudWatch. If you wish to automatically truncate the history of the logs retained in CloudWatch, you can also set the retention period to between 1 and 10 years.

Statistics

Over time, AWS creates statistics of all metrics, with the following aggregation approach:

- ▶ **Minimum:** The lowest value within a certain period

- ▶ **Maximum:** The highest value within a certain period

- ▶ **Sum:** The sum of all values within a certain period

- ▶ **Average:** An average of all values within a certain period

- ▶ **SampleCount:** The number of values within a certain period

- ▶ **pNN.NN:** The value of the percentile (for example, up-time percentage) up to 2 decimal points

These metrics can be used to understand the normal operational pattern of your application and to detect issues or even possible cost optimization opportunities.

Percentiles

Percentiles are available for some AWS services. They enable you to understand where in a particular percentile of the service a specific dimension lies. This information allows you to find outliers and use the data in long-term statistical analysis.

CloudWatch Alarms

As we already mentioned, the CloudWatch service enables you to trigger alerts when a certain condition is present for a certain number of CloudWatch checks. An example is the CPU usage of an EC2 instance. If the instance usage is above the 90 percent threshold for a period of three CloudWatch checks, you trigger a notification to an administrator. Because the number of checks depends on the collection interval of the metric, this would represent 10 minutes with standard metrics (first check at 0 minutes, second at 5 minutes, and third at 10 minutes) and 2 minutes for detailed metrics with a 1-minute interval (first check at 0 minutes, second at 1 minute, and third at 2 minutes).

CloudWatch Logs

The beauty of CloudWatch is the ability to apply the same features mentioned in the preceding section to logs. When collecting logs to CloudWatch, you can easily view them in the AWS Management Console, perform analytics, and create alarms based on the patterns you define. Logs are stored in Cloud-Watch indefinitely; however, you can automatically truncate them by setting the retention period to between 1 and 10 years. Logs can also be exported to S3 and then archived to Glacier for more cost-effective storage. We cover S3 and Glacier in more detail in Chapter 6, "Backup and Restore Strategies."

CloudWatch Logs Insights

When working with logs, CloudWatch treats every log entry as streaming data that is available for processing shortly after it is delivered to CloudWatch. CloudWatch Logs Insights provides a simple-to-use interface where you can run SQL-like queries to search and filter through the log content, run simple transformations, and visualize the data. The service enables you to discover causes for past issues and run continuous validation of the platform state after each change or application deployment.

You can also use CloudWatch Logs Insights to search for operational information for services that log such information. For example, you can search for the number of email messages that were sent or received via the WorkMail service during a certain period of time, as shown in Figure 2.2.

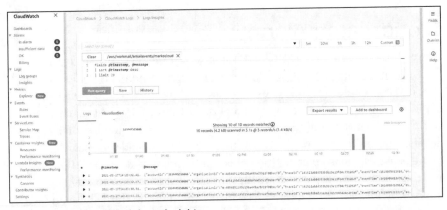

FIGURE 2.2 CloudWatch Logs Insights

Cram Quiz

Answer these questions. The answers follow the last question. If you cannot answer these questions correctly, consider reading this section again until you can.

1. You have been put in charge of designing a monitoring platform for an application for a large enterprise. The monitoring system needs to be highly available and should allow for collecting metrics from your custom application running on EC2 with an interval of one second. Which of the following solutions would be the easiest to implement the required monitoring environment?

    ○ **A.** Unfortunately, this is not possible in AWS due to the high availability and metric collection frequency.

    ○ **B.** Use a custom monitoring solution on two or more EC2 instances in two availability zones to make the monitoring system highly available. Configure the custom agent to send the specific application metrics with a one-second interval.

    ○ **C.** Use CloudWatch. Install CloudWatch agents on the EC2 instance that hosts the application. Configure the agents to send the specific application metrics with the default interval.

    ○ **D.** Use CloudWatch. Install CloudWatch agents on the EC2 instance that hosts the application. Configure the agents to send the specific application metrics with a one-second interval.

2. Which of the following services would you recommend to use for security incident alerting?

    ○ **A.** Store the logs to CloudWatch Logs. Use an alert pattern in CloudWatch Alarms and send the alerts via SNS.

    ○ **B.** Store the logs to CloudWatch Logs. Use an alert pattern in CloudWatch Logs Insights to trigger security incident alerts.

    ○ **C.** Store the logs to CloudWatch Logs Insights. Use an alert pattern in CloudWatch Logs Insights to trigger security incident alerts.

    ○ **D.** Store the logs to CloudWatch Logs Insights. Use an alert pattern in CloudWatch Alarms and send the alerts via SNS.

Cram Quiz Answers

1. Answer: D is correct. CloudWatch is inherently highly available due to its regional scope. The CloudWatch agent needs to be configured to send custom metrics in a one-second interval to comply with the application requirements.

2. Answer: A is correct. CloudWatch Logs stores logs. CloudWatch Alarms can be configured to trigger on a pattern-matching condition (for example, a certain number of failed login attempts in a certain amount of time). CloudWatch Logs Insights can be used later to determine the cause of the issue; however, it cannot be used in the real-time alerting chain.

CloudTrail

This section covers the following official AWS Certified SysOps Administrator - Associate (SOA-C02) exam domains:

▶ Domain 1: Monitoring, Logging, and Remediation

▶ Domain 4: Security and Compliance

CramSaver

If you can correctly answer these questions before going through this section, save time by completing the Cram Quiz at the end of the section.

1. What information is captured in a CloudTrail log?

2. What is the default retention of the default CloudTrail trail?

Answers

1. Answer: CloudTrail logs record information about who requested the action, where the request originated from, when it was requested, what was requested, and the full response.

2. Answer: The default CloudTrail trail tracks events for the past 90 days.

The AWS CloudTrail service performs continuous monitoring of the actions being performed against the AWS API, by creating an auditable log of all requests. By default, your newly created account has a 90-day CloudTrail trail created and enabled to capture all actions against the AWS APIs. If you are required to trail specific services with a longer retention, you can create a custom CloudTrail trail in which you can include the services to monitor, types of actions to record, and the retention period. Note that not all AWS services support full CloudTrail integration, but most do. You can also configure CloudWatch Alarms for CloudTrail events and thus forward information on any critical CloudWatch events to a notification email, text message, or another service that will perform remediation.

CloudTrail logs record information that helps you establish the following:

▶ Who requested the action?

▶ Where did the request originate from and when?

▶ What was requested?

▶ The full API response

Figure 2.3 shows a CloudTrail log with the formatting of the aforementioned information.

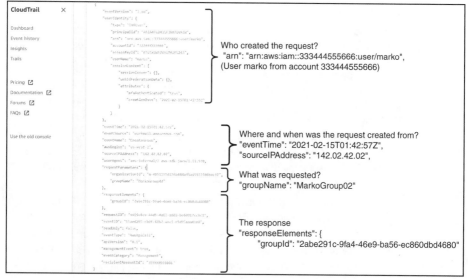

FIGURE 2.3   CloudTrail log

You can designate a specific S3 location to store the logs that can belong to your account or another account. This allows you to configure a trail to a centralized logging account to ensure the data is stored in accordance with the strictest compliance standards and guidelines. CloudTrail also enforces automatic encryption at rest and in transit by default and is configurable with a custom KMS key for even more control over key management. CloudTrail log file integrity validation can also be enabled. This creates MD5 hashes of files delivered to S3 and stores them in a hash file. The hashes can then be compared and the integrity of the logs verified.

Cram Quiz

Answer these questions. The answers follow the last question. If you cannot answer these questions correctly, consider reading this section again until you can.

1. Due to a recent security incident where several EC2 instances were terminated by a rogue employee, your CISO has tasked you with ensuring all destructive requests against the EC2 service are logged and maintained for a long period of time. You also need to ensure the logs are stored securely in a centralized S3 bucket. Your CISO is also worried about tampering with the logs and would like to prevent that. You have chosen to use CloudTrail as the service to provide this feature. How would you configure CloudTrail to comply with the requirements?

   ○ **A.** Configure a new CloudTrail trail. Select EC2 as the service and WRITE as API for the activity. Point the trail to the default S3 location. Cloud-Trail ensures all EC2 actions use integrity validation on the default S3 bucket.

   ○ **B.** Configure a new CloudTrail trail. Select EC2 as the service and WRITE as API for the activity. Point the trail to the default S3 location. Enable integrity validation on the trail.

   ○ **C.** Configure a new CloudTrail trail. Select EC2 as the service and WRITE as API for the activity. Point the trail to the designated central S3 location. Enable integrity validation on the trail.

   ○ **D.** Set the default CloudTrail. CloudTrail ensures all default actions use integrity validation by default.

2. Which service would you use to notify a security response team of a critical CloudTrail event?

   ○ **A.** CloudWatch Logs Insights

   ○ **B.** CloudWatch Alarms

   ○ **C.** CloudTrail Notifications

   ○ **D.** CloudTrail Alarms

Cram Quiz Answers

1. Answer: C is correct. You need to configure a new CloudTrail trail and capture all WRITE API operations. You also need to point the trail to the designated central bucket and enable integrity validation on the trail.

2. Answer: B is correct. CloudTrail can be integrated with CloudWatch Alarms that can be triggered when an event or a specific pattern of events is captured by CloudTrail.

What Next?

If you want more practice on this chapter's exam objectives before you move on, remember that you can access all of the Cram Quiz questions on the Pearson Test Prep software online. You can also create a custom exam by objective with the Online Practice Test. Note any objective you struggle with and go to that objective's material in this chapter.

CHAPTER 3

Troubleshooting and Remediation

This chapter covers the following official AWS Certified SysOps Administrator - Associate (SOA-C02) exam domains:

▶ Domain 1: Monitoring, Logging, and Remediation

▶ Domain 4: Security and Compliance

(For more information on the official AWS Certified SysOps Administrator - Associate [SOA-C02] exam topics, see the Introduction.)

As a general rule, you should consider the services, instances, and objects you deploy to AWS to "just work." Of course, you need to take this rule with a grain of salt because back-end issues might cause impairment of services in an availability zone, thus impairing the application's functionality. However, if there is impairment on the AWS side, you can just examine the API response and determine whether the issue is at your end or at the provider's end.

In this chapter, we discuss the three aspects of troubleshooting and remediation and introduce AWS services that can help you detect and remediate issues.

ExamAlert

Remember that proper troubleshooting and remediation can be done only if you have already set up your monitoring and log collection in advance. The tools and services discussed in this section rely heavily on the services discussed in Chapter 2, "Monitoring Services in AWS." For this reason, the exam usually ties troubleshooting, monitoring, and remediation into one question, so services from both this and the preceding chapter could be included in a specific question in the exam.

Responding to Alarms

This section covers the following official AWS Certified SysOps Administrator - Associate (SOA-C02) exam domains:

▶ Domain 1: Monitoring, Logging, and Remediation

▶ Domain 4: Security and Compliance

CramSaver

If you can correctly answer these questions before going through this section, save time by skimming the Exam Alerts in this section and then completing the Cram Quiz at the end of the section.

1. You have issued a request to download an object on an S3 bucket. Your request receives a 403 HTTP response. What could be the cause of the bad response?

2. True or False: You need to enable the EC2 instance health monitoring first before you can create a CloudWatch Alarm based on the state of the instance check.

Answers

1. Answer: There is an issue in the user, group, role, or bucket policy. All polices in AWS combine with equal weight, and a denial to a resource in one policy has a global effect on the request.

2. Answer: False. EC2 instances have the automatic health check configured; health monitoring can be used directly in CloudWatch Alarms to trigger an alert based on the health check.

In any IT environment, alarms can be triggered by specific issues, breaches of certain monitoring metric thresholds, or detection of changes in a specific defined log stream. Generally, in AWS these issues take three different forms:

▶ Infrastructure issues

▶ Application issues

▶ Security issues

Infrastructure Issues

Generally, you should follow AWS best practices and deploy any unmanaged system across two availability zones, as discussed in Chapter 1, "Introduction to AWS." Anytime you deploy, you expect the infrastructure to just work. If you have a deployment issue, you can easily resolve the issue by trying a redeployment. We call this approach the "rinse and repeat" approach. The approach is useful both for the initial deployment as well as development testing and upgrades.

Troubleshooting infrastructure issues in AWS then usually refers to resolving either a misconfiguration or a fault that was introduced from the configuration or deployment side. For example, let's say you deploy a new version of a security group for EC2 instances. The new version was incorrectly configured, and due to the incorrect configuration, the application front end becomes unavailable. Errors don't just happen when performing manual changes; they can leak into scripts, templates, and automation configurations.

You can also set up infrastructure triggers in CloudWatch Alarms to try to prevent any possible issues with the infrastructure or detect any unusual metric and try to preemptively remediate. For example, you can monitor the state of these instances, and if any health issues are detected, you can perform automatic remediation. Many different factors can constitute infrastructure health issues, including but not limited to

- ▶ **EC2 instance health check failure:** All instances have an automatic health check configured. This can be monitored with CloudWatch, and you can create an alarm that informs you of any issues of this type.

- ▶ **Change in number of EC2 instances:** An availability zone failure could cause the number of reachable instances in an EC2 environment to drop suddenly. You can track the number of active instances and perform remediation. This is usually done through autoscaling. The number could also increase dramatically due to a runaway automation script. That is also an important factor to monitor and alert on.

- ▶ **Infrastructure performance:** The performance of instances, networks, and disks can also indicate issues. You should always set thresholds for performance alarms that encompass the range of performance expected within your environment and trigger alarms when performance metrics are out of spec.

ExamAlert

Infrastructure performance is correlated with the performance of the application, and the application security is coupled with the overall data security. An infrastructure performance alarm often can be triggered by an application or security issue. The exam focuses on a holistic view of troubleshooting, so expect to see questions that include all levels of troubleshooting and remediation in one.

Application Issues

After you set up the infrastructure monitoring and alarming, you need to deal with the application layer. Tracking internal application metrics and logs and creating alarms to respond to should be done in the same exact manner as with the infrastructure. The application often can trigger an infrastructure issue; for example, an infinite loop in code can cause a CPU spike to 100 percent. This means that when troubleshooting your application, you should not expect it to "just work," and you need to compare the aforementioned collection of monitoring and logs to the infrastructure data to determine if the issues are infrastructure related or stem from the application itself.

The simplest practice for metric and log collection when running your application on EC2 instances or on-premise servers would be using the CloudWatch agent. The agent can collect data from any source within the operating system and forward that data to CloudWatch as metric or log data. An even better approach is coding API calls to the CloudWatch API within the application code so that the application is able to self-report metrics regardless of the environment where it runs.

Security Issues

At the top layer of the monitoring and alerting stack are security issues. These issues also encompass a wide range of aspects that need to be determined for each application beforehand. A range of different alerts can be configured for security issues, including but not limited to

▶ **Large numbers of failed login attempts:** These could indicate brute-force break-in attempts to the application.

▶ **Sudden spikes in data transfer out:** These could indicate a breach or data leak.

▶ **Attempts to assume roles from unknown locations:** These could indicate a breach of credentials.

▶ **Large number of failed access attempts:** These could indicate reconnaissance by a rogue actor.

Error Handling in AWS

The AWS infrastructure exposes a public HTTP API, and all calls either receive a 200-type HTTP response if the action is accepted and will be processed, or a 400-type or 500-type HTTP response, indicating the problem is with the query. All 400-type responses indicate there is an issue with the request. All 500-type responses indicate that there is an issue with the AWS infrastructure. In case of infrastructure issues, always make sure to repeat the request with an exponential back-off approach, meaning that you wait for an increasingly longer period of time before reissuing the request.

Here are some examples of HTTP 400-type and 500-type responses:

▶ **400 - bad request:** Any 400 error includes a message like InvalidAction, MessageRejected, or RequestExpired. Specific responses by some services also indicate throttling. In case of throttling, you should retry the requests with exponential back-off.

▶ **403 - access denied:** All IAM polices apply with equal weight, and a deny in one policy denies an action across all policies. Check all the policies attached to the user, group, or role. Check any inline policies and resource policies attached to buckets, queues, and so on.

▶ **404 - page not found:** This error indicates the object, instance, or resource specified in the query does not exist.

▶ **500 - internal failure:** This error indicates an internal error on an operational service on the AWS side. You can immediately retry the request and will probably succeed on the second try. If not, retry with exponential back-off.

▶ **503 - service unavailable:** These errors are rare because they indicate a major failure in an AWS service. You can retry your request using exponential back-off. This way you ensure the request will succeed at some point after the issue is resolved.

CramQuiz

Answer these questions. The answers follow the last question. If you cannot answer these questions correctly, consider reading this section again until you can.

1. You are the administrator of a hybrid-cloud application that uses S3 as the central store for all the data being shared across the platforms. The Internet users are always directed to the AWS portion of the application, whereas the on-premises users are always directed to the local application running on the on-premises servers. Recently, the security team has pointed out that user credentials are hard-coded in the application, and an update was made to the application to use roles instead of the user access key and secret key coded into the application. Your team has already updated and tested the role that will be used within your application and found no issues. The last step is to update the S3 bucket policy to reflect the change. After you update the bucket policy, the on-premises users report receiving a 403 response when trying to retrieve documents from within the application. Interestingly, the Internet users don't seem to have any issues accessing those same documents. What would be the most likely cause for this issue based on the problem description?

   ○ **A.** The S3 bucket policy is incorrectly written.

   ○ **B.** The application on the on-premises servers needs to be updated.

   ○ **C.** The role needs to be assumed on the on-premises servers.

   ○ **D.** The role is not attached to the EC2 instances.

2. You have been asked to collect the 400-type and 500-type errors from a third-party application running on your Linux on-premises servers. Your company would like you to deliver the errors to AWS and tie them into a CloudWatch Alarm. What would be the simplest way to achieve this?

   ○ **A.** Install the AWS CLI and copy the logs to an S3 bucket with the **aws s3 cp** command. Create an S3 trigger to a Lambda function that forwards the logs to CloudWatch for analysis and configure a CloudWatch Alarm to trigger on the specific log pattern.

   ○ **B.** Install the S3 CLI and copy the logs to an S3 bucket with the **s3 cp** command. Create an S3 trigger to a Lambda function that forwards the logs to CloudWatch for analysis and configure a CloudWatch Alarm to trigger on the specific log pattern.

   ○ **C.** Install the CloudWatch agent and point the logs to an S3 bucket. Create an S3 trigger to a Lambda function that forwards the logs to CloudWatch for analysis and create a CloudWatch Alarm to trigger on the specific log pattern.

   ○ **D.** Install the CloudWatch agent and point it to the application logs. Create a CloudWatch Alarm to trigger on the specific log pattern.

Cram Quiz Answers

1. Answer: C is correct. The issue is a 403 – permission denied. Because the web users are able to access the document and the issue is isolated to the on-premises servers, the on-premises servers are not correctly authenticated. The policy now allows the role to access the bucket instead of the user and is correctly configured. The role must have been attached to the EC2 instances because they allow web users to access the document. The most likely issue is that the role has not been assumed on the on-premises servers.

2. Answer: D is correct. Installing the CloudWatch agent is the simplest way to deliver the logs to CloudWatch. The metrics or logs collected can then be used directly on CloudWatch Alarms. It would also be possible to create the solution as described in A, but that approach is unnecessarily complicated.

Amazon EventBridge

This section covers the following official AWS Certified SysOps Administrator - Associate (SOA-C02) exam domain:

▶ Domain 1: Monitoring, Logging, and Remediation

CramSaver

If you can correctly answer these questions before going through this section, save time by skimming the Exam Alerts in this section and then completing the Cram Quiz at the end of the section.

1. In what way do CloudWatch Events and EventBridge differ from each other?

2. True or false: In AWS you can build both serverless and traditional, instance-based applications that can respond to infrastructure, application, and third-party events.

Answers

1. Answer: EventBridge offers integration of AWS events as well as any application and third-party provider events on the event bus. CloudWatch Alarms only supports AWS events by default; however, custom event patterns can be established.

2. Answer: True. With EventBridge and Systems Manager Automation, you can build traditional, instance-based applications and create automation scenarios that are able to respond to real-time events from the EventBridge.

Amazon EventBridge is a new service built on the same API structure as the Amazon CloudWatch Events service. CloudWatch Events enables you to collect events from your AWS services, instances, and objects. The EventBridge service is an evolution of the CloudWatch Events platform and is slated to replace it entirely because at this point the CloudWatch Alarms service is still available but deprecated.

EventBridge is more than just an internal event collection platform because it enables you to build your own serverless event bus, helping you design a seamless platform where events from your own application can be combined with events from AWS. These events can also trigger actions on services within AWS and your application, enabling you to build event-driven applications at any scale. Another benefit of EventBridge is that third-party Software as a Service

(SaaS) providers are able to publish their integration to EventBridge, thus making EventBridge a unified platform for tracking and relaying events in a diverse environment of multiple coordinated platforms.

> **ExamAlert**
>
> The new exam questions are typically written to reflect the change in monitoring and possibly mention solutions with both CloudWatch Events and EventBridge. If you find yourself with two questions, both describing a solution based on the two services, consider selecting EventBridge as the correct answer due to the fact that EventBridge fully replaces CloudWatch Alarms because CloudWatch Alarms is being deprecated.

With EventBridge, you can create applications that emit streams in real time and create routing rules to send your data for consumption to another service, also in real time. The EventBridge bus also completely decouples the publisher and consumer and complies with a loosely coupled, cloud native, serverless, event-based approach to computing.

Integration with AWS Systems Manager Automation

Systems Manager is a set of AWS tools that offers comprehensive configuration management of fleets of servers. We discuss AWS Systems Manager in more detail in Chapter 7, "Provisioning Resources."

An important part of Systems Manager is Systems Manager Automation, which allows you to perform the following common IT tasks:

▶ Automating provisioning and configuration of instances

▶ Performing complex and disruptive operations such as replacing an image for your instances in a scalable, secure, and orchestrated manner

▶ Enhancing the security of your environment by implementing automated responses to security-related events

▶ Reacting to changes in your environment through integration with Amazon EventBridge support

You can select Systems Manager as a target type when creating an EventBridge rule by simply specifying the automation document that will be targeted based on the event pattern.

Having the ability to tie the EventBridge service with Systems Manager is invaluable in any systems operations environment because it enables you to treat the infrastructure as a programmatically addressable resource that can respond to events in a similar manner that serverless applications do. You therefore can create much more flexible, resilient, and reliable infrastructure even when your application is not ready to go entirely serverless.

CramQuiz

Answer this question. The answer follows the question. If you cannot answer the question correctly, consider reading this section again until you can.

1. You need to be able to detect a change in the number of EC2 instances running in your application and send the information about the change to your Zendesk ticketing platform. Which service would allow you to achieve this functionality? (Choose all that apply.)

   - ○ **A.** EventBridge
   - ○ **B.** CloudWatch Events
   - ○ **C.** EC2 AutoScaling
   - ○ **D.** Systems Manager Automation

Cram Quiz Answer

1. Answer: A is correct. A third-party SaaS provider like Zendesk provides the ability to integrate AWS events with their applications through EventBridge.

AWS Config

This section covers the following official AWS Certified SysOps Administrator - Associate (SOA-C02) exam domains:

▶ Domain 1: Monitoring, Logging, and Remediation

▶ Domain 4: Security and Compliance

CramSaver

If you can correctly answer these questions before going through this section, save time by completing the Cram Quiz at the end of the section.

1. Your organization requires you to capture a comprehensive auditable log of the state of your AWS account over time. What would be the simplest way to capture the state for auditing purposes?

2. What would be the easiest way to perform remediation of an issue found in AWS Config?

Answers

1. Answer: Enable AWS Config Configuration Recorder to start collecting configuration snapshots on your account. AWS Config snapshots allow you to maintain an auditable record of the state of your infrastructure in AWS.

2. Answer: You can enable remediation directly in AWS Config if the remediation is supported as an action for the config rule. In case there is no remediation supported, you can create a notification to another service that will perform remediation or notify an administrator for human intervention.

So far, we have covered how to monitor, troubleshoot, and react to alarms and events at the infrastructure and account level. However, there is a missing aspect to the troubleshooting and reaction story that is needed in any IT environment: the state. Capturing the state of your application is a crucial part of tracking how your application changes over time and for ensuring you have a manageable audit trail. Recording the state of your application environment is also a crucial factor in determining compliance and increasing the security of your platform over time; this is where AWS Config comes in.

With AWS Config, you can create a configuration snapshot of your environment so you can easily assess, audit, and evaluate the state of all the AWS resources within your account or organization. Over time, configuration snapshots can be compared against a desired state, thus allowing you to maintain an auditable record of compliance for your application infrastructure in AWS.

AWS Config also can detect any resource changes by continuously performing checks against the infrastructure through preconfigured or custom AWS Config rules. When a rule is created, you can also define a remediation action for the rule, thus enabling you to alert or autoremediate the state of the environment when remediation is supported by AWS Config.

CramQuiz

Answer these questions. The answers follow the last question. If you cannot answer these questions correctly, consider reading this section again until you can.

1. Your company was recently a target of a malicious actor due to a misconfiguration of an S3 bucket ACL, making it publicly accessible. The CISO has instructed you that all S3 buckets need to be private. How would you discover public S3 buckets in your account and automatically remediate this issue?

   ○ **A.** Use AWS Config with the built-in s3-bucket-public-read-prohibited rule and enable automatic remediation.

   ○ **B.** Use AWS Config with the built-in s3-bucket-public-read-prohibited rule and use an AWS Lambda for remediation.

   ○ **C.** Use AWS Config with the built-in s3-bucket-public-read-prohibited rule and use an AWS Systems Manager for remediation.

   ○ **D.** Use AWS Config with the built-in s3-bucket-public-read-prohibited rule and remediate the buckets manually.

2. You have been asked to perform that inventory of EC2 instances in your AWS account. What would be the simplest way to determine the number and types of instances and which Amazon Machine Image (AMI) is being used across all regions?

   ○ **A.** Use AWS Systems Manager Automation to create a snapshot of the environment.

   ○ **B.** Use AWS Config to create a snapshot of the environment.

   ○ **C.** Use the AWS CLI and issue a **list-instances** command. Repeat for all regions.

   ○ **D.** Use the AWS SDK to write code to perform the list-instances API call. Create a Lambda function and invoke it. Repeat for all regions.

Cram Quiz Answers

1. Answer: A is correct. AWS Config with the built-in s3-bucket-public-read-prohibited rule allows for automatic remediation of S3 buckets that have a publicly accessible ACL or policy attached.

2. Answer: B is correct. An AWS Config snapshot is the simplest way to capture the number, type, and AMI being used by your EC2 instances across all regions.

What Next?

If you want more practice on this chapter's exam objectives before you move on, remember that you can access all of the Cram Quiz questions on the Pearson Test Prep software online. You can also create a custom exam by objective with the Online Practice Test. Note any objective you struggle with and go to that objective's material in this chapter.

CHAPTER 4

Implementing Scalability and Elasticity

This chapter covers the following official AWS Certified SysOps Administrator - Associate (SOA-C02) exam domains:

▶ Domain 2: Reliability and Business Continuity

▶ Domain 3: Deployment, Provisioning, and Automation

▶ Domain 5: Networking and Content Delivery

(For more information on the official AWS Certified SysOps Administrator - Associate [SOA-C02] exam topics, see the Introduction.)

Ensuring your application's infrastructure is scalable and elastic delivers a double benefit for the application. First, by adding more resources dynamically when required, you can adapt to any amount of traffic to ensure you do not leave any request unanswered. Second, by removing resources, you ensure the application is cost-effective when little or no requests are being received. However, designing a scalable/elastic application is not always an easy task.

In this chapter, we examine scaling, request offloading, and loose coupling as strategies that can enable an application to meet demand while maintaining cost-effectiveness. Ensuring your application is scalable and elastic also builds a good underlying foundation to achieve high availability and resilience, which we discuss in Chapter 5, "High Availability and Resilience."

Scaling in the Cloud

This section covers the following official AWS Certified SysOps Administrator - Associate (SOA-C02) exam domains:

▶ Domain 2: Reliability and Business Continuity

▶ Domain 3: Deployment, Provisioning, and Automation

CramSaver

If you can correctly answer these questions before going through this section, save time by skimming the Exam Alerts in this section and then completing the Cram Quiz at the end of the section.

1. You are operating a forum application that consists of three layers: a web front end on EC2, an application on EC2, and a database layer RDS. The web front end delivers the static forum content and formatting, the application layer stores the session information for each user, and the database layer stores all the user preferences. Assess the scalability of this deployment, identify any issues, and propose a solution.

2. You have been tasked with troubleshooting an image-processing platform. The application resides on a single-layer ECS container deployment that accepts requests for image processing from an incoming S3 bucket and deposits the processed image in an output S3 bucket. Lately, a spike in usage has caused the ECS application to reach its maximum scale. Users using the paid platform have reported that bulk image uploads complete successfully to S3, but some images are never processed. As a result, users are left searching for unprocessed images and need to resubmit them for processing. How could you ensure that the application works as intended?

3. Your developers have updated the forum application as per your previous comments. Your application is now growing, and you have been tasked with ensuring the application maintains scalability to millions of users. To assess the scalability, you have been given more information on the deployment. The web front end uses Apache2 HTTPS servers on Ubuntu Linux on EC2. The application layer runs custom Python code on EC2 that connects to a DynamoDB table to store session data. The database layer is deployed on a Multi-AZ RDS MySQL cluster with two instances (primary and secondary). Assess the scalability of this deployment and identify any potential bottlenecks.

4. After you optimize the application, your clients report highly improved performance. After receiving the latest AWS bill, the CFO has questions about additional cost of the application. While examining the cost report, you find that the application layer seems to still be deployed with a static number of servers like it was before the session state was offloaded. How can you further optimize the application to reduce the cost?

Answers

1. Answer: Both the web and database layers are scalable. The application layer is limited in elasticity due to the persistence of the session data on the EC2 instances. Session data should be moved off the EC2 instances.

2. Answer: The bulk image uploads seem to exceed the capacity of the ECS cluster. The application needs to be redesigned with a buffer for the image-processing requests. Implementing a message queue service could offload the requests so that the back end can process them in a more predictable manner.

3. Answer: The only issue to identify is with the database layer. A Multi-AZ RDS deployment is only vertically scalable with an upper limit of the maximum size of the RDS instance. The maximum size of the instance could potentially bottleneck the whole forum application.

4. Answer: Find a good metric on which to scale the application layer and implement AWS Autoscaling. The application should shut down some of the instances when usage is low and power them on when traffic increases.

For any application to be made elastic and scalable, you need to consider the sum of the configurations of its components. Any weakness in any layer or service that the application depends on can cause the application scalability and elasticity to be reduced. Any reduction in scalability and elasticity can potentially introduce weaknesses in the high availability and resilience of your application. At the end of the day, any poorly scalable, rigid application with no guarantee of availability can have a tangible impact on the bottom line of any business.

The following factors need to be taken into account when designing a scalable and elastic application:

▶ **Compute layer:** The compute layer receives a request and responds to it. To make an application scalable and elastic, you need to consider how to scale the compute layer. Can you scale on a metric-defined amount of CPU, memory, and number of connections, or do you need to consider scaling at the smallest scale—per request? Also consider the best practice for keeping the compute layer disposable. There should never be any persistent data within the compute layer.

▶ **Persistent layer:** Where is the data being generated by the application stored? Is the storage layer decoupled from the instances? Is the same (synchronous) data available to all instances, or do you need to account for asynchronous platforms and eventual consistency? You should always ensure that the persistent layer is designed to be scalable and elastic and take into account any issues potentially caused by the replication configuration.

▶ **Decoupled components:** Are you scaling the whole application as one, or is each component or layer of the application able to scale independently? You need to always ensure each layer or section of the application can scale separately to achieve maximum operational excellence and lowest cost.

▶ **Asynchronous requests:** Does the compute platform need to process every request as soon as possible within the same session, or can you schedule the request to process it at a later time? When requests are allowed to process for a longer amount of time (many seconds, perhaps even minutes or hours), you should always decouple the application with a queue service to handle any requests asynchronously—meaning at a later time. Using a queue can enable you to buffer the requests, ensuring you receive all the requests on the incoming portion of the application and handle the processing with predictable performance on the back end. A well-designed, asynchronously decoupled application should almost never respond with a 500-type HTTP (service issue) error.

Assessing your application from these points of view should give you a rough idea of the scalability and elasticity of the platform. When you have a good idea of the scalability/elasticity, also consider any specific metrics within the defined service-layer agreement (SLA) of the application. After both are defined, assess whether the application will meet the SLA in its current configuration. Make a note if you need to take action to improve the scalability/elasticity and continuously reassess because both the application requirements and defined SLA of the application are likely to change over time.

After the application has been designed to meet the defined SLA of the application, you can make use of the cloud metrics provided in the platform at no additional cost to implement automated scaling and meet the demand in several different ways. We discuss how to implement automation in the AWS Autoscaling later in this section.

ExamAlert

Remember, one of the crucial factors that enables scalability and elasticity is ensuring your resources are disposable. That means any data is always written outside the processing layer. All databases, files, logs, and any kind of output the application generates should always be decoupled from the processing layer. In the exam, different services might be part of the proposed solution. When analyzing the proposed answer, always ensure the data being output by the application doesn't stay on the EC2 instance for a longer time and that the solution has the lowest cost. For example, one answer could propose that logs be sent to CloudWatch logs via the CloudWatch agent, whereas another answer might propose logs be written to S3 every hour. Although the second solution will probably be more cost-effective, you should consider the first solution if the defined SLA of the application requires that all logs need to be captured.

Horizontal vs. Vertical Scaling

The general consensus is that there are only two ways (with minor variance, depending on the service or platform) to scale a service or an application:

▶ Vertically, by adding more power (more CPU, memory, disk space, network bandwidth) to an application instance

▶ Horizontally, by adding more instances to an application layer, thus increasing the power by a factor of the size of the instance added

A great benefit to vertical scaling is that it can be deployed in any circumstance, even without any application support. Because you are maintaining one unit and increasing its size, you can vertically scale to the maximum size of the unit in question. The maximum scaling size of an instance is defined by the maximum size that the service supports. For example, at the time of writing, the maximum instance size supported on EC2 (u-24tb1.metal) offers 448 CPU cores and 24 TB (that's 24,576 GB!) of memory, while the smallest still-supported size (t2.nano) has only 1 CPU core and 0.5 GB of memory. Additionally, there are plenty of instance types and sizes to choose from, which means that you can horizontally scale an application the exact size you need at a certain moment in time. This same fact applies to other instance-based services such as EMR, RDS, and DocumentDB. Figure 4.1 illustrates vertical scaling of instances.

Vertical Scaling

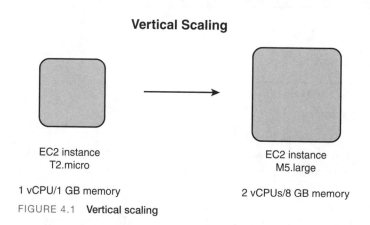

EC2 instance
T2.micro

EC2 instance
M5.large

1 vCPU/1 GB memory

2 vCPUs/8 GB memory

FIGURE 4.1 **Vertical scaling**

However, when thinking about scalability, you have to consider the drawbacks of vertical scaling. We mentioned maximum size, but one other major drawback is what makes horizontal scaling impractical—a single instance. Because all of AWS essentially operates on EC2 as the underlying design, you can take EC2 as a great example of why a single instance is not the way to go. Each instance you deploy is deployed on a hypervisor in a rack in a datacenter, and this datacenter can only ever be part of one availability zone. In Chapter 1, "Introduction to AWS," we defined an availability zone as a fault isolation environment—meaning any failure, whether it is due to a power or network outage or even an earthquake or flood, is always isolated to one availability zone. Although a single instance is vertically scalable, it is by no means highly available, nor does the vertical scaling make the application very elastic, because every time you scale to a different instance type, you need to reboot the instance.

This is where horizontal scaling steps in. With horizontal scaling, you add more instances (scale-out) when traffic to your application increases and remove instances (scale-in) when traffic to your application is reduced. You still need to select the appropriate scaling step, which is, of course, defined by the instance size. When selecting the size of the instances in a scaling environment, always ensure that they can do the job and don't waste resources. Figure 4.2 illustrates horizontal scaling.

Auto Scaling group

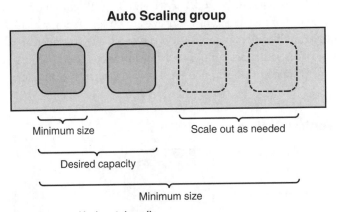

FIGURE 4.2 **Horizontal scaling**

In the ideal case, the application is stateless, meaning it does not store any data in the compute layer. In this case, you can easily scale the number of instances instead of scaling one instance up or down. The major benefit is that you can scale across multiple availability zones, thus inherently achieving high availability as well as elasticity. This is why the best practice on AWS is to create stateless, disposable instances and decouple the processing from the data and the layers of the application from each other. However, a potential drawback of horizontal scaling is when the application does not support it. The reality is that you will sooner or later come upon a case where you need to support an "enterprise" application, being migrated from some virtualized infrastructure, that simply does not support adding multiple instances to the mix. In this case you can still use the services within AWS to make the application highly available and recover it automatically in case of a failure. For such instances you can now utilize the AWS EC2 Auto Recovery service, for the instance types that support it, which automatically re-creates the instance in case of an underlying system impairment or failure.

Another potential issue that can prevent horizontal scalability is the requirement to store some data in a stateful manner. Thus far, we have said that you need to decouple the state of the application from the compute layer and store it in a back-end service—for example, a database or in-memory service. However, the scalability is ultimately limited by your ability to scale those back-end services that store the data. In the case of the Relational Database Service (RDS), you are always limited to one primary instance that handles all writes because both the data and metadata within a traditional database need to be consistent at all times. You can scale the primary instance vertically; however, there is a maximum limit the database service will support, as Figure 4.3 illustrates.

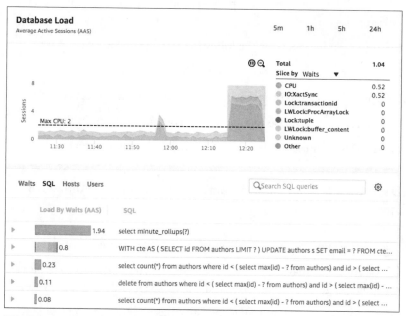

FIGURE 4.3   Database bottlenecking the application

You can also create a Multi-AZ deployment, which creates a secondary, synchronous replica of the primary database in another availability zone; however, Multi-AZ does not make the application more scalable because the replica is inaccessible to any SQL operations and is provided for the sole purpose of high availability. Another option is adding read replicas to the primary instance to offload read requests. We delve into more details on read replicas later in this chapter and discuss database high availability in Chapter 5.

> **ExamAlert**
>
> If the exam question is ambiguous about scalability or elasticity, you should still consider these as an important requirement of the application. Unless specific wording indicates cost as the primary or only driver, always choose the answer with the solution that will scale and is designed with elastic best practices in mind.

AWS Autoscaling

After you design all the instance layers to be scalable, you should take advantage of the AWS Autoscaling service to automate the scale-in and scale-out operations for your application layers based on performance metrics—for example, EC2 CPU usage, network capacities, and other metrics captured in the CloudWatch service.

The AutoScaling service can scale the following AWS services:

▶ **EC2:** Add or remove instances from an EC2 AutoScaling group.

▶ **EC2 Spot Fleets:** Add or remove instances from a Spot Fleet request.

▶ **ECS:** Increase or decrease the number of containers in an ECS service.

▶ **DynamoDB:** Increase or decrease the provisioned read and write capacity.

▶ **RDS Aurora:** Add or remove Aurora read replicas from an Aurora DB cluster.

To create an autoscaling configuration on EC2, you need the following:

▶ **EC2 Launch template:** Specifies the instance type, AMI, key pair, block device mapping, and other features the instance should be created with.

▶ **Scaling policy:** Defines a trigger that specifies a metric ceiling (for scaling out) and floor (for scaling in). Any breach of the floor or ceiling for a certain period of time triggers autoscaling.

▶ **EC2 AutoScaling group:** Defines scaling limits and the minimum, maximum, and desired numbers of instances. You need to provide a launch configuration and a scaling policy to apply during a scaling event.

Dynamic Scaling

Traditionally, scaling policies have been designed with dynamic scaling in mind. For example, a common setup would include

▶ An AutoScaling group with a minimum of 1 and a maximum of 10 instances

▶ A CPU % ceiling of 70 percent for scale-out

▶ A CPU % floor of 30 percent for scale-in

▶ A breach duration of 10 minutes

▶ A scaling definition of +/– 33 percent capacity on each scaling event

The application is now designed to operate at a particular scale between 30 and 70 percent aggregate CPU usage of the AutoScaling group. After the ceiling is breached for 10 minutes, the Autoscaling service adds a third more instances to the AutoScaling group. If you are running one instance, it adds another because it needs to meet 33 percent or more of the capacity. If you are running two instances, it also adds one more; however, at three instances, it needs to add two more instances to meet the rules set out in the scaling policy. When the application aggregate CPU usage falls below 30 percent for 10 minutes, the AutoScaling group is reduced by 33 percent, and the appropriate number of instances is removed each time the floor threshold is breached. Figure 4.4 illustrates dynamic scaling.

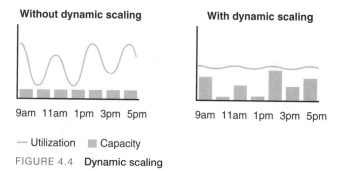

Without dynamic scaling

9am 11am 1pm 3pm 5pm

With dynamic scaling

9am 11am 1pm 3pm 5pm

— Utilization   ▣ Capacity

FIGURE 4.4   **Dynamic scaling**

Manual and Scheduled Scaling

The AutoScaling configuration also has a desired instance count. This feature enables you to scale manually and override the configuration as per the scaling policy. You can set the desired count to any size at any time and resize the

AutoScaling group accordingly. This capability is useful if you have knowledge of an upcoming event that will result in an increase of traffic to your site. You can prepare your environment to meet the demand in a much better way because you can increase the AutoScaling group preemptively in anticipation of the traffic.

You can also set up a schedule to scale if you have a very predictable application. Perhaps it is a service being used only from 9 a.m. to 5 p.m. each day. You simply set the scale-out to happen at 8 a.m. in anticipation of the application being used and then set a scale-in scheduled action at 6 p.m. after the application is not being used anymore. This way you can easily reduce the cost of operating intermittently used applications by over 50 percent. Figure 4.5 illustrates scheduled scaling.

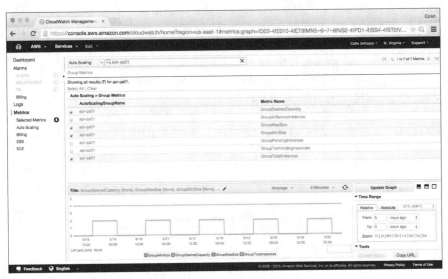

FIGURE 4.5 Scheduled scaling

Predictive Scaling

Another AutoScaling feature is predictive scaling, which uses machine learning to learn the scaling pattern of your application based on the minimum amount of historical data. The machine learning component then predicts the scaling after reviewing CW data from the previous 14 days to account for daily and weekly spikes as it learns the patterns on a longer time scale. Figure 4.6 illustrates predictive scaling.

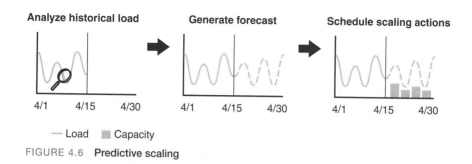

FIGURE 4.6   Predictive scaling

Cram Quiz

Answer these questions. The answers follow the last question. If you cannot answer these questions correctly, consider reading this section again until you can.

1. Which of the following are not characteristics of a scalable/elastic application?

   O **A.** Synchronous request handling in the compute layer

   O **B.** Session persistence in an external database

   O **C.** Session persistence in the compute layer

   O **D.** Asynchronous request offloading to a message queue

2. Which of the following are required to enable the application to scale automatically with AWS AutoScaling? (Choose three.)

   O **A.** EC2 Launch Configuration

   O **B.** Scaling Policy

   O **C.** EC2 User Data

   O **D.** DynamoDB

   O **E.** CloudWatch Alarm

   O **F.** AutoScaling Group

3. True or False: After you assess that your application is fully scalable and elastic, you only need to maintain the application as is in the cloud.

4. True or False: AutoScaling supports only dynamic, scheduled, and predictive scaling.

Cram Quiz Answers

1. Answer: C is correct. The compute layer should be made stateless. Any persistence in the compute layer hinders scalability and elasticity and potentially causes disruption in the application operation. If an instance in a cluster is lost, all the sessions on the instances are lost with it, meaning all the users connected to that particular instance have to log in and start working with the application from scratch.

2. Answer: A, B, and F are correct. To create an autoscaling configuration on EC2, you need an EC2 Launch Configuration that defines how to configure the EC2 instances that are launched; a scaling policy that determines the scaling thresholds; and an autoscaling group that determines the minimum, maximum, and desired numbers of instances.

3. Answer: False. The application should periodically be reassessed for scalability and elasticity because both the application requirements and the SLA might have changed.

4. Answer: False. Autoscaling also supports manual scaling by setting the desired number of instances in the autoscaling group.

Caching

This section covers the following official AWS Certified SysOps Administrator - Associate (SOA-C02) exam domains:

▶ Domain 2: Reliability and Business Continuity

▶ Domain 5: Networking and Content Delivery

CramSaver

If you can correctly answer these questions before going through this section, save time by skimming the Exam Alerts in this section and then completing the Cram Quiz at the end of the section.

1. You have implemented autoscaling on both the web and app tier of your three-tier application, but in times of high read requests, the application seems to be performing slowly or even times out. What could you do to make the application more responsive?

2. You have been tasked with deploying a reliable caching solution that can handle multiple different data types and deliver microsecond to millisecond response performance. Which AWS service would you recommend?

3. True or False: To deliver static content to the user in the fastest possible manner, use a web server with lots of memory and utilize server-side caching.

Answers

1. Answer: Implement the read cache to offload the database that seems to be bottlenecking the read requests.

2. Answer: ElastiCache Redis would support all the required features.

3. Answer: False. Static content should be delivered via a content delivery network (CDN). In AWS, you can use CloudFront to deliver static content through more than 200 geographically distributed locations across the globe.

Now that you have seen how to create an application that is highly scalable and elastic, you need to also consider the scaling impact on the persistent layer. As mentioned in the previous section, you need to consider the scalability of the persistent layer and include it in the overall assessment of the elasticity of the application. It serves no purpose to make an application highly elastic when the database back end is rigid and introduces a bottleneck for the whole application.

This is where caching comes in as a good way to ensure the data in the application is accessible in the fastest manner possible. When delivering an application from the cloud, you can use several different caching strategies to deliver and reuse frequently used data and offload the need to request the same data over and over again.

A simple analogy to caching is your refrigerator. It takes a minute for you to walk to the fridge (the cache) and grab some milk (cache hit). However, when there is no milk (cache miss) in the fridge, you need to go to the store (the origin), grab a few cartons, and take them home to put them in the fridge. The journey to the store and back is many times longer, so it makes sense to buy items that you frequently use and put them in the fridge. The fridge does have a limited capacity, just like cache usually does, and you will typically find a much greater variety of items at the store.

Types of Caching

There are several different types of caching that you can use in your application.

Client-Side Caching

When a client requests the contents of the application from a server, you should ensure that components that are static or change infrequently are reused with client-side caching. Modern browsers have this capability built in, and you can use it by specifying cache control headers within your web server or the service that delivers the content, such as S3.

Edge Caching

When content is delivered frequently to multiple users, you can employ edge caching or what is more commonly referred to as a content delivery network. In AWS, you can use the Amazon CloudFront service to deliver frequently used content in a highly efficient manner to millions of users around the globe while at the same time offloading multiple same requests off the application or back end.

Server-Side Caching

When a feature, a module, or certain content stored within the web service is requested frequently, you typically use server-side caching to reduce the need for the server to look for the feature on disk. The first time the feature is requested and the response assembled, the server caches the response in memory so it can be delivered with much lower latency than if it were read from disk and reassembled each time. There is a limitation to the amount of memory the server has, and of course, server-side caching is traditionally limited to each instance. However, in AWS, you can use the ElastiCache service to provide a shared, network-attached, in-memory datastore that can fulfill the needs of caching any kind of content you would usually cache in memory.

Database Caching

The last layer of caching is database caching. This approach lets you cache database contents or database responses into a caching service. There are two approaches to database caching:

▶ **In-line caching:** This approach utilizes a service that manages the reads and writes to and from the database.

▶ **Side-loaded caching:** This approach is performed by an application that is aware of the cache and database as two distinct entities. All reads and writes to and from the cache and the database are managed within the application because both the cache and database are two distinct entities.

An example of an in-line caching solution is the DynamoDB Accelerator (DAX) service. With DAX, you can simply address all reads and writes to the DAX cluster, which is connected to the DynamoDB table in the back end. DAX automatically forwards any writes to DynamoDB, and all reads deliver the data straight from the cache in case of a cache hit or forward the read request to the DynamoDB back end transparently. Any responses and items received from DynamoDB are thus cached in the response or item cache. In this case the application is not required to be aware of the cache because all in-line cache operations are identical to the operations performed against the table itself. Figure 4.7 illustrates DAX in-line caching.

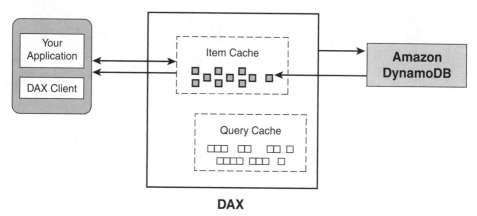

DAX

FIGURE 4.7   **DAX in-line caching**

An example of a sideloaded caching solution is ElastiCache. First, you set up the caching cluster with ElastiCache and a database. The database can be DynamoDB, RDS, or any other database because ElastiCache is not a purpose-built solution like DAX. Second, you have to configure the application to look for any content in the cache first. If the cache contains the content, you get a cache hit, and the content is returned to the application with very low latency. If you get a cache miss because the content is not present in the cache, the application needs to look for the content in the database, read it, and also perform a write to the cache so that any subsequent reads are all cache hits.

There are two traditional approaches to implement sideloaded caching:

▶ **Lazy loading:** Data is always written only to the database. When data is requested, it is read from the database and cached. Every subsequent read of the data is read from the cache until the item expires. This is a lean approach, ensuring only frequently read data is in the cache. However, every first read inherently suffers from a cache miss. You can also warm up the cache by issuing the reads you expect to be frequent. Figure 4.8 illustrates lazy loading.

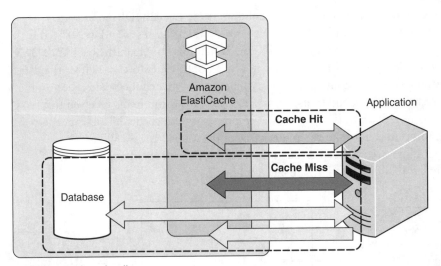

FIGURE 4.8 **Lazy loading**

▶ **Write through:** Data is always written to both the database and the cache. This avoids cache misses; however, this approach is highly intensive on the cache. Figure 4.9 illustrates write-through caching.

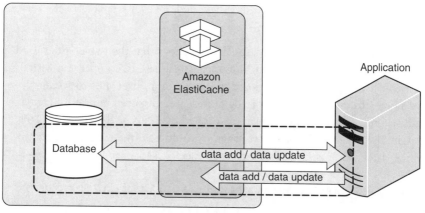

FIGURE 4.9 **Write-through caching**

Because the application controls the caching, you can implement some items to be lazy loaded but others to be written through. The approaches are in no way mutually exclusive, and you can write the application to perform caching based on the types of data being stored in the database and how frequently those items are expected to be requested.

> **ExamAlert**
>
> When choosing a caching strategy, always consider the rate of data change and choose the correct time-to-live (TTL) of the data in the cache, to match the rate of change of the data. Data on an e-commerce site such as item descriptions, reviews, and images are unlikely to change frequently, but data such as item stock and price might not be suitable for caching at all. Always keep this in mind when selecting an answer on the exam.

ElastiCache

ElastiCache is a managed service that can deploy clusters of in-memory data stores. They can be used to perform server-side and database caching.

A typical use case is database offloading with an application-managed side-loaded cache, as described in the previous section. Most applications that work with a database have a high read-to-write ratio—somewhere in the range of 80–90 percent reads to 10–20 percent writes. This means that offloading the reads from the database could save as much as 60–80 percent of the load on the database. For example, if the read-to-write ratio is 90–10 percent, each write (10 percent resources) requires a subsequent read (at least 10 percent resources), and if the rest of the reads are cached, up to 80 percent of the read load can be offloaded to the cache.

An additional benefit of caching with ElastiCache is that the two engines used, Memcached and Redis, are both in-memory datastores. In comparison with databases where response latencies are measured in milliseconds to seconds, the response times from in-memory databases are measured in microseconds to milliseconds. That can mean that any cached data can be delivered 10, 100, or potentially even 1000 times faster than it would be if the request were read from the database. Figure 4.10 contrasts latency of Redis versus S3.

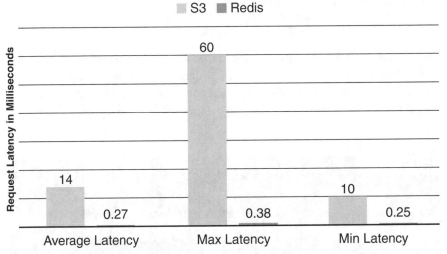

FIGURE 4.10 **Redis vs. S3 GET latencies**

Memcached

One of the engines supported by ElastiCache is Memcached, a high-performance, distributed, in-memory key-value store. The service has a simple operational principle in which one key can have one or many nested values. All the data is served out of memory; thus, there is no indexing or data organization in the platform. When using Memcached, you can design either a single instance cache or a multi-instance cache where data is distributed into partitions. These partitions can be discovered by addressing the service and requesting a partition map. There is no resilience or high availability within the cluster because there is no replication of partitions.

Memcached is a great solution for offloading frequent identical database responses. Another use for Memcached is as a shared session store for multiple web instances. However, the lack of resilience within the Memcached design means that any failure of a node requires the application to rebuild the node from persistent database data or for the sessions with the users to be re-established. The benefit of Memcached is that it is linearly read and write scalable because all you need to do is add nodes to the cluster and remap the partitions.

Redis

The other engine supported by ElastiCache is Redis, a fully-fledged in-memory database. Redis supports much more complex datasets such as tables, lists, hashes, and geospatial data. Redis also has a built-in push messaging feature that can be used for high-performance messaging between services and chat. Redis also has three operational modes that give you advanced resilience, scalability, and elasticity:

▶ **Single node:** A single Redis node, not replicated, nonscalable, and nonresilient. It can be deployed only in a single availability zone; however, it does support backup and restore.

▶ **Multinode, cluster mode disabled:** A primary read-write instance with up to five read replicas. The read replicas are near synchronous and offer resilience and read offloading for scalability. Multinode clusters with cluster mode disabled can also be deployed in one or more availability zones.

▶ **Multinode, cluster mode enabled:** One or more shards of multinode deployments, each with one primary and up to five read replicas. By enabling cluster mode, you retain the resilience and scalability but also add elasticity because you can always reshard the cluster and horizontally add more write capacity. Cluster mode always requires the database nodes to be deployed across multiple availability zones. However, sharding means that multiple primary nodes are responsible for multiple sets of data. Just like with database sharding, this increases write performance in ideal circumstances, but it is not always guaranteed and can add additional complexity to an already-complex solution. Figure 4.11 illustrates Redis multinode cluster mode, both disabled and enabled.

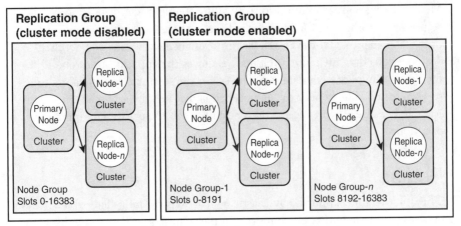

FIGURE 4.11   Redis multinode, cluster mode disabled vs. enabled

The features of Redis give you much more than just a caching service. Many businesses out there use ElastiCache Redis as a fully functional in-memory database because the solution is highly resilient, scalable, elastic, and can even be backed up and restored, just like a traditional database.

> **ExamAlert**
>
> If an exam question indicates the database is overloaded with reads, caching should be the main strategy to enable scalability of reads. The benefit of caching is that the data in the cache, when configured correctly, is highly likely to be current and synchronous with the database. However, always be careful when scaling the caching cluster because too many caching instances can add additional unnecessary cost to the application.

Amazon CloudFront

Now that the database and server-side caching are sorted, you need to focus on edge caching. CloudFront is a global content delivery network that can offload static content from the data origin and deliver any cached content from a location that is geographically much closer to the user. This reduces the response latency and makes the application feel as if it were deployed locally, no matter which region or which physical location on the globe the origin resides in.

CloudFront also can terminate all types of HTTP and HTTPS connections at the edge, thus offloading the load to servers or services. CloudFront also works in combination with the Amazon Certificate Manager (ACM) service, which can issue free HTTPS certificates for your domain that are also automatically renewed and replaced each year.

CloudFront enables you to configure it to accept and terminate the following groups of HTTP methods:

▶ **GET and HEAD:** Enables standard caching for documents and headers. Useful for static websites.

▶ **GET, HEAD, and OPTIONS:** Enables you to cache OPTIONS responses from an origin server.

▶ **GET, HEAD, OPTIONS, PUT, PATCH, POST, and DELETE:** Terminates all HTTP(S) sessions at the CloudFront Edge Location and can increase the performance of both the read and write requests.

One of the better features is the ability to rewrite the caching settings for both the cache held within the CloudFront CDN as well as the client-side caching headers defined within servers. This means that you can customize the time-to-live of both the edge and client-side cache. CloudFront distributions can be configured with the following options for setting TTL:

▶ **Min TTL:** Required setting when all HTTP headers are forwarded from the origin server. It defines the minimum cache TTL and also determines the shortest interval for CloudFront to refresh the data from the origin.

▶ **Max TTL:** Optional setting. It defines the longest possible cache TTL. It is used to override any cache-control headers defined at the origin server.

▶ **Default TTL:** Optional setting. It allows you to define cache behavior for any content where no TTL is defined at the origin server.

CloudFront Security

CloudFront is also inherently secure against distributed denial-of-service (DDoS) attacks because the content is distributed to more than 200 locations around the globe. An attacker would need to have a massive, globally distributed botnet to be able to attack your application. On top of the benefit of the distributed architecture, CloudFront is also resilient to L3 and L4 DDoS attacks with the use of AWS Shield Standard service. Any CloudFront distribution can also be upgraded to Shield Advanced, a subscription-based service that provides a detailed overview of the state of any DDoS attacks as well as a dedicated 24/7 response team, which can help with custom DDoS mitigation at any OSI layer.

CloudFront also supports integration with the AWS Web Application Firewall (WAF) service that can filter any attempts at web address manipulations, SQL injections, CSS attacks, and common web server vulnerabilities as well as filter traffic based on IP, geography patterns, regular expressions, and methods.

CloudFront also enables you to limit access to content by

▶ Restricting access to your application content with signed URLs or cookies

▶ Restricting access to content based on geolocation

▶ Restricting access to S3 buckets using Origin Access Identity (OAI)

Cram Quiz

Answer these questions. The answers follow the last question. If you cannot answer these questions correctly, consider reading this section again until you can.

1. Which AWS service enables you to easily deploy a horizontally scalable in-memory caching cluster?

   ○ **A.** ElastiCache Memcached

   ○ **B.** ElastiCache Redis, Cluster mode enabled

   ○ **C.** ElastiCache Redis, Cluster mode disabled

   ○ **D.** CloudFront

2. You have configured a CloudFront distribution to cache static content from an Apache2 web server. The content on the web server is refreshed every 15 minutes when the application is updated. However, the users are complaining that they seem to see updates only every 2 hours or so. What is most likely the problem, and how would you resolve this issue?

   ○ **A.** CloudFront TTL is too long. Set the Min TTL to 15 minutes. This will ensure the content is refreshed every 15 minutes.

   ○ **B.** Origin TTL is too long. Set the Max TTL to 15 minutes. This will ensure the content is refreshed every 15 minutes.

   ○ **C.** Origin TTL does not exist. Set the Default TTL to 15 minutes. This will ensure the content is refreshed every 15 minutes.

   ○ **D.** CloudFront TTL does not exist. Set the TTL to enabled and Default TTL to 15 minutes. This will ensure the content is refreshed every 15 minutes.

Cram Quiz Answers

1. Answer: B is correct. ElastiCache Memcached is a high-performance, distributed, in-memory key-value store that can scale horizontally.

2. Answer: B is correct. Max TTL defines the longest possible cache TTL and is used to override any cache-control headers defined at the origin server that are likely to be misconfigured.

Read Replicas

This section covers the following official AWS Certified SysOps Administrator - Associate (SOA-C02) exam domain:

▶ Domain 2: Reliability and Business Continuity

CramSaver

If you can correctly answer these questions before going through this section, save time by skimming the Exam Alerts in this section and then completing the Cram Quiz at the end of the section.

1. Your three-tier application has been connected to a business intelligence (BI) forecasting platform. While the forecasts are improving business practices, the users of your application are reporting the performance has decreased. The web and app tier are scaling appropriately, and the caching cluster is at about 40 percent capacity. What could be the cause of the slowdown seen by the users, and how could you resolve it?

2. True or False: Aurora natively supports both MySQL and PostgreSQL.

Answers

1. Answer: The BI platform has introduced additional load on the database. Because the BI forecasting requires access to most or all of the dataset, the cache cannot be used to offload the required reads. To mitigate, implement a database read replica.

2. Answer: True. The two engines are fully supported at the time of writing. Other database engines might be supported in the future.

There are five general approaches to scaling database performance:

▶ **Vertical scaling:** You can add more CPU and RAM to the primary instance.

▶ **Horizontal scaling:** You can add more instances to a database cluster to increase the available CPU and RAM, but this approach is not always supported.

▶ **Sharding:** When horizontal scaling is not supported, you can distribute the dataset across multiple primary database engines, thus achieving higher write performance.

▶ **Caching:** You can add a caching cluster to offload reads, which can be expensive.

▶ **Read replicas:** You can add read replicas to offload read traffic, possibly asynchronous.

Read replicas can potentially offer the same benefit of read offloading that caching can have for your application. One big benefit of read replicas is that the whole database is replicated to the read replica, not just frequently read items. This means that read replicas can be used where the reads are frequently distributed across the majority of the data in the database. As you can imagine, this would be very expensive and resource intensive to achieve in the cache. You would need to provision enough in-memory capacity (potentially terabytes), read the entire database, and write the data into the cache before you could perform any complex operation on the data in the cache. Sometimes complex operations can't even be performed on the caching server; for example, joins of multiple tables for analytics, business intelligence, or data mining purposes are just not possible within the cache.

This is where read replicas excel. You can introduce read replicas in most instance-based AWS database services, including RDS, Aurora, DocumentDB, and Neptune.

In the RDS service, up to five read replicas can be deployed in any MySQL, MariaDB, PostgreSQL, or Oracle database. Because the data resides on the volume attached to the instance, built-in database replication tools are used to replicate the data across the network to the read replica. This means that read replicas introduce additional load on the primary instance and that the replication is always asynchronous with a potential lag of a few seconds to potentially a few minutes in extreme cases. Figure 4.12 illustrates RDS read replicas.

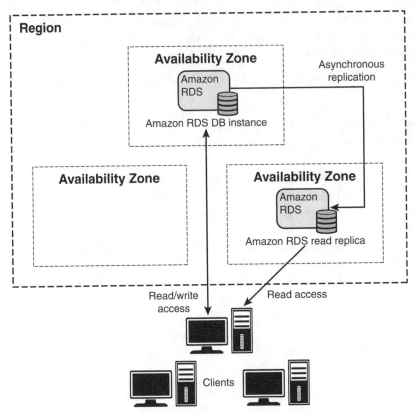

FIGURE 4.12   **RDS read replicas**

The replica can be placed in any availability zone in the same region as the primary database or can be deployed in a cross-region deployment. A read replica can also be promoted to a primary instance, which means that establishing a read replica can be an easy way to clone a database. After the replica is promoted to primary only, a sync of all the missing data is required.

> **ExamAlert**
>
> Traditional RDS database read replicas are a very cost-efficient way to provide data for small (terabyte)-scale analytics and should be selected as a preferred option when the entire dataset needs to be read offloaded. Always evaluate whether the question requires you to offload a certain portion of the data (with caching) or the entire dataset is required (with read replicas).

Other AWS database services employ a decoupled compute–datastore approach. For example, the AWS Aurora service stores all the data on a cluster volume that is replicated to six copies across (at least) three availability zones. The primary instance has read and write access. All writes are sent as changelogs directly to the six nodes of the storage volume, and the commit to the database page is done at the storage cluster. This means that the replication is near synchronous with potentially no more than a few milliseconds of replication lag due to the network distance between the cluster volume nodes in other availability zones and several hundred milliseconds if the replication is done across regions. Additionally, Aurora supports up to 15 read replicas per region and can be deployed to multiple regions with an additional 16 read replicas in other regions. All of the read replicas read from the same cluster volume, meaning they can deliver near synchronous data for each read request. The read replicas can also be seamlessly scaled because there is no requirement to replicate the data on to the replica. When a replica is started, it is simply connected to the cluster volume. This allows the cluster to avoid initial replication lags that you would see in traditional databases. This feature can be used both for elasticity and vertical as well as horizontal scaling of the cluster. Figure 4.13 illustrates an Aurora cluster design.

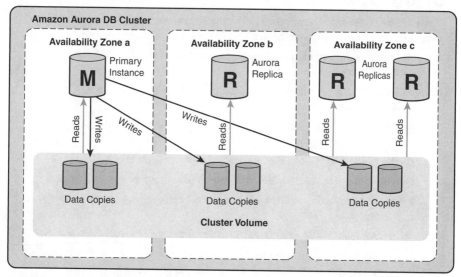

FIGURE 4.13   Aurora cluster design

A similar approach to decoupling the storage volume and the database nodes is used in DocumentDB, Neptune, and so on.

On top of this capability, Aurora can forward some read-heavy analytical operations to the cluster volume nodes and offload the primary from having to perform the reads for any JOIN, GROUP BY, UNION, and such operations across approximately a million or more rows. This capability extends the lightweight analytics capabilities of RDS read replicas to deliver much more power to your analytics queries.

Aurora natively supports MySQL and PostgreSQL databases and is slightly more expensive than RDS MySQL and RDS PostgreSQL.

ExamAlert

When an exam question indicates that high performance at high scale is required for MySQL or PostgreSQL, always evaluate whether the answer includes Aurora as an option. We recommend you select RDS MySQL or RDS PostgreSQL only if any cost considerations are explicitly stated in the question. Also, consider reducing the number of read replicas by powering them off or terminating them if they are not in use.

Cram Quiz

Answer these questions. The answers follow the last question. If you cannot answer these questions correctly, consider reading this section again until you can.

1. You have been instructed to eliminate any inefficiencies in the following deployment:

   Web tier: EC2 autoscaling group scaling on CPU usage, 30% floor, 70% ceiling, minimum 1, maximum 10.

   App tier: EC2 autoscaling group scaling on CPU usage, 20% floor, 80% ceiling, minimum 1, maximum 6.

   Cache tier: 1 ElastiCache Memcached cluster with 2 partitions

   Database tier: Multi-AZ MySQL RDS with 3 read replicas

   Which of the following would allow you to cost optimize the cluster? (Choose all that apply.)

   - ○ **A.** Evaluate whether all RDS read replicas are required.
   - ○ **B.** Evaluate the maximum on the App and Web EC2 autoscaling groups.
   - ○ **C.** Evaluate the partition configuration of the ElastiCache cluster.
   - ○ **D.** Evaluate the network performance if the app tier matches the network performance of the database tier.

2. You have been asked to propose a solution to scale the read portion of an application database back end in the most cost-effective manner possible. Your application runs Linux LAMP stack with a 30 GB MySQL RDS Multi-AZ back end. The read-heavy operations are very predictable and occur during a particularly heavy four-hour operation each week and require the whole dataset. Which option would you recommend?

○ **A.** Replace the RDS MySQL with Aurora MySQL and let Aurora add read replicas automatically as needed.

○ **B.** Point the read-heavy operation at the RDS Multi-AZ replica in the other availability zone.

○ **C.** Deploy a read replica in RDS. Point the application at the RDS read replica. Terminate the read replica after the read-heavy operation is complete. Repeat the process with a script next week.

○ **D.** Deploy a read replica in RDS. Point the application at the RDS read replica. Create a script that powers off the read replica after the read-heavy operation is complete and powers it on before the next operation with enough time to synchronize the changes.

Cram Quiz Answers

1. Answer: A and C are correct. You should always evaluate whether the read replicas and caching clusters you deployed are required and properly scaled.

2. Answer: C is correct. Although A and D are possible solutions, deploying a read replica on a weekly basis would be the most cost-effective way to achieve this goal because the operation is sparse in nature and lasts for only four hours. Deploying a read replica is performed from a snapshot and can be just as fast or even faster than replicating a week's worth of data to the powered-off replica. Although the charges of powered-off instances are reduced, they are not zero. Remember also that you can stop a DB instance for up to seven days. If you don't manually start your DB instance after seven days, your DB instance is automatically started so that it doesn't fall behind any required maintenance updates. B is impossible because a Multi-AZ replica is not accessible for any SQL operations.

What Next?

If you want more practice on this chapter's exam objectives before you move on, remember that you can access all of the Cram Quiz questions on the Pearson Test Prep software online. You can also create a custom exam by objective with the Online Practice Test. Note any objective you struggle with and go to that objective's material in this chapter.

CHAPTER 5

High Availability and Resilience

This chapter covers the following official AWS Certified SysOps Administrator - Associate (SOA-C02) exam domains:

▶ Domain 2: Reliability and Business Continuity

▶ Domain 5: Networking and Content Delivery

(For more information on the official AWS Certified SysOps Administrator - Associate [SOA-C02] exam topics, see the Introduction.)

CramSaver

If you can correctly answer these questions before going through this section, save time by skimming the Exam Alerts in this section and then completing the Cram Quiz at the end of the section.

1. You operate a 99.9 percent HA application in an AWS region. You have received an SLA update for your application that has raised the three nine requirements to a four nine requirement. What would be the correct course of action in this scenario?

2. When is an application considered to be both highly available and resilient?

Answers

1. Answer: Establish another full replica of the application to increase the availability to four nines.

2. Answer: The application requires at least two complete replicas to be deployed. Each replica must be able to handle the failure of the other replica and accept 100 percent of the network traffic at all times.

An application can be made elastic and scalable if you can easily increase or decrease the capacity when required to meet the demand. However, high availability and resilience are not guaranteed even if an application is fully scalable and elastic. High availability and resilience depend on how you deploy and operate the application, and both of these factors need to be considered independently of scalability and elasticity.

High availability is defined as a factor of availability, and resilience is defined as the ability to maintain the application's availability in case of failures and errors in the application or the infrastructure. High availability is commonly referred to as "one nine"—meaning 90 percent; "two nines"—meaning 99 percent; "three nines" —meaning 99.9 percent; "four nines"—meaning 99.99 percent; and so on. Table 5.1 provides a breakdown of high availability definitions.

TABLE 5.1 **Uptime Percentage Chart**

Availability	Downtime Per Day	Downtime Per Month	Downtime Per Year
90%, "one nine"	2.4 Hours	72 Hours	36.5 Days
95%	1.2 Hours	36 Hours	18.25 Days
98%	28.8 Minutes	14.4 Hours	7.30 Days
99%, "two nines"	14.4 Minutes	7.20 Hours	3.65 Days
99.5%	7.2 Minutes	3.60 Hours	1.83 Days
99.9%, "three nines"	1.44 Minutes	43.8 Minutes	8.76 Hours
99.95%	43.2 Seconds	21.56 Minutes	4.38 Hours
99.99%, "four nines"	8.66 Seconds	4.38 Minutes	52.56 Minutes
99.999%, "five nines"	0.86 Seconds	25.9 Seconds	5.26 Minutes
99.9999%, "six nines"	0.086 Seconds	2.59 Seconds	31.5 Seconds

As you can see, the chart could extend to seven nines, eight nines, and so on; however, in reality it becomes impractical to measure downtime beyond five nines in a cloud-connected application because the application is usually connected over the Internet and the typical expected response times of the application might be measured in up to tens of milliseconds. In most cases, a five nines application is considered to essentially be available "all the time."

When defining a service-layer agreement (SLA), you need to typically define an uptime that your application will theoretically be able to deliver. But what is the projected uptime for a complex, multilayer application? The easiest way to define it is to take the weakest component with the lowest SLA and define the whole application according to that SLA. However, if your application is now below the threshold defined in the SLA, you need to establish another replica of the application and combine the uptimes of both to deliver the new uptime.

For example, an application has a 99.9 percent uptime. To increase the overall uptime, you need to spin up another replica of the application in a different availability zone (AZ) and divide the traffic among them. This second copy also has 99.9 percent uptime. The combined uptime is 100 percent minus a multiple of the failure rates.

In this example, the uptime would be defined as

$$\text{Uptime} = 100\% - (0.1\% \times 0.1\%) = 100\% - 0.01\% = 99.99\%$$

The combined uptime of two three-nines application replicas can deliver an uptime of four nines. However, this considers that both of the applications are capable of receiving the full 100 percent of the network traffic at any time and that any requests to both replicas can be handled and distributed without loss, meaning they are also designed with full resilience.

ExamAlert

▶ Not all scalable applications are inherently elastic—for example, an application that only supports vertical scaling.

▶ Not all elastic applications are inherently highly available—for example, a horizontally scalable application in one availability zone.

▶ Not all highly available applications are inherently resilient—for example, an application distributed across two availability zones with each location able to handle only 50 percent of the traffic.

Availability Zones in AWS

This chapter covers the following official AWS Certified SysOps Administrator - Associate (SOA-C02) exam domains:

▶ Domain 2: Reliability and Business Continuity

▶ Domain 5: Networking and Content Delivery

CramSaver

If you can correctly answer these questions before going through this section, save time by completing the Cram Quiz at the end of the section.

1. You are required to deploy an application with a highly available persistent datastore. In how many availability zones must you deploy your application storage system to achieve this at a minimum?

2. What distinguishes a private subnet from a public one?

Answers

1. Answer: You can use the EBS service to create a highly available persistent volume. The service maintains two replicas in one availability zone. Although you meet the high availability defined in the question, the application is not resilient to availability zone outages.

2. Answer: A public subnet has a route to an Internet gateway that allows inbound and outbound traffic to any instance in that subnet with a public or Elastic IP attached. There is no way to let incoming traffic into a private subnet, but outgoing requests can be forwarded via a NAT instance or gateway to the Internet.

Availability zones are fault isolation environments within AWS regions. We already discussed the basic design where one or more datacenters are grouped in two availability zones and that each region is typically designed to hold two or more availability zones. For more information, refer to the "AWS Global Architecture" section in Chapter 1, "Introduction to AWS."

When you choose to use managed services, AWS always manages the availability of the service and typically those are deployed across at least three availability zones for full resilience. Most of the time the service also has a defined uptime, and sometimes there is a definition for the durability of data within the service. For example, the S3 standard service has uptime defined as 99.99 percent (four nines) and durability defined as 99.999999999 percent (eleven nines), due to the fact that all objects on S3 standard are replicated to at least three devices in at least three availability zones within a region by default.

In the case of unmanaged services like EC2 and EBS and some managed services that require high network performance, such as Elastic Map Reduce (EMR) and Redshift, you need to handle the high availability and resilience by adopting the AWS design best practices. There are three ways of making the application highly available:

▶ **Single AZ high availability:** Maintaining two or more replicas in the same availability zone

▶ **Multi-AZ high availability:** Maintaining two or more replicas across two or more availability zones

▶ **Multiregion high availability:** Maintaining two or more replicas across two or more AWS regions

Single AZ high availability is built into some services like EBS. Because an EBS volume cannot exist in more than one availability zone at a time, the design ensures the volume is synchronously mirror-replicated on another device within the availability zone. This allows the EBS service to withstand failures of hardware within an availability zone.

However, due to a more widespread power or network issue, whole availability zones can go down, so it is up to you to replicate the data from one EBS volume to another availability zone. This can be done in two ways:

▶ Create another EBS volume in another AZ and use software replication.

▶ Create frequent snapshots of the EBS volume that are stored to S3.

The third option is cross-region replication, which allows the service to survive a regional outage and can also be used to mitigate any disaster situation. Cross-region replication does, however, carry additional cost due to the fact that data will transit the AWS backbone or the Internet to the other region. Transfer out charges always apply when performing cross-region replication.

VPC

Any applications where high availability needs to be deployed and maintained by the customer must be deployed in the AWS Virtual Private Cloud (VPC) service. The network service enables you to define both public and private network environments, with complete control over the routing and granular security of the network.

A VPC requires you to define a network address range and segment it into subnets. The network and subnets are defined with classless interdomain routing (CIDR) notation where each address is composed of

▶ **The network address:** The number of static bits at the beginning of the address, recorded with a notation slash-number at the end of the address. For example, 10.10.0.0/16 defines that the first 16 bits (10.10) are reserved for the network and do not change.

▶ **The host address:** The remaining bits not in use by the network. For example, 10.10.0.0/24 defines that only the last 8 remaining bits are dynamic and can have a value of .0 to .255.

The VPC network range is divided into one or more subnets. Each subnet defined resides in exactly one availability zone. Always choose to size the subnets appropriately to accommodate all possible instance IP addresses. This must include room for scaling and future expansion. The number of instance addresses is a factor of two on the power of available network bits minus five, which are required for the subnet basic functionality. The five addresses reserved by AWS for their use are

▶ The network address (for example, 10.10.0.0/24)

▶ The broadcast address (for example, 10.10.0.255)

▶ The router at the first usable host address (for example, 10.10.0.1)

▶ The IPAM service (DHCP/DNS) on the second usable address (for example, 10.10.0.2)

▶ An AWS reserved address on the third usable address (for example, 10.10.0.3)

The VPC and subnet ranges are restricted to sizes between /16 and /28. This means that the VPC has support for quite a wide range of network sizes. Let's calculate a few examples:

▶ **192.168.0.0/28:** 4 bits are available for addresses. According to the definition, the number of available addressees is $2^4 - 5$. That is 16 − 5, which means 11 addresses are available for hosts.

▶ **10.20.30.0/24:** 8 bits are available for addresses. According to the definition, the number of available addressees is $2^8 - 5$. That is 256 − 5, which means 251 addresses are available for hosts.

▶ **192.168.10.0/22:** 10 bits are available for addresses. According to the definition, the number of available addressees is $2^{10} - 5$. That is 1024 − 5, which means 1019 addresses are available for hosts.

▶ **172.16.0.0/17:** 15 bits are available for addresses. According to the definition, the number of available addressees is $2^{15} - 5$. That is $32,768 - 5$, which means $32,763$ addresses are available for hosts.

For high availability, ensure that you have created at least two subnets for each purpose or tier, with each subnet in its own availability zone. Two types of subnets can be defined within a VPC network:

▶ A private subnet

▶ A public subnet

Private Subnets

A private subnet within a VPC has no access to or from the Internet; however, it is by default accessible and can access all other private and public subnets in the VPC because the default routing in the VPC targets the entire VPC CIDR range. You can connect private subnets via VPN or Direct Connect connections to on-premises environments or other VPCs via VPC peering. You can also allow indirect access from the private network to the Internet via a NAT gateway or NAT instance or appliance that will allow instances in the private subnet to reach the Internet while remaining private and inaccessible from the Internet.

Public Subnets

Any private subnet can also be easily converted into a public subnet, by creating a route table entry to an Internet gateway (IGW) attached to the VPC where the subnet is created. The IGW automatically allows traffic to be sent to and from all instances running in the public subnet that have a public or Elastic IP attached.

Public IP addresses can be attached to the instance automatically at startup, but they are selected randomly from an AWS-owned pool of public addresses and are changed every time the instance is shut down or restarted. If you would like to assign a static public IP to an instance and have the public IP assigned to the instance or application persistently through reboots, you can also choose to assign and attach an Elastic IP address to an instance. Elastic IPs are persistent regardless of the state of the instance, and they can also be detached and reattached to any instance in your VPC. This capability can be very useful in case of a failure of a stateful application that needs to be accessed via IP. When a replacement of the failed instance is deployed, the same Elastic IP can be detached from the failing instance and reattached to the new instance, and the application can be recovered with minimal downtime.

Figure 5.1 demonstrates the differences in the routes of a public subnet, a private subnet, and a subnet connected to the VPN.

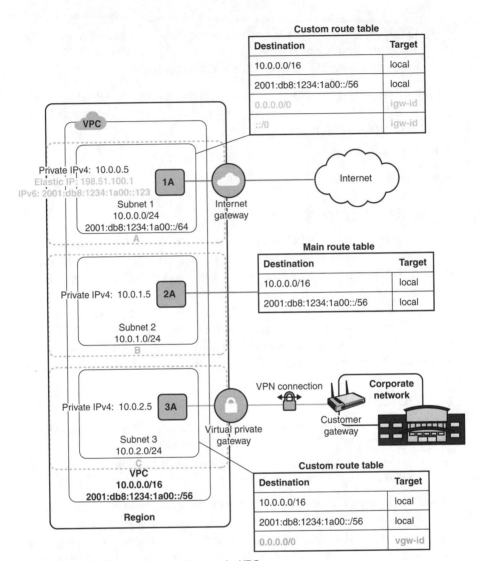

Custom route table

Destination	Target
10.0.0.0/16	local
2001:db8:1234:1a00::/56	local
0.0.0.0/0	igw-id
::/0	igw-id

Main route table

Destination	Target
10.0.0.0/16	local
2001:db8:1234:1a00::/56	local

Custom route table

Destination	Target
10.0.0.0/16	local
2001:db8:1234:1a00::/56	local
0.0.0.0/0	vgw-id

FIGURE 5.1 Public and private subnets of a VPC

Cram Quiz

Answer these questions. The answers follow the last question. If you cannot answer these questions correctly, consider reading this section again until you can.

1. Which of the following subnets would you use to deploy a highly available application running on a maximum of 2000–3000 hosts?

   ○ **A.** 10.20.30.0/23

   ○ **B.** 10.20.30.0/22

   ○ **C.** 10.20.30.0/21

   ○ **D.** 10.20.30.0/20

2. You have been asked to deploy an application into production. The production requirement is that four nodes must always be available in the VPC. Which of the following deployments would ensure you meet the requirements?

   ○ **A.** Deploy four instances into two VPC subnets and span them across two availability zones.

   ○ **B.** Deploy four instances into three VPC subnets. Ensure subnets are created in two availability zones.

   ○ **C.** Deploy six instances into four VPC subnets in one availability zone.

   ○ **D.** Deploy six instances into three VPC subnets. Ensure the subnets are created in three availability zones.

Cram Quiz Answers

1. Answer: C is correct. Although multiples of any of the network subnets could be used to achieve this goal, a /21 range would be appropriate in this scenario. In a /21, 2043 addresses are available for hosts. To be highly available, you need two subnets, which will give you more than 4000 addresses combined. The application should comfortably fit into these two subnets plus leave a bit of room for future growth or changes. You could argue that three /22 addresses would be close enough, but with just barely over 3000 addresses, it leaves little room to grow the application within the existing subnets. The /23 addresses in A would introduce at least six subnets, whereas a minimum highly available deployment of /20 in D would give you over 8000 addresses, meaning it could be wasteful.

2. Answer: D is correct. Having six instances across three availability zones ensures you always have four instances available, even if a complete availability zone is lost.

High Availability with Elastic Load Balancers and Route 53

This section covers the following official AWS Certified SysOps Administrator - Associate (SOA-C02) exam domains:

▶ Domain 2: Reliability and Business Continuity

▶ Domain 5: Networking and Content Delivery

CramSaver

If you can correctly answer these questions before going through this section, save time by skimming the Exam Alerts in this section and then completing the Cram Quiz at the end of the section.

1. You have deployed a set of 10 EC2 instances with the intention to make your application highly available. Your instances have been evenly deployed into us-west-2a. You would like to use the Network Load Balancer to make the application highly available. What would be the result of this configuration?

2. You have been asked to ensure your application is able to withstand a regional outage. Which service can be used in AWS to load-balance traffic between two regions in a 50–50 percent fashion?

Answers

1. Answer: Deploying the instances in only one availability zone (us-west-2a) is not optimal because it would make the application highly available but not resilient to an availability zone outage. Deploy the instances into two availability zones in us-west-2.

2. Answer: Route 53 with weighted routing would be the correct solution to allow for sending traffic to both regions. Because 50–50 is required, both region endpoints need to be added to the weighted record with equal weights.

One of the key AWS services that enables you to deploy highly available applications is the Elastic Load Balancing (ELB) service. ELB integrates with EC2, ECS, EKS, and other AWS services and enables you to distribute traffic across multiple instances of your application for high availability. The ELB service can also work together with the AutoScaling service to enable higher resilience of your application. When a failure occurs, the AutoScaling service can automatically scale the number of instances to meet the traffic demands that were previously handled by the file instance(s).

Four types of load balancers are available in AWS:

▶ Classic Load Balancer

▶ Application Load Balancer (ALB)

▶ Network Load Balancer (NLB)

▶ Gateway Load Balancer (GLB)

ELB Classic is the previous-generation load-balancing service that still provides a robust and simple-to-use load balancer to forward traffic to one or more availability zones within a region. ELB Classic is also supported on the EC2 Classic network. Neither one of these services is intended for use with modern, highly available, resilient architectures, and they are provided at this point merely for backward compatibility. Most modern applications should be designed to use the ALB or NLB service because the plan is to retire the Classic Load Balancer in August 2022.

The ALB is the next-generation layer 7 load-balancing solution from AWS that can handle HTTP and HTTPS traffic. The service can understand the application request, and based on the pattern of the request, can route the request to multiple back ends. This capability is useful when running microservices or other distributed solutions within an application. The ALB service automatically handles high availability of the service by deploying a redundant endpoint in each availability zone that it serves, with a minimum of two.

The NLB is the next-generation layer 4 load-balancing solution from AWS that can handle TCP, UDP, and SSL/TLS traffic.

ExamAlert

Although many services support Secure Sockets Layer (SSL), you should avoid using SSL in your applications because it is not considered secure anymore due to a flaw in its design. When SSL is referenced in the documentation, this might also be used as a general placeholder for "in-transit encryption." Most AWS services fully support Transport Layer Security (TLS) even when the term *SSL* is used. TLS is essentially an updated version of SSL and can easily be upgraded to, most of the time solely with the right software changes. Most modern applications support at least TLS 1.2 and higher and do not use SSL as the underlying security protocol.

The NLB is designed to deliver very high network throughput and very low latencies with the capability to serve tens of millions of responses per second. The NLB can also be operated with a static IP address, which enables integration with both high-performance microservices as well as legacy applications.

The GLB is designed to distribute traffic across third-party virtual appliances. The GLB can be used to seamlessly scale third-party virtual appliances and make third-party applications much more elastic.

The ELB service can deliver both single zone and multizone application high availability, but the load balancer service cannot be deployed across regions.

To make an application available across regions, you can utilize the Route 53 DNS service. The Route 53 service is a next-generation managed DNS cloud solution that enables you to manage DNS through the AWS API. Route 53 is the only AWS service that has a 100 percent SLA defined.

Route 53 provides much more than just the standard DNS request-response functionality. Within Route 53, you can register public domains, create public and private zones, and provide traffic-shaping functionalities through orchestrated DNS responses.

Route 53 can perform health checks of target IPs and CNAMEs as well as measure latency from the user to the target. The Route 53 service has the following routing policies that help you shape the traffic:

- **Simple routing:** Provides one response for each DNS request.

- **Weighted routing:** Provides responses based on the weight of the values for each record. This policy is useful for DR, testing, and deployment.

- **Failover routing:** Provides responses based on the health of two or more DNS targets.

- **Latency-based routing:** Measures the latency from the client to the DNS target and delivers the response with the lowest latency target.

- **Geolocation:** Can force users from certain regions or countries into specific AWS regions. This policy is great for compliance and custom regional traffic shaping.

- **Geoproximity:** Can route users from locations nearby to the closest region. This policy is independent of the country of region and merely depends on the distance to the region.

- **Multivalue answer routing:** Returns up to eight (validated and healthy) responses for each request.

Cram Quiz

Answer these questions. The answers follow the last question. If you cannot answer these questions correctly, consider reading this section again until you can.

1. Which of the following Route 53 routing approaches could you use to send customers from a country to a region within that country?

   ○ **A.** Geolocation

   ○ **B.** Geoproximity

   ○ **C.** Weighted routing

   ○ **D.** Static routing

2. Which of the following services can you use to make your application highly available within a region? (Choose all that apply.)

   ○ **A.** ELB Classic

   ○ **B.** NLB

   ○ **C.** ALB

   ○ **D.** Route 53

Cram Quiz Answers

1. Answer: A is correct. Geolocation can determine the country where the request originated and respond with the endpoint address that resides in the appropriate region within that country.

2. Answer: A, C, and D are correct. The NLB can balance traffic within only one availability zone. ALB and ELB Classic can both send traffic to multiple AZs. Route 53 can be used to balance traffic across two endpoints in two availability zones with weighted routing as well.

Highly Available Datastores

This chapter covers the following official AWS Certified SysOps Administrator - Associate (SOA-C02) exam domain:

▶ Domain 2: Reliability and Business Continuity

CramSaver

If you can correctly answer these questions before going through this section, save time by skimming the Exam Alerts in this section and then completing the Cram Quiz at the end of the section.

1. True or False: To make an S3 bucket on a standard tier highly available, you must ensure it is replicated across at least one more availability zone.

2. True or False: Moving an object from S3 Standard to S3 Infrequent Access requires you to download and delete the object from S344 Standard and upload it to S3 Infrequent Access.

Answers

1. Answer: False. The S3 Standard tier is automatically replicated across at least three availability zones.

2. Answer: False. The object can be life-cycled based on time, or intelligent tiering can be used to move the object automatically.

Amazon S3

Amazon S3 is a fully managed, serverless object storage service accessible via HTTP and HTTPS. The service has a 99.99 percent regional high-availability SLA and guarantees 99.999999999 percent of data durability. In more human terms, the durability SLA means there is a probability of losing 1 file out of 10 million every 10,000 years.

Any content stored on S3 must be stored within a bucket. Each bucket serves as a unique endpoint for objects, and each object has a unique key within the bucket. Each key is composed of the filename and one or more prefixes. Prefixes can be used to structure the files even further and to represent a directory-like view of the files because S3 has no concept of directories. Two types of URLs can be used to access an S3 bucket:

▶ Virtual-hosted-style URLs (current)

▶ Path-style URLs (currently expecting deprecation)

Virtual-hosted-style URLs are now the default way of accessing S3 buckets and have the following format:

```
{bucket-name}.s3.{region-id}.amazonaws.com}/{optional key prefix}/
{key-name}
```

In this case the bucket name is a subdomain of s3.{region-id}.amazonaws.com, which means you can create a CNAME record in your DNS service that can point directly to the S3 bucket.

> **ExamAlert**
>
> The S3 service previously supported a global S3 region virtual-hosted-style URL where you were able to omit the region parameter completely, and the format allowed requests to bucket URLs with the following format:
>
> ```
> {bucket-name}.s3.amazonaws.com
> ```
>
> Any buckets created after March 20, 2019, do not support the legacy global endpoint anymore.

The path-style URL is currently being deprecated. Deprecation was scheduled for September 30, 2020, but due to client requests, AWS has delayed the deprecation. Any buckets created after September 30, 2020, cannot be accessed via path-style URLs. The structure of a path-style URL is as follows:

```
http{s}://s3.{region-id}.amazonaws.com/{bucket-name}/
{optional key prefix}/{key-name}
```

S3 Storage Tiers

To store data with efficiency while maintaining high availability, you can also select from several storage classes in S3. The following storage classes are available:

▶ **S3 Standard:** Provides general-purpose online storage with 99.99 percent availability and 99.999999999 percent durability (aka "11 nines").

▶ **S3 Infrequent Access:** Provides the same performance as the S3 standard but is up to 40 percent cheaper with 99.9 percent availability SLA and the same "11 nines" of durability.

▶ **S3 Intelligent Tiering:** Can automatically determine whether to maintain the object stored on the S3 standard or S3 Infrequent Access based on the access pattern of the object. Intelligent tiering tries to optimize the location of the object and thus automatically reduce the cost of storing large amounts of data on S3.

▶ **S3 One Zone-Infrequent Access:** Provides a cheaper data tier in only one availability zone that can deliver an additional 25 percent saving over S3 Infrequent Access. It has the same durability with 99.5 percent availability.

▶ **S3 Glacier:** Costs less than one-fifth of the price of S3 and is designed for archiving and long-term storage. Restore times are between 1 minute and 7 hours, depending on the type of request.

▶ **S3 Glacier Deep Archive:** Costs four times less than Glacier and is the cheapest storage solution at about $1 per terabyte per month. This solution is intended for very long-term storage and has the longest restore times of up to 12 hours.

▶ **S3 Outposts:** Delivers the content from an on-premises AWS Outpost deployment of the S3 service.

S3 also supports life-cycling and expiry of objects. Lifecycle rules can help move objects between storage tiers based on a scenario that you define. For example:

▶ Any object older than 60 days is migrated to S3 Infrequent Access (S3 IA).

▶ After 120 days the object is moved to Glacier.

▶ After one year the object is deleted.

S3 Security

The bucket also acts as a security endpoint for the data because you can apply a bucket policy to the bucket and granular control access to the bucket and objects within it. To control access, you can also use access control lists (ACLs) at the bucket level or for each object. However, ACLs only allow for coarse-grained permissions such as read or read/write to be assigned to the bucket or object. This is why a bucket policy is the preferred method of managing security in S3.

> **ExamAlert**
>
> All new buckets are created with a no public access setting that prevents applying any public access via policies or ACLs. To enable public access, you need to remove the "no public access" setting in the bucket.

A bucket policy is a JSON-formatted document with the same structure as inline IAM polices. It allows you to granularly control each API action against the bucket or object. The ability to control each API call means that you can create permissions for users to read files (GetObjects API) but not list them (ListObjects API). In the same example, you can have a write-only policy, and so on. The owner of a bucket (the user who created it) always has all permissions/full control. Figure 5.2 illustrates the policy evaluation logic in AWS.

ExamAlert

Always consider all polices in line to the S3 bucket when troubleshooting S3 access. Remember that on top of S3 bucket policies and ACLs, the IAM policies can also have S3 permissions defined for users, groups, and roles being used to access S3. The policy evaluation flow is shown in Figure 5.2.

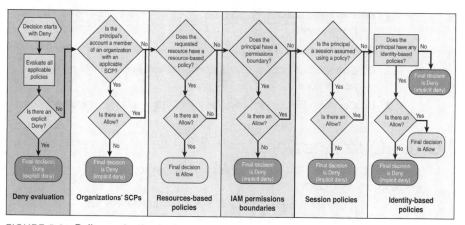

FIGURE 5.2 Policy evaluation logic

Cram Quiz

Answer these questions. The answers follow the last question. If you cannot answer these questions correctly, consider reading this section again until you can.

1. Which of the following S3 tiers is most appropriate for archives that need to be restored in less than seven hours?

    ○ **A.** S3 Infrequent Access

    ○ **B.** S3 Infrequent Access–One Zone

    ○ **C.** Glacier

    ○ **D.** Glacier Deep Archive

2. You have been asked to select a security approach for an S3 bucket. The bucket has two types of users: an owner with unlimited security and writers who deposit work results with a unique filename based on the node name and time. Writers are not allowed to ever read any of the files on S3, even the ones they created.

    ○ **A.** This is not possible on S3 because all writers would need read/write permissions.

    ○ **B.** Create an S3 bucket ACL for the writers with write-only permissions.

    ○ **C.** Create S3 object ACLs for each possible object with write-only permissions.

    ○ **D.** Create an S3 bucket policy for the writers with write-only permissions.

Cram Quiz Answers

1. Answer: C is correct. The Glacier service can restore any number of archives in less than seven hours.

2. Answer: D is correct. A bucket policy allows you to create a write-only (PutObjects API) rule that allows the writers to only create new files.

Highly Available Databases

This chapter covers the following official AWS Certified SysOps Administrator - Associate (SOA-C02) exam domain:

▶ Domain 2: Reliability and Business Continuity

CramSaver

If you can correctly answer these questions before going through this section, save time by completing the Cram Quiz at the end of the section.

1. What is the maximum number of primary nodes supported in a Multi-AZ RDS MySQL cluster?

2. How many read replicas are supported on DynamoDB global tables?

Answers

1. Answer: One. A Multi-AZ has the primary replica for SQL reads and writes in one AZ and a secondary inaccessible synchronous replica in another AZ.

2. Answer: None. DynamoDB global tables are designed with replica tables, which are all primary. Any writes to any of the regions are replicated to all other regions across the globe within one second.

As mentioned in the previous chapter, you can generally sort databases into two categories: relational or SQL and nonrelational or NoSQL (Not only SQL).

Although there are many benefits of using NoSQL databases, such as built-in elasticity, horizontal scalability, high availability, and built-in resilience, many applications still do require the capability to store data in a traditional relational database.

So why are traditional databases so difficult to make highly available and resilient? Any relational database needs to comply with the ACID requirements, which stand for

▶ **Atomicity:** Transactions need to be atomic. If any suboperation within the transaction fails, the whole transaction needs to fail and be rolled back.

▶ **Consistency:** Data must be consistent at all times. When written to, data must not be available until the write transaction has completed in its entirety.

▶ **Isolation:** Concurrent transactions can never interfere with each other and are isolated with unique IDs.

▶ **Durability:** Data must be stored durably. All operations must be recoverable (transactions can be rolled back; tables or the entire database can be restored from backups).

These requirements mean that there needs to be a central location that validates all the write operations and maintains session isolation and consistency. Essentially, in a traditional application, only one node (the primary) can ever be permitted to perform writes. This means that the database write performance can only scale to the maximum size of that one node. Although mechanisms available out there enable you to design multiprimary databases (for example, Aurora multimaster clusters), they can be difficult to manage and also have a limit of scalability due to the fact that more replication across primaries requires additional resources.

Amazon RDS

In AWS the Amazon Relational Database Service (RDS) allows you to deploy, manage, and operate traditional relational databases with managed options for elasticity, scalability, as well as high availability and resilience.

You can easily make these databases highly available by deploying them in a Multi-AZ deployment. When running Multi-AZ, the service maintains a synchronous replica of the database in another availability zone. This means that any data that has been written to the primary is sent over to the replica. The replica stores the data and sends a successful response. Only then will a successful response be provided within the SQL transaction. Thus, any transaction committed to the primary is guaranteed to be stored on the secondary as well. If the primary fails, the service detects the failure and promotes the secondary into the primary role. A new secondary is deployed in another AZ from the most recent snapshot and synchronized with the new primary. Figure 5.3 demonstrates a resilient database design.

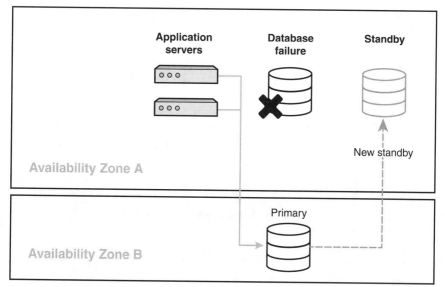

FIGURE 5.3   **RDS Multi-AZ**

Remember that the secondary Multi-AZ replica is never available for any read or write operations while in the secondary role. Its sole purpose is to enable almost instant failover in case of the primary's failure.

As mentioned in the previous chapter, read replicas can be added to a primary database whether it utilizes Multi-AZ or not. A read replica can also be manually promoted to a primary, but you should not expect the data to be synchronous on read replicas. The promotion of a read replica to a primary can be useful if you are replicating the database across the region and intend to promote the replica in case of a regional outage or other type of disaster recovery.

Amazon Aurora

Amazon Aurora is the next-generation open-source engine with native support for both MySQL and PostgreSQL engines. Aurora has a decoupled architecture with all data being stored on a volume that is replicated six times across three AZs. The SQL front end resides on the Aurora nodes. Aurora supports one primary node for read/write access and up to 15 Aurora replicas in the same region. Aurora clusters can also be replicated to other regions with up to 16 replicas of the database in each of the other regions. Figure 5.4 demonstrates the Aurora cluster design.

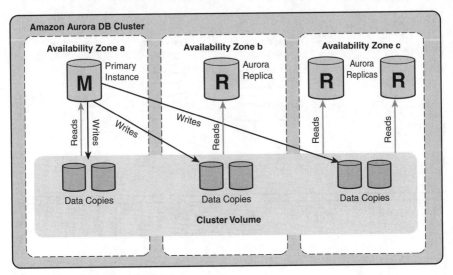

FIGURE 5.4 **Aurora architecture**

Because all nodes of the Aurora cluster access the same cluster volume, the state of the replication across the cluster is near synchronous and depends on the performance of the underlying cluster volume rather than the instances themselves. This means that there is no overhead when calculating the performance required for the read replicas like there is with RDS. The primary and the replicas also have different DNS names provided, so you can easily configure your application to send all writes to the primary and all read requests to the read replicas. Any Aurora read replica can also instantly be promoted into the primary role. This capability is useful in case of a failure of the primary instance or when you want to increase the size of the primary instance.

Amazon DynamoDB

DynamoDB is a serverless NoSQL solution that uses a standard HTTPS access model to access table data. A table in DynamoDB is a collection of items that is regionally bound. A table must also have a unique name in the region where it was created. DynamoDB supports storing any amount of data and is distributed and replicated across three or more availability zones in the region. DynamoDB is also scalable and can be autoscaled by default using the AWS AutoScaling service.

The DynamoDB distributed back end allows the performance of each table to linearly scale, but the dataset distribution is what determines if scaling is possible. When you are creating a table, you need to define a primary key.

The primary key is used to distribute the data on the back end. You should choose a primary key that has a lot of variety and is known to the application (the application uses it to address data) to get the most performance out of DynamoDB. DynamoDB now also supports ACID transactions.

DynamoDB Global Tables

A DynamoDB global table is a collection of DynamoDB regional tables (called replica tables) that are replicated multidirectionally. To create a global table, you need to first create replica tables in each of the regions where you want to run your application. The replica tables are connected to the global table, and each replica is now subscribed to all other replicas' changes. All changes are replicated across the globe with a consistency window of one second. A write to one of the tables is replicated across all other regions within one second.

DynamoDB global tables can be used for any application that needs to share data across the global audience or for any application that is distributed across two or more regions nearby. Because the application always works with the local replica, all typical features of DynamoDB are available to the local instances (ACID transactions [reads and writes], batching, standard writes, strongly consistent reads, and eventually consistent reads). Instances can, however, also access the replica tables in the other region(s), but only standard writes and eventually consistent reads are supported in this scenario.

Cram Quiz

Answer these questions. The answers follow the last question. If you cannot answer these questions correctly, consider reading this section again until you can.

1. You have been asked to make an application highly available across us-east-1 and us-west-2 AWS regions. The application currently uses a MySQL RDS Multi-AZ back end. What would be the most cost-effective solution to support the application requirements?

- ○ **A.** Set the Multi-AZ primary replica to us-east-1a AZ and the secondary replica to us-west-2a AZ.

- ○ **B.** Create a read replica of the primary in the other region.

- ○ **C.** Convert the database to Aurora multiregional deployment. Deploy the primary instance in us-east-1a AZ and a secondary instance in us-west-2a AZ.

- ○ **D.** Convert the database to DynamoDB global tables.

2. You have deployed an Aurora database primary instance in availability zone us-east-1a. What steps need to be taken to make the data in the Aurora database highly available?

   ○ **A.** None.

   ○ **B.** Deploy a read replica to us-east-1b.

   ○ **C.** Turn on Multi-AZ.

   ○ **D.** Create a snapshot of the database volume.

Cram Quiz Answers

1. Answer: B is correct. The application can easily be made highly available by creating a read replica in the other region. If the primary region fails, the read replica can be promoted to primary and the application requests redirected to the other region.

2. Answer: A is correct. The Aurora database has a cluster volume that is replicated six times across three availability zones. After a database is created, the volume itself is automatically made highly available. If the single instance fails or the availability zone where the single instance resides is unavailable, a new instance creation is attempted by the Aurora service. However, there is no guarantee that the launch will succeed; this is why in production it is recommended to keep an Aurora read replica instance in another AZ so that it can be quickly promoted to primary in case of failure.

What Next?

If you want more practice on this chapter's exam objectives before you move on, remember that you can access all of the Cram Quiz questions on the Pearson Test Prep software online. You can also create a custom exam by objective with the Online Practice Test. Note any objective you struggle with and go to that objective's material in this chapter.

CHAPTER 6

Backup and Restore Strategies

This chapter covers the following official AWS Certified SysOps Administrator - Associate (SOA-C02) exam domains:

▶ Domain 2: Reliability and Business Continuity

▶ Domain 4: Security and Compliance

(For more information on the official AWS Certified SysOps Administrator - Associate [SOA-C02] exam topics, see the Introduction.)

At this point you should be familiar with how to make an application scalable, elastic, highly available, and resilient to failures. So you might be asking yourself: "If my application has all of the aforementioned features, why even consider backing up?" Well, the simple answer is that backups are for times when things go very wrong.

A backup represents a point-in-time recovery that you can return to. It's not just failures of hardware and errors in software that take applications down. Most of the time it is human-initiated actions, which could be mistakes or malicious actions. Either can take the application down, corrupt the data, destroy the database, and so on. Regardless of whether the issue is caused by hardware, software, or a human, a backup—or even multiple backups—ensures you can recover to a point in time when everything was working.

In this chapter, we discuss how to implement a good backup strategy in AWS and which services to use to ensure all your data is backed up.

Backup in the Cloud

This section covers the following official AWS Certified SysOps Administrator - Associate (SOA-C02) exam objectives for Domain 2: Reliability and Business Continuity and Domain 4: Security and Compliance:

▶ Domain 2.3: Implement backup and restore strategies

▶ Domain 4.2: Implement data and infrastructure protection strategies

CramSaver

If you can correctly answer these questions before going through this section, save time by skimming the Exam Alerts in this section and then completing the Cram Quiz at the end of the section.

1. Which components need to be considered as dynamically changing over time when backing up your application?

2. How often must a backup be taken, and how quickly must the application be recovered if it has a recovery-point objective (RPO) of 30 minutes and a recovery-time objective (RTO) of 1 hour?

3. Is it possible to retain a backup of an RDS database for an indefinite amount of time?

Answers

1. Answer: The state of the application and the data. All stateful services should be backed up regularly. If a service is stateless, no backup is required because the objects in that service can be re-created with either an original image or an orchestration template.

2. Answer: The application needs to be backed up at least once every 30 minutes (more is recommended if financially viable) to meet the RPO. The application needs to be recovered and operational within 1 hour to meet the RTO.

3. Answer: Manual RDS snapshots can be taken of the RDS database and retained indefinitely.

In the cloud you can consider all backups as point-in-time records of the state of an application. This means that any stateful environment requires backing up, whereas any stateless platforms can simply be re-created.

One of the core best practices in AWS is to keep as many components of an application as stateless as possible. This also reduces the scope of backups because you really need to focus only on the components that dynamically change over time.

For example, a well-architected multitier application has a load balancer, a web front end, one or more application back ends, and one or more datastores. The datastores could consist of databases, object storage, file storage, and other block devices. In AWS, these are always represented by services. Some services contain stateful data, but others do not. If a service is stateless, in the case of failure, the objects within the service can simply be re-created. Most infrastructure services are completely stateless and can be redeployed using orchestration.

For example, you can use a CloudFormation template to deploy all network components. If a failure or human error occurs during an update, you can simply roll back any changes or even redeploy the entire environment through the original CloudFormation template to recover the objects. Other examples are EC2 instances. They can be either stateless or stateful. Stateless applications do not store any state inside the compute environment, whereas stateful applications do. For example, a stateful web server sources its session information in the memory of the server instance. If the instance fails, the session information is lost. A stateless server stores the state information outside the instance—for example, into a database or caching platform. The best practice for compute environments is thus keeping them stateless. In case of failure, a stateless instance can simply be redeployed using the AMI it was originally deployed from.

Table 6.1 shows which services are stateful and the backup/recovery strategy you can employ.

TABLE 6.1 **AWS Services of a Multitier Application and Their State**

Service	Type	Stateful	Backup/Restore
VPC, subnets, IGW...	Network	No	Re-create/orchestration
ELB	Network	No	Re-create/orchestration
EC2	Compute	No	Redeploy/AMI
EBS	Block Storage	Yes	Snapshot/AWS Backup
RDS	Database	Yes	Snapshot/AWS Backup
EFS/FSx	File	Yes	Replicate/AWS Backup
S3	Object Storage	Yes	Versioning

Backups and Snapshots

Those services that do need to be backed up have a few options. If the service runs on an EBS volume, a point-in-time snapshot of that EBS volume can be taken. All snapshots in AWS are incremental. This means that each snapshot captures only the blocks that have changed since the last snapshot. If this is the initial snapshot, all blocks of the volume that contain data are recorded, of course. Snapshots on some services such as EC2, RDS, ElastiCache, and Redis also ensure consistency, but in others you need to ensure a consistent state is created on the volume before you execute a snapshot.

These two snapshot modes of operation can be represented by the differences in the EBS volume and RDS database snapshots. Because the RDS service is fully managed, AWS manages the operating system of the database server instance. When a snapshot request is issued, the RDS service can ensure that all writes are momentarily paused, all data currently still in memory is committed to disk, and a consistent state is created. This ensures any snapshot will always have usable data on the volume. RDS also allows you to automate backups and direct the RDS service to retain the automated snapshots for up to 35 days. Manual snapshots can be initiated at any time by each customer and will be retained indefinitely.

The same is not true for the EBS service. When an EBS volume is attached to the EC2 instance, AWS does not have access into the operating system of the instance. The customer is in full control of the instance and must ensure that if a snapshot is taken of the EBS volume, writes to the selected EBS volume must be momentarily paused, and all data in memory is committed to disk before the snapshot is started. This can easily be done with a script that runs internally within the EC2 operating system.

Although snapshots provide a way for a volume-based service to be backed up, using them is not always an option. Some applications might require a backup of multiple components to take place at the same time, ensuring a distributed state of the application is captured exactly. In this case, you can deploy a traditional agent-based backup solution deployed in the operating system or use the AWS Backup service, which we discuss later in this chapter.

Finally, there are those services that do not support volume-based snapshots. Shared file systems like EFS and FSx, DynamoDB tables, and S3 buckets are not accessible via volumes because they are distributed across a set of AWS managed instances. For these services, you need to employ either a built-in strategy or a time-based replication of the service contents to a separate location.

With DynamoDB, the built-in solution is table backups. A table backup is a point-in-time copy of the DynamoDB table that can be used to restore both the complete table and specific items. The backup schedule can be automated, and up to 35 days of retention is available.

In contrast, S3 does not have a backup solution; instead, you can version objects; this means that when an object is re-uploaded and has changed, a complete copy of that object is created in S3 with an incremented version identifier. S3 is also highly durable and is able to life-cycle data to Glacier. This means that S3 itself can also be used as a backup solution. We discuss S3 as a backup solution and versioning later in this chapter.

With EFS/FSx, things get a bit trickier. The file system is controlled by the tenant, and the service is managed by AWS. Although AWS ensures that the service is as highly available as possible, it does not have any access into the volume and does not guarantee any durability of the data, like with S3. This means that you are required to select and maintain a backup scenario for EFS/FSx. One way to back up the file system is to create a copy of the file system contents to S3. In this scenario, you can use the AWS DataSync service because it can incrementally copy any changes to S3, where you can enable versioning and life-cycling of old versions into Glacier. You can also choose the AWS Backup service to perform backups of the file system, which we discuss later in this chapter.

RPO and RTO

Whenever you are choosing any backup strategy, you need to also define the recovery-point objective (RPO) and the recovery-time objective (RTO). The RPO is used to define how much data can be lost during an event that requires you to restore data, and the RTO defines the time allowed to recover the data and bring it fully online.

For example, an RPO of one hour means that you can lose no more than one hour's worth of data. You should thus select a backup procedure that will capture data every hour at a minimum. If possible, capturing more frequently than each hour ensures that you have not one but several recovery points to return to because the latest one might be incomplete, corrupted, or not reflect a valid point to return to.

An RTO of one hour means that you need to bring the application back to the state before the event within at most one hour. To achieve the lowest possible RTO, you need to employ a good recovery strategy that is simple to execute and as automated as possible.

Figure 6.1 represents the RPO and RTO and how these two factors relate to an event that disrupts an application.

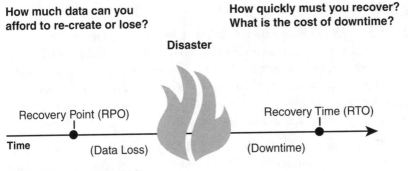

How much data can you afford to re-create or lose?

How quickly must you recover? What is the cost of downtime?

Disaster

Recovery Point (RPO)

Recovery Time (RTO)

Time (Data Loss) (Downtime)

FIGURE 6.1 **RTO and RPO**

Disaster Recovery

Another term that we need to cover when discussing backups is *disaster recovery*. The idea of disaster recovery stems from traditional datacenters, where computing was done in one location (usually due to cost and proximity to the clients/workforce). Traditionally, disaster recovery outlines a plan to recover the primary operating environment from remotely stored backups. These backups could be represented by any type of data storage, ranging from tapes or disks, cold-stored in a remote location, that can be returned to the primary environment and restored, to online storage and standby servers in a remote location that can be activated to take the production load at any moment, and everything in between.

The traditional concept implies that there are so-called cold resources—tapes, disks, storage, servers that are not in use in day-to-day operations because they need to be made available at all times in case of a disaster. This can lead to expensive hardware being unused and can dramatically increase the operating expenses of any application.

In AWS, there is no concept of cold datacenters. All of the equipment is online at all times to deliver AWS services; however, the load on the equipment is never even close to 100 percent. This means that there is always some spare capacity across each AWS datacenter, availability zone, and region that you can use for the purpose of disaster recovery. Because AWS services are pay-per-use, this implies that you never have to pay for any resources that are "waiting" for you to fail over to.

Overview of Backup Strategies

One thing to consider in AWS is that any backup can also be used as a seed for disaster recovery. To ensure you can both recover data and restore a complete environment in case of disaster, you have to select a backup strategy. There are four general ways to set up the backup of your environment that will also support full disaster recovery:

▶ Backup and restore

▶ Pilot light

▶ Warm standby

▶ Multisite active-active

Regardless of whether your primary environment is on-premises or AWS, the design of these strategies works exactly the same. In the following sections, we refer to the *production environment*, which represents the primary site or primary AWS region, and the *backup environment*, which represents an AWS region where backups are stored and where disaster recovery can be initiated.

Backup and Restore

The simplest option is backup and restore. All stateful AWS services support some sort of backup. Backup and restore can be a great strategy when the RPO and RTO are long (typically hours) because the approach is very low cost and also very easy to implement. The cheapest backup and restore approach can be implemented within one region, but we recommend that you always replicate a copy of regional backups to another region, which gives you peace of mind in case of a regional outage due to a major disaster. A simple way is to copy production data with a predefined schedule (once an hour, for example) to S3. If there is a need to restore, you can simply recover the object from S3. In case of a disaster recovery, you can deploy a new instance in the backup environment and restore the data on to the newly deployed instance. The built-in disaster recovery in this scenario has negligible cost.

Pilot Light

Pilot light builds on the backup and restore approach, by providing some services that can be easily and quickly started in case of a disaster. The RPO can be lowered from hours to minutes by ensuring you replicate data more often or even by replicating a database to a cross-region read replica. This approach ensures that the loss of data is minimal and could be as low as a few minutes or even seconds, but the RPO/RTO goal of a pilot light should always be set to the "worst-case scenario" of perhaps tens of minutes. To speed up the RTO, you can prepare images or even set up powered-off EC2 instances in the backup environment. In case of a disaster, the deployment can optimally be done within minutes because the instances are redeployed from the AMI or even just started up. The cost of the pilot light strategy can be very low; in addition to the backups, you need to consider any running resources such as a read replica of your production database.

Warm Standby

A warm standby elaborates on the pilot light strategy by having a small subset of AWS services operational at all times. This is particularly important when the RPO and RTO are very low and the whole application needs to be up and running within a few minutes at worst. In case of a disaster, the warm standby can be made primary and scaled out to support production traffic. There will be some outage when you redirect the traffic and during scale-out because the DNS of the application will take tens of seconds to reflect the change and the scale-out process might take another minute or two on top of that. This solution is rather costlier because it does require you to have an active, lower-capacity site always up and running. However, you can always also trickle a subset of traffic through the warm standby, thus continuously verifying that the application can be failed over at any time.

Multisite Active-Active

Last but not least is the multisite active-active approach. In this scenario, there is more than one production site in more than one region. All of the production sites are able to receive traffic and respond to requests at any time and can be balanced to ensure that the application never experiences any downtime. The real trick in this scenario is not the implementation nor the strategy for recovery; rather, it is the correct approach to data replication across regions. Replicating data to another region can be difficult to do in a consistent manner, due to the distances across regions. Replicating to another region can also be costly. On top of cost, you need to consider that sometimes replicating out-of-country could carry legal consequences as well. However, multisite active-active is the best solution to ensure zero downtime for your application.

Figure 6.2 compares the backup strategizes from the point of view of RPO/RTO, cost, and downtime.

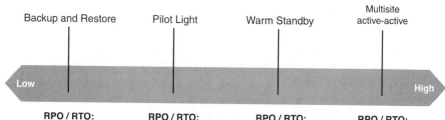

Backup and Restore	Pilot Light	Warm Standby	Multisite active-active

Low   High

RPO / RTO: Hours	RPO / RTO: 10s of minutes	RPO / RTO: Minutes	RPO / RTO: Real-time
• Lower-priority use cases • Restore data after event • Deploy resources after event • Cost $	• Less-stringent RTO and RPO • Core services • Start and scale resources after event • Cost $$	• More-stringent RTO and RPO • Business-critical services • Scale resources after event • Cost $$$	• Zero downtime • Near-zero loss • Mission-critical services • Cost $$$$

FIGURE 6.2   Comparison of backup strategies

ExamAlert

You are bound to have at least one question concerning the backup strategies. Often exam takers select the most powerful backup strategy; however, you should always consider that the lower the RPO/RTO, the higher the cost will be.

Cram Quiz

Answer these questions. The answers follow the last question. If you cannot answer these questions correctly, consider reading this section again until you can.

1. You have been asked to operate an existing application with a pilot light backup/DR strategy. Production is in us-west-2, and the pilot light is deployed in eu-west-1. Your complete customer base resides in the continental US. The application has an RPO of 90 minutes and RTO of 1 hour. The budget for the application regularly breaches 90 percent of allocated cost before the end of month. You do not know much else about the application. Based on the information provided, which of the following changes should be implemented in your opinion?

   ○ **A.** The RPO can be improved by using warm standby.

   ○ **B.** The backup/DR region should be changed.

   ○ **C.** The cost can be improved by moving to backup/restore.

   ○ **D.** Leave the application as is.

2. You have been asked to select a backup/DR strategy for a mission-critical application. The RPO for the application is defined as 5 minutes, and the RTO is defined as 10 minutes. You have already set up an RDS read replica that shows a lag of less than 45 seconds in a secondary region. The design must meet the requirements and be cost-effective. What approach would you use to deploy the application components?

- ○ **A.** Deploy a multisite active-active design to minimize the disruption of the mission-critical application.

- ○ **B.** Deploy a warm standby to fail over the mission-critical application in case of a disaster.

- ○ **C.** Deploy a pilot light scenario with powered-off copies of the production EC2 instances. Powering them on always meets or exceeds the RTO of the mission-critical application.

- ○ **D.** Deploy a pilot light scenario with the same AMIs being used by the production EC2 instances. Deploying the AMIs into EC2 always meets or exceeds the RTO of the mission-critical application.

Cram Quiz Answers

1. Answer: B is correct. The region should be changed to a US region. Because all the clients reside in the continental US, replicating to an EU region might breach possible data residency laws and make the application less functional in the case of a disaster, due to the network distance and increased latency from the US to EU.

2. Answer: C is correct. The RPO is ensured with the RDS read replica. The most cost-effective solution to meet the RTO is to use a pilot light with powered-off instances. They boot up within minutes and ensure the application can be recovered and online within the RTO. Powered-off instances can also be started and updated during regular update periods, ensuring that they are up to date in case of a disaster. Deploying from an AMI might take longer than 10 minutes during recovery, due to the fact that the AMI might be out of data. Because the RTO is 10 minutes, A and B are not cost effective.

S3 as a Backup Service

This section covers the following official AWS Certified SysOps Administrator - Associate (SOA-C02) exam objective from Domain 2:

▶ Domain 2.3: Implement backup and restore strategies

CramSaver

If you can correctly answer these questions before going through this section, save time by completing the Cram Quiz at the end of the section.

1. True or False: The only way to synchronize files to S3 is to maintain a list of changed files and then issue an S3 copy operation of the changed files to backup changes to S3.

2. Which service offers the cheapest option for data storage in AWS?

Answers

1. Answer: False. You can use S3 sync or AWS DataSync to synchronize files in a local directory with S3 or vice versa.

2. Answer: Glacier Deep Archive offers the lowest-cost storage at less than $1 per terabyte per month. However, the retrieval times of Deep Archive are longer, so it might not be a viable solution for backups with short RTOs.

S3 is the perfect service to use when backing up objects or files. The service is an inexpensive solution that allows you to store unlimited amounts of data with extremely high durability. On top of that, the S3 service supports life-cycling of data into cheaper tiers automatically, so you can easily migrate your data from the fastest online storage into a cold archive.

There are several ways to integrate S3 as a backup solution. Most notably, S3 is the industry standard for object storage, and most other object storage solutions out there tout compatibility with S3. For this same reason, most backup software providers have developed plug-ins that allow you to store the backups directly to S3 as well. However, there are many other ways to easily copy data to S3.

S3 Sync

S3 sync is an AWS CLI feature that can be a great option when you simply want to copy a large number of files from your production server to AWS. S3 sync creates a synchronization list of files on the local directory with an S3 bucket. The synchronization can also be done in both directions. All you need is a single AWS CLI command, and the data can easily be synchronized.

For this example, let's say you have a bucket called mylittlesyncbucket and five files called sync01-05.txt in the local directory. Now you can run the **S3 sync** command:

```
aws s3 sync . s3://mylittlesyncbucket
```

The result should look like this output. Note that the files are uploaded in random sequence:

```
upload: .\sync03.txt to s3://mylittlesyncbucket/sync03.txt

upload: .\sync01.txt to s3://mylittlesyncbucket/sync01.txt

upload: .\sync04.txt to s3://mylittlesyncbucket/sync04.txt

upload: .\sync05.txt to s3://mylittlesyncbucket/sync05.txt

upload: .\sync02.txt to s3://mylittlesyncbucket/sync02.txt
```

When you log in to the AWS console, you can see the bucket has been synced with the local directory, as shown in Figure 6.3.

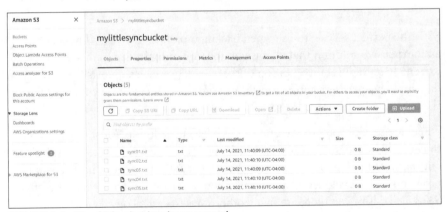

FIGURE 6.3   The S3 bucket has been synced

If you add more files to the directory or change the content of those files and then rerun the **s3 sync** command, only the files that have changed are copied over.

To ensure all file versions are stored on S3, you can enable versioning on the S3 bucket you are syncing to; thus, you can prevent any corruption of the production files from corrupting the backups in S3.

AWS DataSync

The S3 sync approach requires you to do a bit of scripting, and this can be difficult to manage at scale. To avoid having to create your own scripting, you can use the AWS DataSync service. DataSync can synchronize file systems in the production location with other file systems in the backup location or with S3. The DataSync service requires you to use a DataSync agent that has access to the source file system. The DataSync agent uses a secure connection to the DataSync service and employs traffic optimization when transferring data. DataSync can be up to 10 times faster than other solutions for transferring data, making it a great solution to choose when syncing data from on-premises file systems to AWS.

Versioning and Life-Cycling Rules

To maintain a record of all changes to a file in AWS S3, you can enable bucket versioning. Versioning forces every change to an object (insert, upload, delete, patch) with the same key to be stored as a separate copy under the same key with an incremented version identifier. Figure 6.4 demonstrates this process.

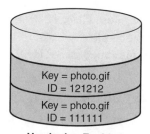

Versioning Enabled

FIGURE 6.4   **S3 versioning**

All S3 buckets are created without versioning. Versioning can be enabled, meaning all copies of all objects are retained, but a versioned bucket also can be suspended. When bucket versioning is suspended, all objects have a "null" version generated, and this null version is overwritten. However, all older versions in a suspended bucket persist, as demonstrated in Figure 6.5.

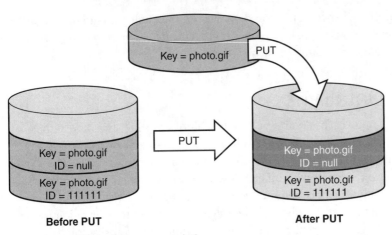

Before PUT   **After PUT**

FIGURE 6.5 **S3 versioning suspended**

Any request for the object in the versioned bucket returns the latest version; however, you can also retrieve a specific version of an object in the versioned bucket by specifying the version identifier.

As discussed in the preceding chapter, any objects and versions of those objects can also be life-cycled to a cheaper S3 storage tier. This means that you can either move any older versions to the archive or delete them entirely.

Glacier

Glacier is the archiving tier of S3 in AWS; however, you can use Glacier directly through the API as well. Many different backup tools allow you to store data onto Glacier directly. When using Glacier, be mindful of the RTO because the retrieval times in Glacier fall into three categories:

▶ **Expedited retrieval:** Retrieval of archives up to 250 MB takes 1–5 minutes.

▶ **Standard retrieval:** Retrieval of archives takes 3–5 hours.

▶ **Bulk retrieval:** Retrieval of large numbers of archives takes 5–12 hours.

Glacier Deep Archive is the cheapest AWS storage option; it allows you to store data at less than $1 per terabyte per month. Glacier Deep Archive supports only the following two retrieval options:

▶ **Standard retrieval:** Default option for retrieval of archives takes 12 hours.

▶ **Bulk retrieval:** Retrieval of large amounts of archives occurs within 48 hours.

S3 Cross-Region Replication

When using S3 as a backup option, or when you require the same objects to be retrieved multiple times and quickly from more than one region, you can also replicate any data in S3 to another bucket in another S3 region easily by enabling cross-region replication.

To enable replication, you need to set up the replication configuration to the source bucket. You need to specify the destination bucket and which files to replicate. The ability to filter files to be replicated is great because you can specifically choose the prefix that is to be replicated. You can also select the storage class to be replicated to. This is a great solution when you want to replicate any objects in an S3 bucket to another region for disaster recovery. You simply select the secondary region's storage tier as Glacier or even Glacier Deep Archive (depending on the RTO). You can also manage ownership of copies when replicating, meaning you can define that the files, once replicated, will have ownership by the account that owns the bucket. Cross-region replication is also fairly quick and has an SLA of replicating 99.99 percent of the objects in the source bucket to the destination bucket within 15 minutes.

Cram Quiz

Answer these questions. The answers follow the last question. If you cannot answer these questions correctly, consider reading this section again until you can.

1. You are an employee of an insurance company. You have been tasked with selecting a storage solution for scans of legal documents like contracts, terms and conditions, and signature pages that are a required part of any insurance agreement. The documents must be stored with the highest possible durability and must be retained for 10 years. The documents need to be made available within 72 hours for a yearly compliance evaluation and in case of legal proceedings requiring these documents. Which datastore would you choose?

    ○ **A.** S3 Infrequent Access

    ○ **B.** Glacier

    ○ **C.** Glacier Deep Archive

    ○ **D.** S3 Infrequent Access—One Zone

2. You manage an application that creates an output file every second with UNIX date stamp as its name. You have been asked to write a script that will ensure these files are sent to S3 in the order that they were created within 5 seconds of their creation. You have decided to try S3 sync, but it seems S3 sync is not suitable for this task. What is the reason?

   ○ **A.** S3 sync takes longer than 5 seconds to synchronize the files to S3.

   ○ **B.** S3 sync is not suitable for large numbers of unique files.

   ○ **C.** S3 sync uploads files in a random manner.

   ○ **D.** S3 sync changes the filename of the uploaded files.

Cram Quiz Answers

1. Answer: B is correct. Because these documents will only be recovered very rarely, Glacier Deep Archive is the best and most cost-effective solution for storing documents that need to be recovered within 12 hours or more.

2. Answer: C is correct. S3 sync uploads files in a random manner. Because the preservation of order needs to be retained, creating a custom script that will upload files in order is required.

What Next?

If you want more practice on this chapter's exam objectives before you move on, remember that you can access all of the Cram Quiz questions on the Pearson Test Prep software online. You can also create a custom exam by objective with the Online Practice Test. Note any objective you struggle with and go to that objective's material in this chapter.

CHAPTER 7

Provisioning Resources

This chapter covers the following official AWS Certified SysOps Administrator - Associate (SOA-C02) exam domain:

▶ Domain 3: Deployment, Provisioning, and Automation

(For more information on the official AWS Certified SysOps Administrator - Associate [SOA-C02] exam topics, see the Introduction.)

As you can probably imagine, provisioning resources in AWS is a major responsibility within an organization. It can also quickly become overwhelming when your organization embraces the cloud and ends up having thousands of resources in its AWS infrastructure.

This chapter focuses on different solutions related to provisioning resources in AWS. You first learn about the AWS CLI, an alternative to deploying resources directly in the AWS Management Console. You also learn the essentials of managing EC2 AMIs.

To make the process of provisioning AWS infrastructure resources easier, this chapter explores using templates with AWS CloudFormation. By using AWS Elastic Beanstalk, you learn how to make the process of deploying applications in your AWS infrastructure easier.

To gain better visibility of your AWS infrastructure, you explore the AWS Systems Manager. You also learn how to share resources between different AWS accounts and regions by using the AWS Resource Access Manager.

Deployment Tools in AWS

This section covers the following official AWS Certified SysOps Administrator - Associate (SOA-C02) exam topics for Domain 3: Deployment, Provisioning, and Automation:

▶ 3.1 Provision and maintain cloud resources

▶ 3.2 Automate manual or repeatable processes

CramSaver

If you can correctly answer these questions before going through this section, save time by skimming the Exam Alerts in this section and then completing the Cram Quiz at the end of the section.

1. What are the three primary methods to interact with AWS resources and services?

2. Which IaaC AWS tool can you use to configure an EC2 instance using a YAML-formatted configuration file?

Answers

1. Answer: AWS CLI, the Management Console, and SDK

2. Answer: AWS CloudFormation

One of the primary reasons to migrate to a cloud solution is to have access to an easy way to provision resources. The following sections cover a wide variety of tools that are designed to simplify how you provide different AWS resources.

AWS CLI

You can interact with AWS resources and services in three primary ways:

▶ **Management Console:** This tool is often the most common way to interact with AWS resources and services. The Management Console is the web-based interface that allows you to navigate your AWS environment to view, create, modify, and destroy AWS resources and services.

▶ **SDK:** A software developer kit provides software developers with the tools needed to communicate with AWS. SDKs are written for specific languages, and at the time of writing this book, the following languages have an AWS SDK: JavaScript, Python, PHP, .NET, Ruby, Java, Go, Node.js, and C++.

▶ **CLI:** A command-line interface is a tool that allows you to perform actions within AWS using text-based commands. Like an SDK, a CLI enables you to automate processes (using shell scripts, for example). When using the Management Console, you can select options using the web-based interface. When using a CLI, you must be aware of these options and the commands associated with specific AWS operations.

ExamAlert

Expect to see at least a handful of CLI questions on the exam. Some of these questions might focus on just the syntax of AWS CLI commands, but there can be some resource-specific questions. If you want to review CLI commands for a specific resource, visit the following reference: https://awscli.amazonaws.com/v2/documentation/api/latest/reference/index.html.

The AWS CLI can be installed on different environments, including MacOS, Linux, Windows, and within Docker containers. Installing the AWS CLI is not an exam objective, so we don't cover it any further in this book; however, if you want to install the AWS CLI for practice, visit the following site for additional information: https://docs.aws.amazon.com/cli/latest/userguide/install-cliv2.html.

After installing the AWS CLI, you need to configure it so that it can communicate with your AWS environment. This configuration requires information about a user account, including the account access key ID and a secret access key, which is generated while creating the user when choosing the option shown in Figure 7.1.

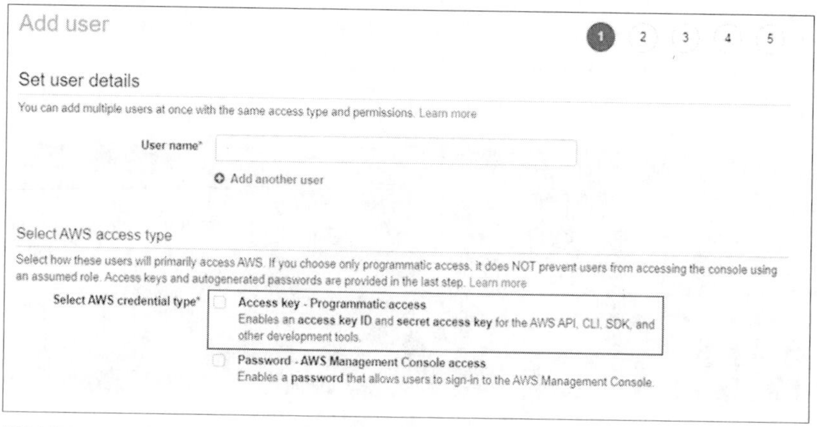

FIGURE 7.1   Setting the access key ID and secret access key

To configure the AWS CLI after installing, execute the **aws configure** command as follows:

```
$ aws configure
AWS Access Key ID [None]: <insert Access Key ID here>
AWS Secret Access Key [None]: <insert Secret Access Key ID here>
Default region name [None]: <insert region name, like us-west-1, here>
Default output format [None]: <insert output format here; json is most
                              common>
```

To understand the basic syntax of an AWS CLI command, consider the following example:

```
aws ec2 terminate-instances --instance-ids <id>
```

The command syntax breaks down into these different components:

▶ **aws:** All AWS CLI commands start with **aws**.

▶ **ec2:** This is called the AWS command or top-level command. Typically, it is associated with an AWS service or resource—**ec2** in this case.

▶ **terminate-instances:** This is called the subcommand. Each AWS command has subcommands that further define the action to take. In this example, the **terminate-instances** command is designed to terminate one or more instances that are currently running.

▶ **--instance-ids:** This is an option to the command. Options are specific to the command or subcommand. In this example, the option **--instance-ids** is used to indicate which instances are to be terminated.

▶ **<id>:** This is the argument that corresponds with the previous option. In this example, **<id>** would be replaced with one or more EC2 instance IDs before actually running this command.

> **ExamAlert**
>
> There are hundreds of **aws ec2** subcommands, too many to memorize for the exam. If you are asked any questions that are specific to **aws ec2** subcommands, they will likely be about listing, launching, or terminating EC2 instances. Consider reviewing the following short guide before taking the exam to become familiar with these subcommands: https://docs.aws.amazon.com/cli/latest/userguide/cli-services-ec2-instances.html.

Managing EC2 AMIs

An EC2 AMI, or Amazon Machine Image, is used to launch an EC2 instance. You can manage AMIs via the Management Console by navigating to **Services > EC2 > Images > AMIs**. Once there, the following options are available:

- ▶ **Launch:** Launch an EC2 instance from a selected AMI.

- ▶ **EC2 Image Builder:** Build an AMI (that is, image) using a guided wizard provided by the Management Console.

- ▶ **Actions:** This provides additional EC2 options, including the ability to copy an existing AMI and deregister an AMI.

- ▶ **Access the AWS Marketplace:** Clicking the Find More Than 500 AMIs of Popular Open Source and Commercial Software From link takes you to the AWS Marketplace where other organizations have provided customized AMIs. These AMIs are broken into different categories, such as Business Applications, DevOps, and Machine Learning. Although some of these AMIs are free to use, many have some sort of fee associated with them.

> **ExamAlert**
>
> For the exam, be aware that you can create your own AMIs or deploy AMIs from the AWS Marketplace. Also, be aware that in addition to the charges incurred for having the AWS instance run, AMIs from the AWS Marketplace often have an additional cost, like a license fee.

AWS CloudFormation

Imagine a scenario in which you must routinely provision a collection of resources. For example, maybe each developer within your organization needs to have an EC2 instance in which to perform their work. The tedious task of managing these resources takes valuable time from your staff, resulting in higher employee costs.

Additionally, manually configuring systems sometimes results in misconfigurations caused by human errors. These misconfigurations are even more likely in a scenario in which a more complex collection of resources needs to be provisioned. For example, imagine your organization needs to routinely provision three EC2 instances within its own VPC, along with a Security Group and a Load Balancer.

AWS CloudFormation, an Infrastructure as Code (IaC) solution, is designed to make the managing of AWS Resources less time consuming. This is handled using CloudFormation templates, which are JSON- or YAML-formatted files that describe the details of the resources that you want to provision. The template is a key component to a CloudFormation Stack, which is the resource in CloudFormation that performs the provisioning operation when executed.

A complete CloudFormation template can contain hundreds of lines to define all of the parameters of the resources that you want to provision. The following simple example using YAML format provisions an EC2 instance:

```
Resources:
  WebAppInstance:
    Type: AWS::EC2::Instance
    Properties:
      ImageId: ami- 6d1c2007f840b45e9
      InstanceType: t2.micro
```

The same resource can be provisioned using a JSON-formatted file, like the following:

```
{
    "Resources": {
        "WebAppInstance": {
            "Type": "AWS::EC2::Instance",
            "Properties": {
                "ImageId": "ami- 6d1c2007f840b45e9",
                "InstanceType": "t2.micro"
            }
        }
    }
}
```

AWS Elastic Beanstalk

With AWS Elastic Beanstalk, you can deploy and manage applications within your AWS infrastructure. Although this might sound similar to AWS Cloud-Formation, remember that CloudFormation provides an IaC solution. In other words, the goal of CloudFormation is to make it easy to manage the infrastructure resources (EC2 instances, database resources, and so on). With Elastic

Beanstalk, the focus is on the application, and the infrastructure is automatically provisioned as needed by Elastic Beanstalk.

> **ExamAlert**
>
> If you are asked an exam question that is related to provisioning infrastructure components, think AWS CloudFormation. If the question is related to deploying applications, think AWS Elastic Beanstalk.

The wizard that is used to create an Elastic Beanstalk resource provides a good idea of the purpose of the service. As with most resources, this wizard asks you to provide a name for the application and (optionally) tags. Figure 7.2 shows the next two sections of this wizard.

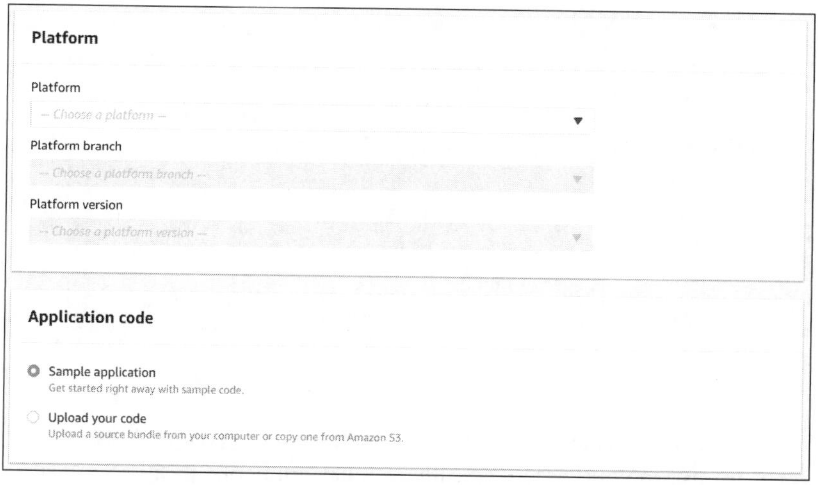

Platform

Platform

-- Choose a platform --

Platform branch

-- Choose a platform branch --

Platform version

-- Choose a platform version --

Application code

◉ Sample application
Get started right away with sample code.

○ Upload your code
Upload a source bundle from your computer or copy one from Amazon S3.

FIGURE 7.2   **AWS Elastic Beanstalk Wizard**

Note that you are prompted to provide a platform (side note: AWS Elastic Beanstalk is a PaaS service). At press time, the following platforms are available:

- ▶ .NET Core on Linux
- ▶ .NET on Windows Server
- ▶ Docker
- ▶ GlassFish
- ▶ Go
- ▶ Java

- ▶ Node.js
- ▶ PHP
- ▶ Python
- ▶ Ruby
- ▶ Tomcat

The preceding are application platforms. For example, the Python platform would mean that you want to execute Python code in the application.

The Platform branch defines the infrastructure where the application is executed. These are defined by AWS, as you can see in Figure 7.3.

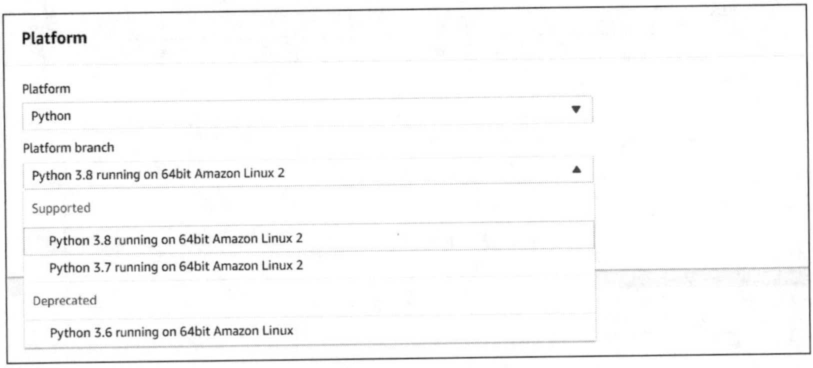

Platform

Platform

| Python | ▼ |

Platform branch

| Python 3.8 running on 64bit Amazon Linux 2 | ▲ |

Supported

Python 3.8 running on 64bit Amazon Linux 2

Python 3.7 running on 64bit Amazon Linux 2

Deprecated

Python 3.6 running on 64bit Amazon Linux

FIGURE 7.3 **Python platform branches**

The platform version allows you to specify which specific version of the platform you want to run your code. Typically, you have only one option because AWS does not support many versions of a platform.

In the last section of this wizard shown in Figure 7.3, you choose what code you want to execute. You can start with a sample application and build your code from the sample. Alternatively, you can write your code in a separate testing environment and upload your code.

CloudFormation StackSets

One of the features of CloudFormation is StackSets, a tool that allows you to manage stacks that manage resources across multiple accounts and AWS regions. A stack is a group or collection of AWS resources that you want to manage as a single unit. The StackSet is created in a single AWS account within a single region. The StackSet uses the template that you provided to create, update, or delete additional stacks in other AWS accounts or regions using the template defined within the StackSet.

The account in which you create the StackSet is referred to as the Administrator account. The accounts where stacks are created by the StackSet are called Target accounts. See Figure 7.4 for a conceptual view of this concept.

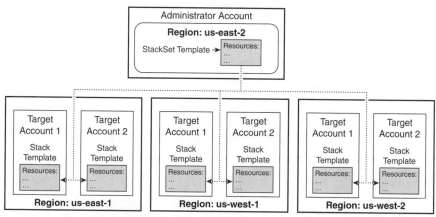

FIGURE 7.4   **AWS CloudFormation StackSets**

On the exam, you likely won't be asked questions regarding creating complete StackSet templates, but you should be familiar with the concept and following prerequisites for using StackSets:

▶ StackSets either make use of service-managed or self-managed permissions on the Target account. Complete steps to configuring these permissions are beyond the scope of this book, but for the exam you should be aware of these requirements.

▶ StackSets use a feature of AWS Organizations called trusted access. AWS Organizations is a tool that allows you to manage multiple AWS accounts. The feature of trusted access must be configured before using StackSets.

AWS Systems Manager

One of the concerns that an organization that migrates to the cloud has is how to see the organization's infrastructure. The AWS Systems Manager provides a single pane of glass that allows for full visibility of the resources within an organization's infrastructure. When using Systems Manager, you can place resources into groups and visualize the aggregated operational data of the group. You can also take actions that are applied to all of the resources in the group.

AWS Systems Manager is really a collection of tools, including the following:

▶ **Explorer:** This dashboard displays analytical data regarding the operational health and performances of resources. This data can be derived from multiple AWS accounts and regions.

▶ **OpsCenter:** When operational issues crop up, the OpsCenter is the place where you can investigate the issues. The OpsCenter provides information from different sources, including CloudTrail logs, CloudWatch alarms, and AWS Config data.

▶ **Incident Manager:** This tool allows you to see incidents related to the availability and performance of applications. The tool also allows you to configure automatic responses to incidents.

Overall AWS Systems Manager provides more than 15 different tools. See https://aws.amazon.com/systems-manager/features/ for a summary of these tools.

AWS Resource Access Manager

Many large organizations have multiple AWS accounts. All these accounts pose difficulties when a resource that has been created in one account needs to be accessible in another account. The AWS Resource Access Manager (RAM) allows you to share resources across multiple AWS accounts.

RAM can be used either with or without AWS Organizations. When RAM is used without AWS Organizations, resources can be directly shared with other AWS accounts. When it is used with AWS Organizations, resources can be shared with an organization unit (OU), individual IAM roles, or individual IAM users.

When sharing resources with RAM, you also specify what permissions the resource share will be allowed. These are similar to the IAM permissions that you can grant roles and user accounts. For example, if you share an EC2 image resource, you can use the AWSRAMDefaultPermissionImageBuilderImage permission to list available images (imagebuilder:ListImages) and retrieve an image (imagebuilder:GetImage).

> **ExamAlert**
>
> It is unlikely that you will be asked questions about specific RAM permissions on the exam, but you should be aware that permissions are used to limit access to resources that are shared by RAM.

Not all resources can be shared with RAM. At press time, the following resources are sharable:

▶ AWS App Mesh

▶ AWS Certificate Manager Private Certificate Authority

▶ Amazon Aurora

▶ AWS CodeBuild

▶ Amazon EC2

▶ EC2 Image Builder

▶ AWS Glue

▶ AWS License Manager

▶ AWS Network Firewall

▶ AWS Outposts

▶ Amazon S3 on Outposts

▶ AWS Resource Groups

▶ Amazon Route 53

▶ AWS Systems Manager Incident Manager

▶ Amazon VPC

Cram Quiz

Answer these questions. The answers follow the last question. If you cannot answer these questions correctly, consider reading this section again until you can.

1. You have been asked to configure the AWS CLI to be used for a new IAM account. Which of the following account parameters need to be generated to correctly configure the AWS CLI? (Choose two.)

    ○ **A.** Access key ID

    ○ **B.** Authorization ID key

    ○ **C.** Secret access key

    ○ **D.** User control key

2. Which of the following are valid AWS CLI commands?

  ○ **A.** **aws ec2 --instance-ids i-1234567890abcdef0 terminate-instances**

  ○ **B.** **aws terminate-instances ec2 --instance-ids i-1234567890abcdef0**

  ○ **C.** **aws ec2 terminate-instances --instance-ids i-1234567890abcdef0**

  ○ **D.** **aws --instance-ids i-1234567890abcdef0 terminate-instances ec2**

Cram Quiz Answers

1. Answer: A and C are correct. The AWS CLI configuration requires information about a user account, including the account access key ID and secret access key, which is generated when creating the user account.

2. Answer: C is correct. The top-level command (**ec2**) should be next after **aws**. The secondary command (**terminate-instances**) should be after the primary command. The options/argument pair (**--instance-ids i-1234567890abcdef0**) follows the secondary command.

What Next?

If you want more practice on this chapter's exam objectives before you move on, remember that you can access all of the Cram Quiz questions on the Pearson Test Prep software online. You can also create a custom exam by objective with the Online Practice Test. Note any objective you struggle with and go to that objective's material in this chapter.

CHAPTER 8

Application Management

This chapter covers the following official AWS Certified SysOps Administrator - Associate (SOA-C02) exam domain:

▶ Domain 3: Deployment, Provisioning, and Automation

(For more information on the official AWS Certified SysOps Administrator - Associate [SOA-C02] exam topics, see the Introduction.)

Resources in the cloud often contain software that needs to be maintained. This includes handling the lifecycle management of software as well as routine operations such as upgrading and patching software.

In this chapter, you learn about these application management processes, as well as the applications and tools that you may utilize in your AWS account to make the process of managing applications easier and more automated.

Lifecycle Management

This section covers the following official AWS Certified SysOps Administrator - Associate (SOA-C02) exam topics for Domain 3: Deployment, Provisioning, and Automation:

▶ 3.1 Provision and maintain cloud resources

▶ 3.2 Automate manual or repeatable processes

CramSaver

If you can correctly answer these questions before going through this section, save time by skimming the Exam Alerts in this section and then completing the Cram Quiz at the end of the section.

1. Which deployment should contain the live solution that your organization uses?

2. What is an LTS build?

Answers

1. Answer: Production.

2. Answer: An LTS build is a stable build that should be supported for a longer than average period of time.

Deploying resources isn't just about provisioning a server or a database. Resources in the cloud cost your organization money, both in direct costs from AWS as well as the money to maintain the resources. Additionally, a mis-deployed resource can cost additional money and can bring an operation to a standstill.

The following sections focus on the different application builds you should consider when planning your deployment. They also cover different upgrade methods that can have an impact on your resources.

Deployment Environments

A major consideration when deciding how to deploy applications in the cloud is to determine which environments you want to create. Each environment plays a specific role in your solution. Not all environments are deployed in every situation, and each environment provides a benefit that must be weighed against the cost (typically budgetary cost, but there are other costs, such as manpower and maintenance costs).

Development

In a development environment, you develop new software or modify existing software that your organization is developing. Although the development environment might be used to prepare for changes to a production environment, its primary purpose is to allow software developers to operate in an environment that doesn't affect any live work.

Quality Assurance (QA)

In a QA environment, testing is performed before migrating changes to a production environment. Initially, the QA environment should mirror the current production environment. In the QA environment, new features and configurations are tested to ensure they meet the needs of the users and organization.

Testing can include having regular users work in the environment to ensure that the environment works as it should. Eventually, after testing is complete, the changes made to the development environment are implemented in the production environment.

Production

The production environment is the live solution that is used by your organization.

Staging

Some organizations utilize a staging environment to replicate the production environment. This staging environment can be used for several different purposes, including determining potential problems in the production environment and as a replacement when the production environment fails or is compromised. It is also used when implementing a blue/green deployment (see the following section for more details).

Blue/Green

When using a blue/green deployment, you have two identical environments: production and staging. The production environment is live and used actively within your organization. The staging area is used in the final phase of deploying a new version of the solution. This means that changes made within your QA environment are applied to the staging environment, and some final tests are performed.

After tests have passed successfully, the staging environment is converted into the production environment, and the production environment is now treated as the staging environment. If the solution still runs smoothly, changes made to the original staging environment are then applied to the new staging environment. The result is the two environments are identical again.

This process is called a blue/green deployment because one environment is traditionally labeled "blue," and the other is traditionally labeled "green." Note that either blue or green can be the production or staging environment at any given time.

The advantages of using this method are smoother upgrades, less downtime, and the ability to quickly roll back a deployment to a previously working environment. The disadvantages of this system are the additional costs and time to maintain both environments.

Disaster Recovery (DR)

A DR environment is used specifically if the production environment is compromised. While a staging area can sometimes be used for DR, it is not an ideal DR solution because there are times during a new deployment that it is not identical to a production environment.

A DR is an identical copy to the production environment that has one specific purpose: a quick way to restore a compromised environment. Typically, the DR environment should be located in a different geographic location than the production environment so a physical disaster cannot disable both environments.

> **ExamAlert**
>
> Expect scenario-based questions designed to test your ability to determine which development environment is the best solution for a given situation.

Application Builds

When an organization develops software and the software is released, either internally or externally, the release is referred to as a build. This section explores different types of builds.

Stable

A stable release is designed to be a release that is ready for a production environment. Typically, if you are a customer who purchases software, that software is considered a stable build.

Prior to a software build being released, earlier releases are called beta builds. Some organizations like to have access to beta builds because this provides them with early insight as to how the software will perform. However, beta builds come with little to no support or warranty. They are considered "use at your own risk" and should not be used in production environments.

Long-Term Support (LTS)

An LTS build is a stable build that should be supported for a longer than average period of time. This can be an important issue for some organizations because moving to a new version of software can pose several challenges, including

▶ Time, effort, and money to ensure that the new version performs within standards.

▶ Potential new licensing costs.

▶ Having to deal with potential inconsistencies or incompatibilities. For example, a newer version of software might not integrate with other software that the organization is already using.

▶ Additional training costs to teach existing employees and customers how the new version of the software behaves.

▶ Reduced production as employees attempt to use the new version of the software.

One disadvantage of utilizing an LTS build is that new features that are released with the regular stable build are not normally implemented in the LTS build.

Canary

You may have heard how miners would take a canary into the mines with them to determine if the air held dangerous levels of toxic gases. The idea was that the bird had a faster breathing rate than humans and would show signs of the presence of toxic gases sooner than humans would.

A canary release works on a similar concept. New features are released to a specific set of beta testers to determine if the new features have any negative impact on the software. The features are provided in the new beta builds in a very specific manner and typically spread out over several beta releases. This allows the developers some insight as to which new features may have caused an issue and allows the developers the time to fix the issues before releasing the software in a stable build.

Upgrade Methods

The following sections describe different upgrade methods that your organization may incorporate when upgrading resources in the cloud.

Rolling Upgrades

Rolling upgrades (also called continuous delivery) is the process of frequently providing updates to software. With this upgrade method, there are not specific release points (although it is common for rolling upgrades to happen nightly), but rather when the developer is ready, a new upgrade is released.

One advantage of a rolling upgrade is that new features are more rapidly released to customers. However, rolling upgrades may be more susceptible to bugs.

Most developers that provide rolling upgrades also provide traditional "release point" upgrades. For example, the popular web browser called Firefox provides a nightly rolling upgrade, but it also provides regular standard releases.

Active-Passive

An active-passive upgrade is similar to using a blue/green deployment. With an active-passive upgrade, the upgrade is deployed to the active environment and the passive environment is not changed.

If any problems occur in the active environment because of the patching, the passive environment is treated temporarily as the active environment. When the problems are worked out in the original active environment, the original passive environment is again treated as passive, and the original active environment is used again as the actual active environment.

If, after testing and a specific period of time, the active environment seems to be functioning properly, the patch is applied to the passive environment. This is different from a blue/green development environment in which the two systems "flip flop" between upgrades as active and passive.

Lifecycle Management

The following sections explore lifecycle management of cloud resources.

Roadmaps

In lifecycle management, roadmaps provide a timeline for the implementation of the product from start to finish. Roadmaps are also used to align the product with business goals and are designed to provide an easy way to visualize the lifecycle management of a project.

Each product may have multiple roadmaps because the visibility of the process may be different for different people. For example, executives may just need to see the "big picture," whereas implementers need to see every detail. Customers may also have a different roadmap because they are focused on when features will be released.

Roadmaps can often be grouped into one of the following categories:

▶ **Features roadmap:** Describes when features will be added to the product.

▶ **Release roadmap:** Describes when each version of the product will be released.

▶ **Portfolio roadmap:** Provides a collection of product lifecycles and how they are related to one another.

▶ **Strategy roadmap:** Defines the overall high-level actions that must take place to meet the goals of the product during its lifecycle.

Versioning

A product's lifecycle management process must include how different versions of the product will be maintained and supported. For example, suppose the current release of a product is version 3.2. In this case, how is version 3.1 handled? Is it still supported by the organization? Is the product still being patched on a regular basis? What are the steps needed to migrate customers from 3.1 to 3.2? And, of course, these same answers (and more) need to be asked for version 3.0 and any previous version.

For new versions, decisions regarding new features and the migration process from older releases need to be made. How does the organization let the customer know about upcoming new features? What happens if a new feature is not available in the release it was originally planned for? Will some features of new versions also be implemented in older versions that are still supported (a process called backporting)?

Upgrading and Migrating Systems

Upgrading a system is the process of enhancing an existing system to provide more features or better performance. For example, you might opt to add more

RAM to an existing system to increase available memory for an operating system.

Migrating a system is the process of moving a resource from one physical location to another. For example, instead of upgrading a system by adding more RAM, you could migrate the operating system to a new hardware platform that has more RAM than the original.

The same concepts apply in cloud computing. Operating systems are placed within virtual machines in the cloud, and these EC2 instances have underlying hardware components. In some cases, you may be able to enhance an existing virtual machine (for example, add more virtual memory), but in other cases, you might find migrating to a new virtual machine to be a better solution. For example, if you need a faster or more powerful CPU, this isn't something that is just added to an existing virtual machine (at least not typical cloud vendor solutions).

Note that this upgrade versus migration doesn't just apply to instances. Any cloud resource, including applications and database software, uses underlying hardware resources that may either be upgraded or require a migration to provide more power and flexibility.

Deprecations or End of Life

Most products will eventually reach a point when they no longer serve a useful purpose or no longer align with the organization's business needs. Typically, an organization takes one of two approaches:

▶ **Specify an end of life for the product:** This involves indicating when the product will no longer be supported and should no longer be used. It is also referred to as "sunsetting" a product.

▶ **Deprecate the product:** This occurs when an organization indicates that the product should no longer be used and is unlikely to be supported in the future. Typically, a deprecated product is being replaced by a newer product, but the organization isn't prepared to force customers to move to the new product. Consider deprecated to be "it is still available, but the developer doesn't recommend you use it anymore."

AWS OpsWorks

AWS provides several tools to help you manage deployments. For the AWS Certified SysOps Administrator – Associate exam, you should focus on AWS OpsWorks, AWS Systems Manager, and AWS CloudFormation because these are the tools specifically mentioned on the exam objectives. Recall that AWS Systems Manager and AWS CloudFormation were covered in Chapter 7, "Provisioning Resources."

AWS OpsWorks consists of three separate products:

- ▶ **AWS OpsWorks for Puppet Enterprise:** Puppet is a third-party product that is used to manage infrastructure resources. It provides a centralized server that performs automated operations on systems, including provisioning, modification, and deprovisioning. Puppet Enterprise also maintains a database of the systems that have been provisioned.

- ▶ **AWS OpsWorks for Chef Automate:** Like Puppet, Chef is a third-party product that allows the central management of infrastructure resources.

- ▶ **AWS OpsWorks Stacks:** Prior to supporting Puppet Enterprise and Chef Automate solutions, AWS OpsWorks Stacks was the only OpsWorks option. OpsWorks Stacks leverages the Chef recipes (the text files that define the infrastructure) but does not require provisioning a Chef server.

Complete coverage of Puppet Enterprise, Chef Automate, and OpsWorks Stacks is beyond the scope of this book. The following are some of the key concepts that you want to know for the exam:

- ▶ AWS OpsWorks for Puppet requires a Puppet server be installed within AWS. Likewise for Chef Automate. In both cases, a wizard is provided to assist with the installation process.

- ▶ AWS OpsWorks is designed to manage the state of a server, including configuration of the server and installation/removal of software on the server.

Cram Quiz

Answer these questions. The answers follow the last question. If you cannot answer these questions correctly, consider reading this section again until you can.

1. You have been asked to deploy some new features in a build for beta testers to review. Which of the following would be the best build environment to utilize for this scenario?

   ○ **A.** Stable.

   ○ **B.** LTS.

   ○ **C.** Canary.

   ○ **D.** Blue/green.

   ○ **E.** None of these answers are correct.

2. Your organization has decided that one of its products should no longer be used and is unlikely to be supported in the future. Which action should the organization take?

   ○ **A.** Deprecate the product.

   ○ **B.** Rename the product.

   ○ **C.** Ignore the product.

   ○ **D.** Re-release the product.

Cram Quiz Answers

1. Answer: C is correct. In a canary release, new features are released to a specific set of beta testers to determine whether the new features have any negative impact on the software.

2. Answer: A is correct. Deprecate the product. In this situation, an organization indicates that the product should no longer be used and is unlikely to be supported in the future.

Patching

This section covers the following official AWS Certified SysOps Administrator - Associate (SOA-C02) exam topic for Domain 3: Deployment, Provisioning, and Automation:

▶ 3.1 Provision and maintain cloud resources

▶ 3.2 Automate manual or repeatable processes

CramSaver

If you can correctly answer these questions before going through this section, save time by skimming the Exam Alerts in this section and then completing the Cram Quiz at the end of the section.

1. A _____ is a collection of hot fixes.

2. For the term *N-1*, *N* refers to the most _____ release of software.

Answers

1. Answer: A rollup is a collection of hot fixes. In some cases, the rollup might contain more than just security updates, but the main focus is to address a collection of security or critical issues with a single update.

2. Answer: For the term *N-1*, *N* refers to the most recent stable release of software, and *N-1* refers to the previous most recent stable release of the software.

In the following sections, you learn about different types of patches that you may deploy on cloud resources. You also explore different patch features.

Security Patches

A security patch is a specific type of software update that is designed to address a vulnerability. Software updates are normally scheduled in advance; for example, an update for a particular software program may come out every three months. When a vulnerability is made known to the software vendor, it is often not near the date of a regular software update. Even if it was near the date for a regular update, the steps to implement the vulnerability fix in the new release may pose a logistical challenge because the update has new changes to the software.

A patch is used instead to create a temporary fix to the problem. Patches are released as needed, often without advance warning. You can keep up with patches by either subscribing to the software vendor's notification system or by viewing Common Vulnerability and Exposure (CVE) notices at https://cve.mitre.org/.

Hot Fixes

When you see the term *hot fix*, think "quick fix." A hot fix isn't intended to be a long-term solution, but rather something to fix the problem while the software vendor works on a more robust and permanent fix. A virtual patch (see the "Virtual Patches" section later) is an example of a hot fix.

Scheduled Updates

As mentioned previously, a scheduled update isn't a patch, but it may contain code that addresses vulnerabilities like a patch does. Most likely the vulnerabilities have been addressed via previous patches, but occasionally a new vulnerability is fixed with a scheduled update.

Virtual Patches

Virtual patches don't really address a vulnerability directly but make use of another tool, like a Web Application Firewall (WAF), to provide a short-term fix to the problem. With a virtual patch, a small application is attached to the software with the goal to block access that the vulnerability currently allows.

Signature Updates

A signature update is associated with antivirus software. A virus signature is much like a fingerprint of the virus. Antivirus programs use this signature to determine whether a virus has infected a system.

Ensuring the antivirus signatures are up to date on a system is a very high priority.

Rollups

A rollup is a collection of hot fixes. In some cases, the rollup might contain more than just security updates, but the main focus is to address a collection of security or critical issues with a single update.

Patching Cloud Components

Although many patches are designed to fix an issue with a product, some patches are designed to provide additional features or enhancements to the software. This is typically performed in a full product upgrade, but in some cases a new feature is requested by a customer and needs to be implemented before the next upgrade cycle.

One of the more common reasons a patch is deployed is to fix a problem in the product. Typically, this is referred to as a *bug fix*, and it is meant to be a temporary fix until the next update of the product.

Because cloud resources are often interrelated, a patch to one resource often requires patches to other resources. The scope of the cloud elements to be patched includes all of the cloud resources that need to be patched to successfully deploy changes.

VMs

Keep in mind that a virtual machine (VM) is a virtual installation of an operating system. Patching VMs in the cloud can pose challenges because the cloud environment doesn't typically include the means to patch operating systems. This is almost always a responsibility of the cloud customer.

OS patches come from the developer of the OS, and there is typically a central location where you can learn about new patches. There are also automation tools that can be used to make the process of patching a large number of systems easier.

Virtual Appliances

A virtual appliance is a type of virtual machine image. The difference between a virtual appliance and a standard virtual machine is that the virtual appliance has been preconfigured to perform a specific task (or set of tasks). This makes the process of patching more difficult because both the operating system and the applications of the virtual appliance require patches on a regular basis.

Some vendors who create virtual appliances also provide patches for the appliance, but this isn't always the case.

Networking Components

When an organization uses a cloud vendor to deploy its cloud infrastructure, the networking components (routers, switches, and so on) are entirely the responsibility of the cloud vendor. If, however, your organization is implementing a private cloud on-premises, patching the network components is the responsibility of your organization.

Modern network components are complex and typically include a full operating system. As with any OS, the vendor who created the network component will occasionally release patches. Typically, these vendors have patch release announcements and may even have a regular patch release cycle.

Applications

In terms of patching applications, the scope depends on the origin of the application as well as the responsibility level associated with the application. For example, if you are using a Software as a Service application, the cloud vendor or the application developer should be 100 percent responsible for patching the application. It is important to review the SLA and other contracts to verify which organization is responsible for patching.

If the application is not SaaS, it is likely the cloud customer's responsibility to patch. This patch may be performed manually or via an automation tool.

Storage Components

A storage component is the underlying device where the data is stored. This can include a magnetic hard drive, a solid-state drive, or a tape device. In terms of patching, the devices themselves may require occasional firmware updates (see the next section on firmware). Additionally, the software used by an operating system to access the storage device (called a device driver) might also need to be patched occasionally.

Firmware

Firmware is software that is designed to provide control over device hardware. In a public cloud, customers rarely have any control over the firmware that is being utilized by the physical hardware (exceptions can include when a customer leases the entire physical system for their use). As a result, the patching of firmware in a public cloud is almost always fully in the scope of the cloud vendor.

In a private cloud environment, where the control of the physical systems is in the hands of the organization using the private cloud, firmware is the responsibility of the organization.

Software

The terms *application* and *software* are often mistakenly used interchangeably, but these terms are not synonymous. An application is a type of software, but software encompasses all types of code that is executed on a system. Often to distinguish between application software and other types of software, the term *systems software* is used.

In the terms of the scope of software patching in a cloud environment, systems software and application software are similar. The biggest difference is that application software is more often SaaS and the patching falls under the responsibility of the cloud vendor or the application developer. Systems software is more often not SaaS and is therefore the responsibility of the cloud customer to ensure the software is properly patched.

Policies

Just because a patch is released doesn't mean that it should be immediately applied. Patches are often temporary fixes and may cause more problems than they fix. Some patches are also minor and unnecessary, at least in terms of the business goals of your organization.

Your organization should have policies on which patches to apply and how they should be applied. For example, you might have a policy that patches are first deployed in a testing environment and tests are performed before releasing in a development environment.

You should also consider which versions of software you wish to deploy. Some organizations opt to have the latest version installed, whereas others tend to stay one version behind. See the next section on N-1 for more details.

N-1

For the term *N-1*, *N* refers to the most recent stable release of software, and *N-1* refers to the previous most recent stable release of the software. There are advantages and disadvantages to always upgrading to the latest release versus staying one release behind the most current release, including

▶ **Features:** The N release typically has newer features that the N-1 release does not.

▶ **Compatibility:** The N-1 release tends to be more compatible with other existing or older software, whereas the N release might work better if you have updated to other related software.

▶ **Security:** The N-1 release tends to require less security patching than the N release because the code is more mature and more of the bugs have been worked out.

Rollbacks

A rollback is a method of undoing the steps taken during a patch. In some cases, a patch may not permit a rollback. In these situations, you want to make sure you test the patch in a testing environment and make sure you back up all related data before patching a live system. You should also have another plan in place to recover the software, which could include performing a full backup on all software before implementing the patch.

> **ExamAlert**
>
> The exam objectives that are related to this section are
>
> ▶ Select deployment scenarios and services (for example, blue/green, rolling, canary)
>
> ▶ Implement automated patch management
>
> Note that these objectives do not list any specific AWS services. However, many of these tools, including OpsWorks, Systems Manager, and CloudFormation, are covered in this chapter and in Chapter 7.

Cram Quiz

Answer these questions. The answers follow the last question. If you cannot answer these questions correctly, consider reading this section again until you can.

1. You have determined that there is a problem with a patch that was recently deployed. Which method would be the best solution to undo the actions that were taken when the patch was deployed?

   ○ **A.** Restore the backup.

   ○ **B.** Perform a rollback.

   ○ **C.** Reinstall software.

   ○ **D.** Delete the patch.

2. Which of the following patch types is most likely to be the responsibility of AWS?

   ○ **A.** VMs

   ○ **B.** Virtual appliances

   ○ **C.** Custom applications

   ○ **D.** Firmware

Cram Quiz Answers

1. **Answer: B is correct.** A rollback is the best method of undoing the steps taken during a patch. In some cases, a patch may not permit a rollback. In these situations, you want to make sure you test the patch in a testing environment and make sure you back up all related data before patching a live system. You should also have another plan in place to recover the software, which could include performing a full backup on all software before implementing the patch.

2. **Answer: D is correct.** Firmware is software that is designed to provide control over device hardware. In a public cloud, customers rarely have any control over the firmware that is being utilized by the physical hardware (exceptions can include when a customer leases the entire physical system for their use). As a result, the patching of firmware in a public cloud is almost always fully in the scope of the cloud vendor.

What Next?

If you want more practice on this chapter's exam objectives before you move on, remember that you can access all of the Cram Quiz questions on the Pearson Test Prep software online. You can also create a custom exam by objective with the Online Practice Test. Note any objective you struggle with and go to that objective's material in this chapter.

CHAPTER 9

Security and Compliance

This chapter covers the following official AWS Certified SysOps Administrator - Associate (SOA-C02) exam domain:

▶ Domain 4: Security and Compliance

(For more information on the official AWS Certified SysOps Administrator - Associate [SOA-C02] exam topics, see the Introduction.)

Managing the security of your AWS account is critical to avoiding a compromised environment. In this chapter, you learn how to manage AWS accounts, including user accounts, group accounts, and roles. You also explore policies to ensure your accounts have the right access to AWS services and resources.

Key topics like access keys, MFA, and security best practices are also covered in this chapter. Finally, you learn how you can use the AWS Trusted Advisor to seek out security issues for your AWS account.

Account Management

This section covers the following official AWS Certified SysOps Administrator - Associate (SOA-C02) exam topics for Domain 4: Security and Compliance:

▶ 4.1 Implement and manage security and compliance policies

▶ 4.2 Implement data and infrastructure protection strategies

CramSaver

If you can correctly answer these questions before going through this section, save time by skimming the Exam Alerts in this section and then completing the Cram Quiz at the end of the section.

1. You have an application hosted on an EC2 instance that needs access to other resources in your AWS account. What IAM feature can you use to provide this access?

2. What is the default password length for AWS accounts?

Answers

1. Answer: A role.

2. Answer: Eight characters.

IAM Essentials

Part of managing accounts on AWS is to have a strong understanding of the different types of accounts provided by AWS Identity and Access Management (IAM). You should understand these account types and know which type of account to use in any given situation.

You also should be aware of other IAM components, such as policies, providers, and settings, which you can see on the IAM page shown in Figure 9.1.

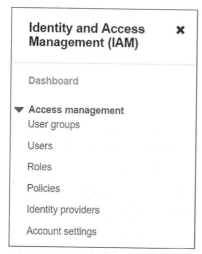

FIGURE 9.1 **IAM components**

IAM Users

User accounts provide access to AWS resources and services. When you first access your AWS account, you use the root user account. This account has full access to perform all operations within the AWS account.

Not all individuals should have full access to all AWS operations. When you create an IAM user account, you should limit access based on the functions that the user should perform.

When you're creating IAM user accounts, the Add User Wizard prompts you to provide information about the new account, including the following key user account attributes:

▶ **AWS credential type:** If your user will use the AWS console only to perform tasks, select **Password - AWS Management Console Access**. If the user will access AWS via application programming interfaces (APIs), the command-line interface (CLI), software development kit (SDK), or another development tool, select **Access Key - Programmatic Access** to generate an access key ID and secret access key.

▶ **Permissions:** This attribute allows you to determine what actions the IAM user can take. You can provide permissions by assigning the IAM user to a group, copying permissions from an existing user, or by using policies.

▶ **Tags:** AWS IAM user accounts can be treated like other AWS resources in that you can apply tags to user accounts. This way, you can view or modify users with similar tags, making administering user accounts easier.

IAM User Groups

You will often find that multiple IAM users have the same permissions. Instead of individually assigning each user specific permissions, you can create a user group, assign the appropriate permissions, and then assign users to the group.

When you're creating group accounts, the Add Group Wizard prompts you to provide information about the new group account, including the following key user account attributes:

▶ **Group name:** The name should indicate the primary function of the group members, such as "S3 administrators."

▶ **Add users to the group:** You can add existing users to the group or add them later.

▶ **Permissions:** Permissions allow you to determine what actions the group members can take.

IAM Roles

AWS services sometimes need to access AWS resources, much like a user. But you can't assign a user account credentials to an AWS service. Instead, you use a role, which provides temporary permissions for an entity when the entity assumes the role.

For example, an EC2 instance may need to access an S3 bucket to store information. You can create a role and then assign the role to the EC2 instance.

When you create a role, the wizard first asks what type of trusted entity the role will be applied to, as shown in Figure 9.2.

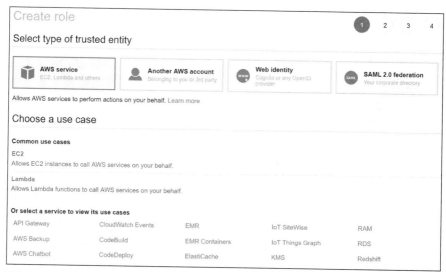

FIGURE 9.2   **Selecting the type of trusted entity**

Note that the trusted entity is not limited to AWS services. User accounts, including AWS accounts and accounts from other sources (Web identities or SAML accounts), can also assume an AWS role.

IAM Policies

IAM Permissions are associated with policies, and policies are applied to user accounts, group accounts, or roles. AWS provides hundreds of premade policies, but you can also create your own custom policies.

ExamAlert

You should know how to view a policy and answer questions regarding what the policy permits.

When you click the **Policies** link on the IAM home page, you can see a list of the premade policies. Each policy is defined as a JSON object. For example, Figure 9.3 shows the JSON object for the AmazonS3ReadOnlyAccess policy.

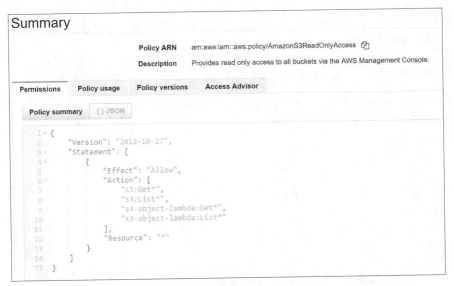

FIGURE 9.3   AmazonS3ReadOnlyAccess policy

There are several components in a policy that you should be aware of, including

▶ **Version:** This component is the version of the policy definition, not of your specific policy. The value associated with the version (in this case, 2012-10-17) is the date of the most recent policy definition, and you should not change this value.

▶ **Statement:** This component is used to define a rule. A rule is used to allow or block access to a resource or service. There can be multiple rules in a policy, so you may see multiple statements in a policy.

▶ **Action:** This component describes the AWS service and level of access. For example, "S3:Get" means "get information from S3 buckets," and "S3:List" means "list the available S3 buckets." There are five access levels for permissions: List, Read, Permissions Management, Write, and Tagging. A value of * means "all five": for example, "S3:*".

▶ **Resource:** This component is used to apply the rule to a specific resource—for example, arn:aws:s3:::examplebucket/test/results.doc. Wildcards can also be used here, such as arn:aws:s3:::examplebucket/*.

If you want to apply a policy to an entity, you can click the Policy Usage tab. This tab displays which entities have the policy attached and allows you to detach or attach this policy to an entity.

Identity Providers

The Identity Providers section of IAM allows you to establish a trust connection between your AWS account and another identity provider (often referred to as an ID). Two standards are currently available:

▶ **SAML:** SAML stands for Security Assertion Markup Language. Identity providers (IDPs) that use SAML include Active Directory and Okta.

▶ **OpenID Connect:** This is another standard that is popular with Google and Salesforce.

Note that some IDPs support both SAML and OpenID Connect. For example, either standard can be used with Okta or Salesforce.

Establishing this trust involves first getting a metadata document from your IDP and uploading this document into the Configure Provider Wizard, as shown in Figure 9.4.

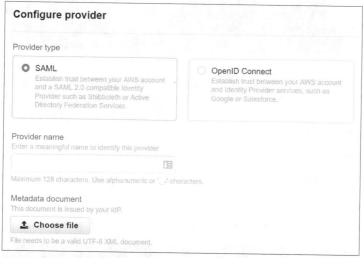

FIGURE 9.4 **Configuring the IDP**

ExamAlert

Configuring an IDP is straightforward when using the Configure Provider Wizard. For the exam, the most important point to remember about IDPs is that AWS supports the SAML and OpenID Connect standards.

Password Policy

Under the Account Settings option of the IAM home page, there is a place where you can modify the password policy. This policy is applied whenever a user attempts to change their password.

AWS provides a default password policy for all AWS accounts, which includes the following rules:

▶ The length of the password must be a minimum of eight characters.

▶ The password must use at least three character types, including uppercase letters, lowercase letters, numbers, and a collection of special characters.

▶ The password cannot be the same as the account name or the email address associated with the account.

ExamAlert

Be familiar with the default password policy because you may be asked a question regarding whether the password policy needs to be changed to match specific criteria.

You can change the password policy, including implementing the following features:

▶ Enable a default expiration of the account password.

▶ Require the administrator to reset an expired password.

▶ Allow users to change their own passwords.

▶ Prevent users from reusing their passwords.

ExamAlert

For the exam, recall that the ability for users to reset their own IAM passwords is not enabled by default.

Access Keys

As previously mentioned, when you create a user account, you have the option to create a key pair for authentication. One key is called the access key ID, and the other is called the secret access key. This is similar to a username and password in the sense that both keys are used to authenticate a user when the user needs programmatic access to their AWS account.

Immediately after the account is created, the key information is displayed, as shown in Figure 9.5.

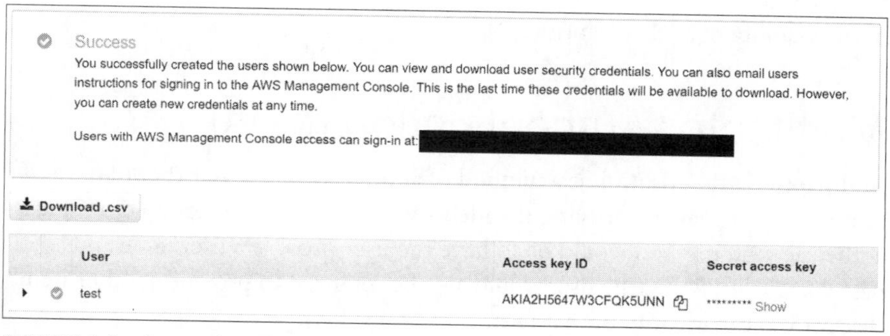

FIGURE 9.5   **Access keys**

Keep this information secure and ensure that your users also keep this information secure. Note that you can download the key information in CSV format, or you can just copy and paste it to a secure location. If you lose this information, new keys need to be generated.

If a user loses their security keys or if the keys are compromised, you should deactivate the current keys and create new keys. You can accomplish this by going to the user's account in IAM and clicking the **Security Credentials** tab, as shown in Figure 9.6.

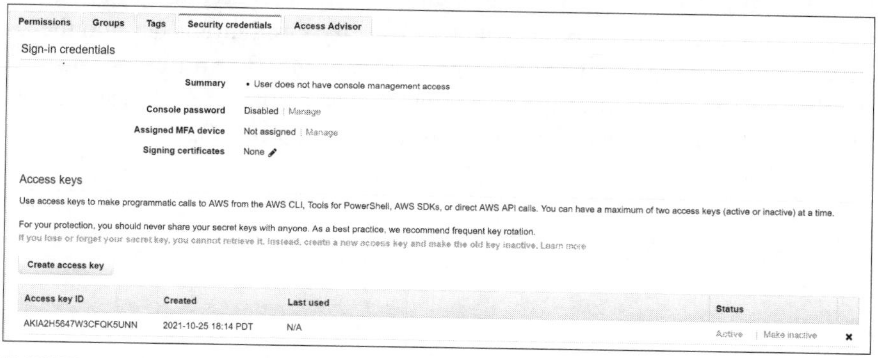

FIGURE 9.6   **Managing access keys**

Your organization may include a policy to rotate access keys. This is similar to requiring that passwords be changed on a regular basis. AWS even suggests rotating keys on a regular basis, which you can see in Figure 9.6 where it states "As a best practice, we recommend frequent key rotation."

AWS doesn't provide an automated method of rotating keys, so you need to manually deactivate older keys and create new keys using this Security Credentials tab for each user. Alternatively, you can consider using a programmatic solution by creating a script that runs AWS CLI commands or creating a program in one of the languages supported by AWS SDKs. Creating this solution is beyond the scope of this book and the exam, but you should at least be aware of the viability of such a solution.

Multifactor Authentication (MFA)

Multifactor authentication is a method of authenticating a user that requires more than one way of verifying the identity of that user. For example, a regular authentication method would be to have the user provide a username and a password. With MFA, the user would also be required to provide another item that proved the identity of that user.

The *factor* in MFA is the other item that is required to authenticate the user. This factor can be something from one of three categories:

▶ **Something that the user has:** This could be a physical object, such as a bank card, a physical key, or a USB stick that contains a unique token.

▶ **Something that the user knows:** This can be another password, a PIN, or some other bit of information that only the user should know.

▶ **Something that the user is:** This can include a biometric-based scan for a fingerprint, voice print, iris (eye), palm, and so on.

For AWS IAM accounts, you can configure MFA for user accounts by going to the user account summary, clicking the **Security Credentials** tab, and then clicking the **Manage** link next to Assigned MFA Device. For the exam, you should be aware of the three types of MFA devices: Virtual MFA device, U2F security key, and Other hardware MFA device (see Figure 9.7).

FIGURE 9.7 **Types of MFA devices**

Best Practices in IAM

AWS has published very specific best practices for securing IAM accounts. This information appears in its User Guide, which is one of the sources for content for exam questions. In other words, you really should be aware of these best practices.

The following list is derived directly from AWS's "Security Best Practices in IAM":

▶ **Secure your root account access keys:** If someone gains access to your root access keys, that person can easily gain control over your AWS account.

▶ **Use roles instead of assigning permissions to user accounts:** Roles are assumed for a limited period of time and are assumed only as needed. This makes roles more secure than assigning permissions to a user account that is always "on."

▶ **Grant least privilege:** It is a lazy habit to provide full access to a service when less access is all that may be needed. For example, you should not apply the AmazonS3FullAccess to an account, group, or role when that entity only needs to view content in S3 buckets. The policy of least privilege would mean that AmazonS3ReadOnlyAccess is a much better solution in this situation.

▶ **Use AWS managed policies:** AWS managed policies are the policies that AWS has created for you. Sometimes a custom policy is a better solution, but when you create a custom policy, there is a greater chance that you might accidentally end up creating security vulnerabilities by granting more access than you intended.

▶ **Validate custom policies:** Policies are written in JSON, so you should use a JSON validator like the one found at https://jsonlint.com after you finish writing your custom policy. AWS also provides a tool called IAM Access Analyzer that automatically appears at the bottom of the JSON tab when you are creating a new policy. This tool provides four features: Security advice, Errors, Warnings, and Suggestions (see Figure 9.8).

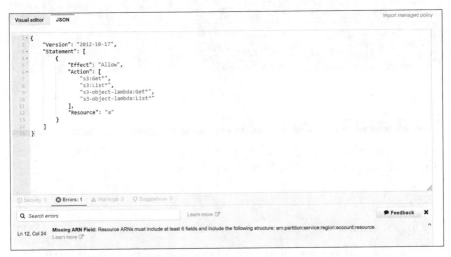

FIGURE 9.8 **IAM Access Analyzer**

▶ **Use your managed policies rather than inline policies:** When you assign permissions to a user or role, you can either first make a policy (managed policy) and then apply the policy, or you can directly create the policy when you create or modify the account (inline policy). Managed policies are better because you can see them when you go to the Policies section of IAM. Inline policies can be seen only by looking at the specific account that they were created for. Also, you can apply managed policies to multiple accounts.

▶ **Review IAM permissions access levels:** The responsibilities of users within an organization change, requiring you to review the access levels for permissions. There are five access levels for permissions: List, Read, Permissions Management, Write, and Tagging.

▶ **Create a strong password policy:** Most organizations have password rules (length of password, how often the password must be changed, and so on). If your organization has a password policy, make sure it applies to your AWS user accounts. If not, determine a policy that best secures the user accounts without creating user headaches (for example, a minimum password length of 40 characters, which is very secure, will likely make life more difficult for your users).

▶ **Enable MFA:** See the "Multifactor Authentication (MFA)" section earlier in this chapter.

▶ **Use roles for any application that is running on an EC2 instance:** See the "IAM Roles" section earlier in this chapter.

▶ **Do not share access keys:** Access keys, like passwords, provide access to an AWS account. As a result, they should never be shared.

▶ **Rotate credentials regularly:** This includes passwords and access keys, as mentioned in the "Access Keys" section earlier in this chapter.

▶ **Remove unnecessary credentials:** This practice may seem like an obvious thing to do, but there are stories of users who left companies only to return later to find their accounts were never deactivated or deleted. Having policies in place with Human Resources should prevent most of these types of situations, but you can also monitor IAM accounts for inactivity by reviewing a user's Console Last Sign-in and the Access Key Last Used value for user accounts.

▶ **Policy conditions:** A policy condition is an option that makes the policy more specific for a given situation. For example, if you include the following condition in a policy rule, the rule would apply only for a user who is working on a system with the IP address 192.168.100.100: **"Condition"** : **{ "StringEquals" : { "aws: SourceIP" : "192.168.100.100" }}**. The more specific the rule, especially Allow rules, the more secure you can make the policy.

▶ **Monitor activity in your AWS account:** AWS provides a large number of tools to help you monitor activity. Many of these tools are covered in this book, including CloudFront, CloudTrail, CloudWatch, Config, and S3 access logging.

Trusted Advisor

AWS Trusted Advisor is a tool that performs checks on five different categories:

- ▶ Cost optimization
- ▶ Performance
- ▶ Security
- ▶ Fault tolerance
- ▶ Service limits

For security and compliance, you should focus on the Security checks. When you go to the Trusted Advisor, you can click the **Refresh All Checks** button to see whether the Trusted Advisor has any suggestions. For example, Figure 9.9 shows a recommendation to enable MFA for the root account.

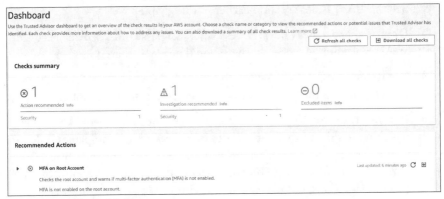

FIGURE 9.9 **Trusted Advisor**

ExamAlert

The number of checks that Trusted Advisor makes is based on your support plan.

Cram Quiz

Answer these questions. The answers follow the last question. If you cannot answer these questions correctly, consider reading this section again until you can.

1. You need to provide permissions to a user account. According to AWS, which type of policy would be considered the best to use?

   ○ **A.** AWS-managed policies

   ○ **B.** Customer-managed policies

   ○ **C.** Inline policies

   ○ **D.** Scoped policies

2. Which of the following is not an MFA category?

   ○ **A.** Something that the user has

   ○ **B.** Something that the user knows

   ○ **C.** Something that the user does

   ○ **D.** Something that the user is

Cram Quiz Answers

1. Answer: A is correct. AWS-managed policies have been vetted and reviewed by multiple individuals. Customer-managed policies are created by you and are more likely to contain errors or allow for unauthorized access. Inline policies apply to a single account and are difficult to see and manage. There is no such thing as scoped policies.

2. Answer: C is correct. Something that the user does is not an MFA category. The rest of the answers are valid categories.

What Next?

If you want more practice on this chapter's exam objectives before you move on, remember that you can access all of the Cram Quiz questions on the Pearson Test Prep software online. You can also create a custom exam by objective with the Online Practice Test. Note any objective you struggle with and go to that objective's material in this chapter.

CHAPTER 10

Data Protection at Rest and in Transit

This chapter covers the following official AWS Certified SysOps Administrator - Associate (SOA-C02) exam domain:

▶ Domain 4: Security and Compliance

(For more information on the official AWS Certified SysOps Administrator - Associate [SOA-C02] exam topics, see the Introduction.)

In this chapter, you learn how to use AWS features to protect data at rest or in transit. You first learn about the different encryption techniques and then learn how the AWS Key Management Service (KMS) can help you manage your encryption keys.

Next, you learn about data classifications and the role of a certificate authority (CA). In that section, you learn how the AWS Certificate Manager (ACM) can be used to manage your public and private certificates.

This chapter ends with a collection of important security tools: AWS Secrets Manager, Amazon GuardDog, Amazon Inspector, and AWS Security Hub.

Protecting Data

This section covers the following official AWS Certified SysOps Administrator - Associate (SOA-C02) exam topic for Domain 4: Security and Compliance:

▶ 4.2 Implement data and infrastructure protection strategies

CramSaver

If you can correctly answer these questions before going through this section, save time by skimming the Exam Alerts in this section and then completing the Cram Quiz at the end of the section.

1. Besides data at rest and data in transit, what is another form of data that needs to be protected?

2. To determine that a web server is valid, a _____ from a CA can be used.

Answers

1. Answer: Data in use

2. Answer: Certificate

Encryption

Encryption is the process of transforming data from its original form to a form that, when viewed, does not reveal the original data. There are three different forms of encryption:

▶ **Data at rest:** Data is encrypted when it is stored. Either you can encrypt the data prior to uploading the data to storage, or in some cases, a function that is provided by the cloud provider can perform this method. When you perform the data encryption, it is your responsibility to decrypt the data when the original data is needed. When the cloud provider encrypts the data, the decryption process must be performed by the cloud provider.

▶ **Data in transit:** Data is encrypted before it is sent and decrypted when received. This form of encryption could involve several different techniques, but in most cases for cloud computing environments, it means that the data is encrypted by a network device that then sends the data across the network.

▶ **Data in use:** Data is encrypted when being actively used, which typically means while it is stored in random-access memory (RAM). Because some exploits may make data in RAM vulnerable, this form of encryption may be very important to ensuring data integrity.

Many different technologies can be used to encrypt data, and which technology you use will depend on several factors, including which cloud provider you utilize. These technologies fall into one of two methods of encryption:

▶ **Symmetric encryption:** With this method, you use the same key (a unique value of some sort) to both encrypt and decrypt the data.

▶ **Asymmetric encryption:** With this method, you use a different key to encrypt and decrypt the data. One key is referred to as the *public key*, and the other is called the *private key*. An example of using this encryption method would be if you wanted someone to send data to you across the network. You provide the public key to this person, and this person then encrypts the data. The only way to decrypt the data is to use the private key, which you would never share with anyone else.

AWS Key Management Service

The Key Management Service (KMS) allows you to create encryption keys and control their access. Both symmetric and asymmetric keys can be created, as you can see in Figure 10.1.

FIGURE 10.1   **KMS**

Key features of AWS KMS include

▶ The ability to create, view, and edit keys

▶ Use policies to control access to keys

▶ The ability to disable (and enable) keys

▶ Automatic key rotation

▶ Key use monitoring

Data Classification

Consider how you would treat data that contains credit card information compared to how you would treat data that contains comments that have been made regarding your company website. The data that contains credit card information is much more sensitive than the data that contains customer comments, so you would want to treat the data differently.

In this situation, data classification becomes important. With data classification, you place data into different categories depending on how you want to treat the data. These categories can be based on rules related to how sensitive the data is, who should be able to read the data, who should be able to modify the data, and how long the data should be available. Unless you are storing data that is related to compliance regulations (like SOC 2, GDPR, PCI-DSS, or HIPAA), the data classification criteria are up to you.

For example, you might consider classifying data based on who is permitted to access it. In this case, you might use the following commonly used categories:

▶ **Public:** This data is available to anyone, including those who are not a part of your organization. This typically includes information found on your public website, announcements made on social media sites, and data found in your company press releases.

▶ **Internal:** This data should be available only to members of your organization. An example of this data would be upcoming enhancements to a software product that your organization creates.

▶ **Confidential:** This data should be available only to select individuals who have the need to access this information. This could include personally identifiable information (PII), such as an employee Social Security number. Often the rules for handling this data are also governed by compliance regulations.

▶ **Restricted:** This data may seem similar to confidential data, but it is normally more related to proprietary information, company secrets, and in some cases, data that is regarded by the government as secret.

In the cloud, there are different techniques to handle different types of data. These techniques could include placing different types of data into different storage locations.

Certificate Management

Consider a situation in which you want to log in to your bank's website and transfer some money. You open a web browser, type in the URL of your bank (or use a browser bookmark), and then log in to the bank. But how do you know that it is really your bank?

It is possible that your browser has been directed to a website that isn't your bank. This redirection might have been done by an individual or group that is trying to steal your login information to gain access to your bank account. You might even have seen this attempt in action. Figure 10.2 shows a message that your web browser will display if it appears that the server you are trying to connect to really isn't the correct server.

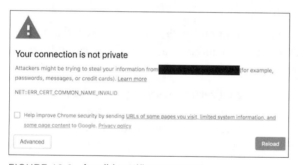

FIGURE 10.2 **Invalid certificate warning**

This discussion brings up another question: how does your web browser know that you are potentially communicating with a rogue server? The answer is by its certificate.

When you communicate using the HTTPS protocol (note that this does not apply to HTTP; the *S* must be in the URL), your browser knows that it must verify the validity of the web server's certificate. It does this by querying a certificate authority (CA), which is a trusted third-party organization that can look at a web server's certificate and verify that it is really the correct web server. You can look at your browser's settings and see a list of the CAs that your browser uses, as shown in Figure 10.3.

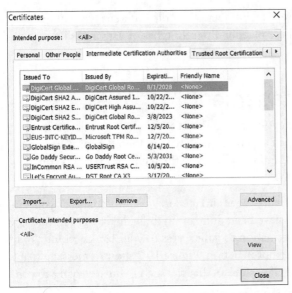

FIGURE 10.3   List of CAs on a Google Chrome Browser

Note that these certificates are also commonly called SSL/TLS certificates in context to HTTP services and functions, and they are based on the public key infrastructure (PKI).

PKI is a standard that defines how digital certificates are created, revoked, managed, stored, used, and distributed. It utilizes a pair of cryptographic keys (public and private), which not only allows the creation and verification of certificates but also provides a way to encrypt the data that is transported between the client and the server.

For the certification exam, you don't need to know all of the details of PKI, but you do need to know some key terms:

▶ **Digital certificate:** A unique value that contains a collection of data that is used to identify an entity (that is, a server). For example, think of certificates in your browser store.

▶ **CA:** Certificate authority; an entity that validates, signs, and issues the digital certificates. For example, Verisign CA and GeoTrust CA are public CAs. Note that AWS provides a tool called AWS Certificate Manager that can manage both public and private certificates.

▶ **Public key:** A unique cryptographic key that is publicly shared. Data encrypted by the public key can be decrypted only by the corresponding private key.

▶ **Private key:** A unique cryptographic key that is never shared. It is used to decrypt data that was encrypted by the corresponding public key.

▶ **CRL:** Certificate revocation list; a list that defines the certificates that the CA no longer considers valid. For example, a certificate that was deemed to be no longer secure but is valid can be declared as void in the CRL.

▶ **CSR:** Certificate signing request; a request to a CA to generate a digital certificate. The CSR must contain specific information, including the public key for the organization, and must be "signed," a process verifying that the organization making the CSR possessed the private key.

AWS Certificate Manager

The AWS Certificate Manager (ACM) allows you to manage certificates. This service provided by AWS allows you to perform the following primary tasks:

▶ **Request a certificate:** This option allows you to request a public certificate from Amazon. If you have configured your AWS account with your organization's CA, you can also request a private certificate from your CA.

▶ **Import a certificate:** If you have a certificate that was created with a non-AWS CA, you can import that certificate into AWS.

▶ **Create a private certificate:** Private certificates are typically used to secure the AWS services and resources within your AWS infrastructure. This feature allows you to create a private certificate.

ExamAlert

A key difference between a public certificate and a private certificate is that public certificates are normally trusted automatically by applications because these applications also trust the public CA. Private certificates are not normally automatically trusted, requiring manual configuration on the application side.

Several AWS services can make use of ACM certificates, including the following:

▶ Elastic Load Balancing

▶ Amazon CloudFront

▶ Amazon API Gateway

▶ AWS Elastic Beanstalk

▶ AWS CloudFormation

▶ AWS App Runner

▶ AWS Nitro Enclaves

ACM certificates are also often used with applications, like web servers, that you deploy on EC2 instances and containers.

> **ExamAlert**
>
> ACM certificates are regional resources and must be imported into each region in which they are used.

AWS Secrets Manager

"Three may keep a secret, if two of them are dead."

—Benjamin Franklin,
Poor Richard's Almanack

While a bit dramatic, this quote from hundreds of years ago illustrates that the importance of keeping a secret can't be overstated. The AWS Secrets Manager is designed to store and manage credential data. This includes several different credential types, including the following AWS services:

▶ AWS RDS databases

▶ AWS DocumentDB databases

▶ AWS Redshift clusters

The AWS Secrets Manager can also be used to manage other types of credentials that are not directly associated with AWS. This includes the following:

▶ Non-AWS databases, including MariaDB, MySQL, PostgreSQL, Oracle database, and Microsoft SQL Server

▶ Application programming interface (API) keys

▶ OAuth tokens

▶ Secure Shell (SSH) keys

You can enable access to secrets by creating an IAM policy that permits an application or resource to access the secret. The technique that is used to access the secret is via the Secrets Manager API.

The AWS Secrets Manager works with encryption keys provided by the AWS Key Management Service to ensure the security of the secrets by encrypting them at rest. You can also configure the AWS Secrets Manager to rotate secrets to provide better security.

By default, secrets are region-based resources. AWS provides a feature called multi-region secrets to allow you to replicate secrets across multiple regions. This feature also allows you to manage these replicated secrets, including deleting secretes in specific regions.

Amazon GuardDuty

Amazon GuardDuty is a tool that performs threat detection functions in your AWS infrastructure. This optional service is not turned on in your AWS account by default.

When GuardDuty is enabled, it actively monitors the following:

- ▶ AWS CloudTrail management events
- ▶ AWS CloudTrail S3 data events
- ▶ VPC flow logs
- ▶ DNS logs

ExamAlert

A feature called GuardDuty for S3 also can be enabled for an additional cost. To enable this feature, you must also enable the standard GuardDuty. However, because GuardDuty can access S3 logs that are stored in CloudTrail, this extra protection may not be necessary.

Costs for GuardDuty are based on the number of events (per million) that are monitored. For logs, the cost is based on per gigabyte per month.

There are several key features for Amazon GuardDuty, including the following:

- ▶ Account-level threat detection to determine whether AWS accounts may have been compromised
- ▶ The ability to create automated threat response actions

▶ Monitoring of potential reconnaissance attempts

▶ Monitoring of possible EC2 instance compromises

▶ Monitoring of possible S3 bucket compromises

Amazon Inspector

Amazon Inspector is a tool that helps you determine security vulnerabilities on applications that you deploy on an EC2 instance within AWS. For example, you might deploy an application on an EC2 instance and want to know whether your application has any potential security risks.

To use Amazon Inspector, you first install an agent on the EC2 instance. Two types of assessments can be configured: network assessments and host assessments. Network assessments are used to determine which network ports of your instance are available from outside of your VPC. Host assessments include the following:

▶ Assessments based on Common Vulnerabilities and Exposures (CVEs)

▶ Assessments based on host-hardening benchmarks from the Center for Internet Security (CIS)

▶ Assessments based on security best practices, such as whether a root login via SSH is permitted or password complexity rules are in place

> **ExamAlert**
>
> You do not need to install the Inspector Agent on the EC2 instance if you just want to perform network assessments. However, if you do, the corresponding service that uses the port is reported.

The Amazon Inspector assessment checks report issues based on how severe they are. The following severity levels are used:

▶ **High:** An alert that indicates a problem that is very likely to result in a security vulnerability. An example would be incorrect permissions on system directories.

▶ **Medium:** An alert that is not critical but still urgent enough to warrant a review. An example would be not having password complexity rules in place.

▶ **Low:** An alert that is not as urgent but should be addressed soon. The recommended way of handling these alerts is to address them the next time the service is updated.

▶ **Informational:** Occasionally, Amazon Inspector provides an informa-tion alert. This doesn't indicate a current issue with the security of your system but might be something to consider when your security policy is reviewed.

AWS Security Hub

The AWS Security Hub allows you to execute security checks across your AWS environment automatically. It also allows you to gather alerts from the follow-ing security policies into a central view:

▶ Amazon GuardDuty

▶ Amazon Inspector

▶ IAM Access Analyzer

▶ Amazon Macie

▶ IAM Firewall Manager

▶ Amazon System Manager

ExamAlert

In-depth knowledge of some of the services that the AWS Security Hub can gather alerts from, such as Amazon Macie, are not specific exam requirements. However, you should be aware that the AWS Security Hub can gather alerts from these services.

Cram Quiz

Answer these questions. The answers follow the last question. If you cannot answer these questions correctly, consider reading this section again until you can.

1. Which of the following AWS services does not make use of ACM certificates?

○ **A.** Elastic Load Balancing

○ **B.** Amazon API Gateway

○ **C.** AWS CloudFormation

○ **D.** AWS CodeCommit

2. Which of the following credentials cannot be stored in the AWS Secrets Manager?

   ○ **A.** IAM passwords

   ○ **B.** AWS RDS databases

   ○ **C.** OAuth tokens

   ○ **D.** Secure Shell (SSH) keys

Cram Quiz Answers

1. Answer: D is correct. ACM certificates are used by the following services: Elastic Load Balancing, Amazon CloudFront, Amazon API Gateway, AWS Elastic Beanstalk, AWS CloudFormation, AWS App Runner, and AWS Nitro Enclaves.

2. Answer: A is correct. The AWS Secrets Manager can store credentials for the following: AWS RDS databases, AWS DocumentDB database, AWS Redshift clusters, Non-AWS databases, application programming interface (API) keys, OAuth tokens, and Secure Shell (SSH) keys.

What Next?

If you want more practice on this chapter's exam objectives before you move on, remember that you can access all of the Cram Quiz questions on the Pearson Test Prep software online. You can also create a custom exam by objective with the Online Practice Test. Note any objective you struggle with and go to that objective's material in this chapter.

CHAPTER 11

Networking and Connectivity

This chapter covers content related to the following official AWS Certified SysOps Administrator - Associate (SOA-C02) exam domains:

▶ Domain 4: Security and Compliance

▶ Domain 5: Networking and Content Delivery

(For more information on the official AWS Certified SysOps Administrator - Associate [SOA-C02] exam topics, see the Introduction.)

A strong understanding of networking concepts is an essential skill for system operators working with AWS resources. Many of the networking systems that you are familiar with from a physical datacenter (routers, firewalls, VPNs) also exist in an AWS Virtual Private Cloud (VPC). However, the methods that you use to manage these systems have evolved.

The VPC

This section covers the following objective of Domain 5 (Networking and Content Delivery) from the official AWS Certified SysOps Administrator - Associate (SOA-C02) exam guide:

▶ 5.1 Implement networking features and connectivity

CramSaver

If you can correctly answer these questions before going through this section, save time by skimming the Exam Alerts in this section and then completing the Cram Quiz at the end of the section.

1. What is the largest IPv4 CIDR range that can be configured for a VPC?

2. You have created a VPC and a public subnet and now must provide access to the Internet for EC2 instances within it. You have not created any custom route tables. What tasks must be completed to accomplish this goal?

Answers

1. Answer: /16

2. Answer: You must create an Internet gateway, attach it to the VPC, and configure a default route in the main route table that points to the Internet gateway.

Virtual Private Cloud

A Virtual Private Cloud (VPC) is an isolated virtual network that belongs to an AWS organization. Within the VPC, you have control over how traffic flows. You choose your classless interdomain routing (CIDR) range, establish subnets, configure and associate route tables, and create and attach firewall rules using network access control lists (NACLs) and security groups. Subnets can be configured to host public resources like web servers or private resources like databases.

A default VPC is automatically created in every AWS region for your AWS account. This default VPC is configured so that you can easily set up an application for public access. The default VPC is not ideal for private resources; therefore, you should consider creating your own VPCs so that you can better control security.

When you create a VPC, you configure a CIDR range that must be between a /16 netmask and /28 netmask. Be sure to configure a large enough CIDR range because it cannot be modified after the VPC is created. If you run out of address space, you can add a secondary CIDR range to an existing VPC. The secondary CIDR range can be contiguous to the primary CIDR range. In Figure 11.1, you can see the AWS Management Console screen where you create a VPC and set the CIDR range.

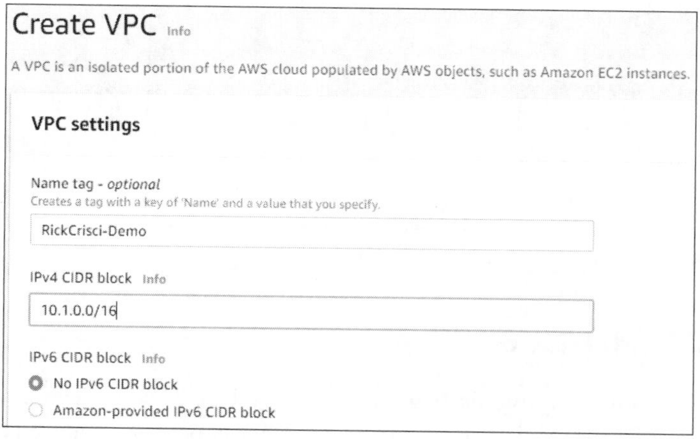

Create VPC Info

A VPC is an isolated portion of the AWS cloud populated by AWS objects, such as Amazon EC2 instances.

VPC settings

Name tag - *optional*
Creates a tag with a key of 'Name' and a value that you specify.

    RickCrisci-Demo

IPv4 CIDR block Info

    10.1.0.0/16

IPv6 CIDR block Info
⦿ No IPv6 CIDR block
◯ Amazon-provided IPv6 CIDR block

FIGURE 11.1   **VPC CIDR range**

Elastic Network Interfaces

An Elastic Network Interface (ENI) is a virtual network interface in a VPC. When EC2 instances are created in a VPC, they automatically get a default network interface (eth0). This interface cannot be detached from this instance. You can choose to have a public IP address automatically assigned to this interface. However, if the instance is stopped, the public IP address is released.

You can create an ENI and attach it to an EC2 instance as a secondary interface. The ENI can be placed in a different subnet than eth0, giving the instance access to multiple subnets, such as management and traffic subnets. Each interface can have different security groups applied as well. Figure 11.2 shows the AWS Management Console screen where you create an ENI.

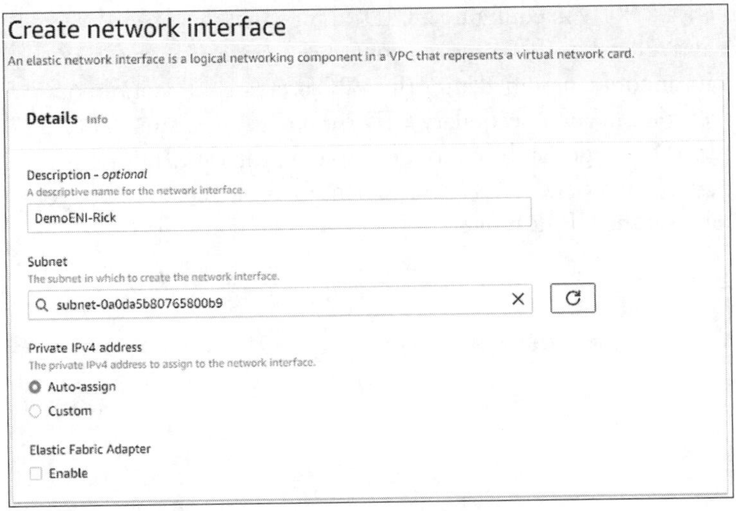

FIGURE 11.2 **ENI**

Elastic IP Address

An Elastic IP (EIP) address is a public IP address that can be associated with an ENI. This dedicated IP address is not released, even if the associated instance is stopped or terminated, as long as the ENI remains. If an EIP is attached to an ENI that is deleted upon termination of an instance, that EIP is automatically released. Figure 11.3 shows an EIP being assigned to an ENI.

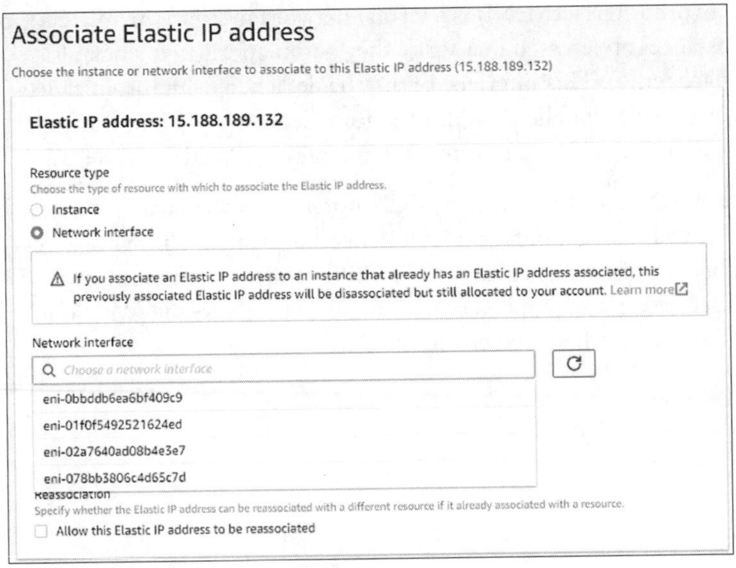

FIGURE 11.3 **EIP**

Internet Gateway (IGW)

An Internet gateway can be attached to a VPC to allow Internet access. The IGW is highly available and does not create any availability risks or bandwidth constraints the way a traditional physical router does.

Your instances are aware of the private addressing scheme only within the VPC. If an instance is configured with a public IP, the IGW provides a one-to-one Network Address Translation (NAT) service when traffic leaves your VPC and goes to the Internet. Figure 11.4 shows the process of attaching an IGW to a VPC.

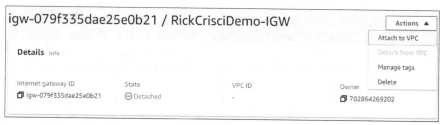

FIGURE 11.4 **Attaching an Internet gateway**

> **ExamAlert**
>
> A VPC has a CIDR range that must be between a /16 netmask and /28 netmask. You can add a secondary CIDR range to an existing VPC to increase the number of usable addresses, but you cannot change an existing CIDR range.

Cram Quiz

Answer these questions. The answers follow the last question. If you cannot answer these questions correctly, consider reading this section again until you can.

1. You have created a VPC with a CIDR range that does not provide enough addresses. Which method should be used to resolve this issue?

   - ○ **A.** Modify the existing CIDR range using the AWS CLI.
   - ○ **B.** Place the VPC in maintenance mode and perform a batch re-addressing using CloudFormation.
   - ○ **C.** Create a new VPC and perform a live migration to relocate EC2 instances to it.
   - ○ **D.** Associate a secondary IPv4 CIDR block with your VPC.

2. You have an EIP associated with a secondary ENI on an EC2 instance. What happens to the EIP if you terminate the instance?

   ○ **A.** The EIP is released.

   ○ **B.** The EIP remains associated with the terminated instance.

   ○ **C.** The EIP is still allocated to your AWS account, and you are still billed for it.

   ○ **D.** The EIP is still allocated to your AWS account, but you are billed for it only if it is associated with a running instance.

Cram Quiz Answers

1. Answer: D is correct. You cannot resize a CIDR block after it has been created. You can add a secondary CIDR block to an existing VPC. Local routes for the secondary CIDR block are automatically generated.

2. Answer: C is correct. The EIP remains associated with your AWS account, and you are billed for it. You must release the EIP to stop incurring charges.

VPC Connectivity

This section covers the following objective of Domain 5 (Networking and Content Delivery) from the official AWS Certified SysOps Administrator - Associate (SOA-C02) exam guide:

▶ 5.1 Implement networking features and connectivity

CramSaver

If you can correctly answer these questions before going through this section, save time by skimming the Exam Alerts in this section and then completing the Cram Quiz at the end of the section.

1. You have a group of EC2 instances in a private subnet. You must configure a NAT gateway to allow these instances to have Internet access. Does the route table of the private subnet need to be modified for this configuration to work?

2. A new subnet has been created within a VPC. The administrator has not assigned a route table to the new subnet. What is the result of this configuration?

Answers

1. Answer: A route entry must be added to the route table associated with the private subnet. You should create a default route that points to the NAT gateway. The NAT gateway must be placed in a public subnet.

2. Answer: The main route table is assigned to this subnet. Every VPC has a main route table that you can modify. The main route table is used by default for all subnets. However, this may create security concerns, especially if the main route table has a route to the Internet gateway.

Subnets

When you create a VPC, you must configure a CIDR range that specifies the entire block of addresses that can be used within the VPC. Subnets are ranges of IP addresses within that CIDR range. For example, if the CIDR range of a VPC is 10.1.0.0/16, you can create a public subnet with the 10.1.1.0/24 address range, as shown in Figure 11.5.

Subnet settings
Specify the CIDR blocks and Availability Zone for the subnet.

Subnet 1 of 1

Subnet name
Create a tag with a key of 'Name' and a value that you specify.

| RickCrisci-Demo-PublicSubnet-AZ3a |

The name can be up to 256 characters long.

Availability Zone Info
Choose the zone in which your subnet will reside, or let Amazon choose one for you.

| Europe (Paris) / eu-west-3a ▼ |

IPv4 CIDR block Info

| Q 10.1.1.0/24 ✕ |

FIGURE 11.5   **Creating a subnet**

A VPC spans all of the availability zones (AZs) in the region but cannot span multiple regions. Each subnet is local to an AZ. In Figure 11.5, eu-west-3a is chosen for the AZ. By creating multiple subnets in different AZs, you can establish highly available applications using a load balancer.

Route Tables

Each VPC is automatically configured with a main route table. This is the default route table associated with subnets. You can also create your own custom route tables. All route tables include a local route that allows traffic to flow within the CIDR range of the VPC.

You modify the route tables for your public subnets with a default route that points all outbound traffic to the Internet gateway. You can see an example of this in Figure 11.6. You could also create a narrow set of specific routes if you don't want to enable general Internet access from your VPC.

FIGURE 11.6   **Public route table**

NAT Gateway

The NAT gateway is an AWS managed service that allows instances in private subnets to connect to the Internet but prevents the Internet from initiating connections to these instances because the NAT service is egress only. Previously, you needed to launch a NAT instance running on EC2 to accomplish this. The NAT gateway must reside in a public subnet and requires a public Elastic IP. You can adjust the route table for your private subnets to use the NAT gateway as a default route, as shown in Figure 11.7.

Destination		Target		Status		Propagated	
10.1.0.0/16		local		⊘ Active		No	
0.0.0.0/0		nat-0d6afda0f726b44fa		⊘ Active		No	

FIGURE 11.7 **Private route table**

ExamAlert

Each subnet is mapped to an AZ. A VPC exists inside a single AWS region and cannot span multiple regions. Instances can be spread across multiple AZs within a region by placing the VMs on different subnets.

Cram Quiz

Answer these questions. The answers follow the last question. If you cannot answer these questions correctly, consider reading this section again until you can.

1. You are examining a route table in your VPC and find the following route entry: "Destination : 10.0.0.0/24 and Target : Local". What type of route is this?

   ○ **A.** An automatically created route entry for traffic within the AZ

   ○ **B.** An automatically created route entry for traffic within the VPC

   ○ **C.** A default route for traffic destined for the Internet

   ○ **D.** A user-defined route for traffic between subnets within a VPC

2. You have created a private subnet in a VPC. Application servers in the private subnet require Internet access for updates. Which statement regarding this configuration is correct?

- ○ **A.** A NAT gateway is automatically created for each private subnet.
- ○ **B.** A NAT instance is automatically created and runs on EC2.
- ○ **C.** To allow Internet access, you should create a NAT gateway within a public subnet and update the route table used by the private subnet.
- ○ **D.** To allow Internet access, you should enable NAT on the Internet gateway and update the route table used by the private subnet.

3. You have public and private subnets in a VPC. In the public subnet, you have a bastion host that is accessible over port 3389. The network for the public subnet is 192.168.10.0/24. In the private network, you have an application server that must be accessible from the bastion host on port 80. The private subnet is network 192.168.20.0/24. A NAT gateway is used to provide Internet access to the private subnet. You are creating a security group for the application servers. Which statements must be manually configured for the security group? (Choose all that apply.)

- ○ **A.** Allow port 80 inbound from the bastion host.
- ○ **B.** Allow ports 80 and 3389 inbound from the bastion host.
- ○ **C.** Allow outbound traffic to the Internet from the application server via the NAT gateway.
- ○ **D.** Allow ports 80 and 3389 outbound to the bastion host.

Cram Quiz Answers

1. Answer: B is correct. Every route table within a VPC is automatically populated with a local route. This route is used for communication within the VPC.

2. Answer: C is correct. To allow Internet access, you should create a NAT gateway. You should modify the route table associated with the private subnet and create a default route that forwards traffic to the NAT gateway.

3. Answer: A is correct. Traffic from the bastion host to the application server is on port 80. You do not need to manually allow any outbound traffic because a security group allows all outbound traffic by default.

VPC Security

This section covers the following objective of Domain 5 (Networking and Content Delivery) from the official AWS Certified SysOps Administrator - Associate (SOA-C02) exam guide:

▶ 5.1 Implement networking features and connectivity

CramSaver

If you can correctly answer these questions before going through this section, save time by skimming the Exam Alerts in this section and then completing the Cram Quiz at the end of the section.

1. Which traffic is allowed by a new security group by default?
2. Is a network access control list stateless or stateful?

Answers

1. Answer: All outbound traffic is allowed, and all inbound traffic is blocked.
2. Answer: An NACL is stateless, which means it does not dynamically allow return traffic for existing connections.

AWS offers multiple security features within the VPC, each of which serves a different purpose. Some of these tools are native to other AWS services. For example, the AWS Application Load Balancer (ALB) features a Web Application Firewall (WAF) that can be used to detect malicious traffic. In this chapter, we focus on security features that are native to the AWS VPC.

VPC Security by Default

In every AWS account, a default VPC is automatically created in every region. This default VPC makes experimentation and initial tasks easy. But beware because the default VPC has very permissive security settings. By default, public access to and from the Internet is not blocked by the network ACLs associated with the default VPC, all subnets are public, and instances get public IPs by default. Ideally, you should create a new custom VPC and configure it in a secure manner. When you create a new VPC, it is isolated by default. This means that no other VPCs have access to the new VPC. There is no public access to or from the Internet unless it is configured.

Security Groups

A security group is a stateful firewall that is applied to individual interfaces on various network-based resources, including EC2 and RDS instances running in a VPC. It can also be applied to interfaces that are used by Lambda functions. A new security group allows all traffic outbound by default. There are no statements regarding inbound traffic. The security group ends in an implicit deny all, meaning that any traffic that is not explicitly allowed will be denied.

Therefore, by default, a new security group allows all outbound traffic and no inbound traffic. However, the security group is stateful and will allow inbound traffic that is a response to an existing connection. In Figure 11.8, you can see the default ruleset for a new security group.

When a security group is assigned to an EC2 instance, it is applied to the first interface by default. When an instance has multiple interfaces, different security groups can be applied to each interface.

| Inbound rules | Outbound rules | Tags | | | |

Inbound rules (0)   Edit inbound rules

Type	Protocol	Port range	Source	Description - optional	
			No rules found		
		This security group has no inbound rules.			

| Inbound rules | Outbound rules | Tags | | | |

Outbound rules (1)   Edit outbound rules

Type	Protocol	Port range	Destination	Description - optional	
All traffic	All	All	0.0.0.0/0	–	

FIGURE 11.8   Default rules for a new security group

Network Access Control Lists (NACLs)

A network access control list is a stateless firewall that is applied to a subnet. Because an NACL is stateless, when a new NACL is created, rules must be configured in both directions to permit traffic to flow. Every subnet must be associated with an NACL. All inbound and outbound traffic is denied by default when a new NACL is created. NACL rules are applied in order from the top down. In Figure 11.9, you can see the default ruleset for a new NACL.

FIGURE 11.9 Default rules for a new network access control list

Public and Private Subnets

Public subnets are associated with a route table that has a default route pointed to an Internet gateway. Instances in a public subnet are usually configured with public IP addresses (though not required). Private subnets are not configured with a route to the Internet gateway and require a Network Address Translation (NAT) gateway or NAT instance to access the Internet.

VPC Flow Logs

VPC Flow Logs are an important tool for VPC security. VPC flow logs can be used to monitor the network traffic in your Amazon VPC. You will learn more about flow logs in Chapter 13, "Troubleshoot Network Connectivity."

> ExamAlert
>
> You must be able to differentiate between security groups and NACLs and their use cases. Security groups are stateful and applied to individual interfaces. NACLs are stateless and are applied to entire subnets.

Cram Quiz

Answer these questions. The answers follow the last question. If you cannot answer these questions correctly, consider reading this section again until you can.

1. You have configured a network access control list to permit inbound traffic to an EC2 web server from a set of customer IP addresses. The NACL is configured to block all outbound traffic. What is the result of this configuration?

   ○ **A.** Users from the permitted IP addresses can access the web server. The web server can also initiate a connection to the customer IP addresses.

   ○ **B.** Users from the permitted IP addresses can access the web server without issues, but the web server cannot initiate a connection to the customer IP addresses.

   ○ **C.** Users from the permitted IP addresses cannot access the web server.

   ○ **D.** Users from the permitted IP address range can access the web server only if a security group rule is created to allow it.

2. You are creating a security group that allows monitoring software to communicate with EC2 instances using ICMP. The monitoring software will initiate communication to the EC2 instances. Which statements regarding this configuration are correct? (Choose two.)

   ○ **A.** You need to configure the security group to allow the necessary incoming traffic.

   ○ **B.** ICMP cannot be tracked by a security group because it is a connectionless protocol.

   ○ **C.** You need to allow outbound ICMP on the security group.

   ○ **D.** You do not need to allow outbound ICMP on the security group.

Cram Quiz Answers

1. Answer: C is correct. Users from the permitted IP addresses cannot establish connectivity with the web server. The NACL is not stateful, and therefore, return traffic from the web server instance can never reach the customer IP addresses because all outbound (return) traffic is blocked.

2. Answer: A and D are correct. ICMP traffic can be tracked by a security group. A security group is stateful and dynamically allows return traffic. Therefore, you do not need to allow outbound ICMP on the security group.

AWS Network Firewall

This section covers the following objective of Domain 5 (Networking and Content Delivery) from the official AWS Certified SysOps Administrator - Associate (SOA-C02) exam guide:

▶ 5.1 Implement networking features and connectivity

Cramsaver

If you can correctly answer these questions before going through this section, save time by skimming the Exam Alerts in this section and then completing the Cram Quiz at the end of the section.

1. You are using the AWS Network Firewall with the AWS Firewall Manager. What is the scope of the policies that you create?

2. Does the AWS Network Firewall protect from DDoS attacks?

Answers

1. Answer: Policies can be applied across multiple VPCs and AWS accounts.

2. Answer: No, the AWS Network Firewall does not mitigate volumetric attacks that generate massive amounts of traffic or requests. The AWS WAF and AWS Shield can be used to mitigate those types of attacks.

About the AWS Network Firewall

The biggest benefit of the AWS Network Firewall is that it can be enabled across an entire AWS environment, with multiple VPCs and accounts, with just a few clicks in the console. Rules can be defined that provide fine-grained control over network traffic. You can also import open-source or partner-created rules. It has a built-in intrusion prevention system (IPS) and can also perform URL filtering. Because it is a managed service, you do not need to manage or deploy EC2 instances or any other AWS resources to enable it.

The AWS Network Firewall can be deployed as in a centralized or distributed configuration. In a centralized deployment, the AWS Network Firewall is attached to a transit gateway. This allows you to filter inbound and outbound traffic to or from Internet gateways, Direct Connect gateways, VPN site-to-site and client gateways, NAT gateways, and even between other attached VPCs. In a distributed deployment, the AWS Network Firewall is deployed within VPCs for enforcement closer to the applications.

AWS Network Firewall activity can be logged to an Amazon S3 bucket or to Amazon Kinesis Firehose. The AWS Network Firewall does not support deep packet inspection for encrypted traffic. Traffic can be decrypted by a Network Load Balancer (NLB) before it is sent to the AWS Network Firewall.

AWS Marketplace

In addition to AWS managed services, a large number of partner solutions are available in the AWS Marketplace. You can deploy a third-party firewall solution on a load-balanced auto scaling group of EC2 instances for a higher level of protection. This also allows you to have consistent solutions on-premises and in the cloud.

> **ExamAlert**
>
> The AWS Network Firewall can provide stateless or stateful firewall rules; intrusion prevention; and filtering of URLs, IP addresses, and domains. It can secure traffic at layers 3–7.

Cram Quiz

Answer these questions. The answers follow the last question. If you cannot answer these questions correctly, consider reading this section again until you can.

1. Which options can be used to monitor logs from the AWS Network Firewall? (Choose two.)

   ○ **A.** Logs can be stored in a DynamoDB table and queried.

   ○ **B.** Logs can be stored in an S3 bucket.

   ○ **C.** Kinesis Firehose can be used to port logs to a third-party provider.

   ○ **D.** Redshift can be used to port logs to a third-party provider.

2. What types of traffic can be inspected by the AWS Network Firewall? (Choose two.)

   ○ **A.** HTTPS (SNI)/HTTP protocol URL filtering

   ○ **B.** Deep packet inspection for encrypted traffic

   ○ **C.** DDoS mitigation

   ○ **D.** Domain, port, protocol, IP addresses, and pattern matching

Cram Quiz Answers

1. Answer: B and C are correct. AWS Network Firewall activity can be logged to an Amazon S3 bucket or to Amazon Kinesis Firehose.

2. Answer: A and D are correct. The AWS Network Firewall supports outbound traffic control using HTTPS (SNI)/HTTP protocol URL filtering, access control lists (ACLs), DNS queries, and protocol detection. AWS Network Firewall rules can be based on domain, port, protocol, IP addresses, and pattern matching.

VPC Endpoints

This section covers the following objective of Domain 5 (Networking and Content Delivery) from the official AWS Certified SysOps Administrator - Associate (SOA-C02) exam guide:

▶ 5.1 Implement networking features and connectivity

CramSaver

If you can correctly answer these questions before going through this section, save time by skimming the Exam Alerts in this section and then completing the Cram Quiz at the end of the section.

1. What is the difference between a gateway endpoint and an interface endpoint?

2. Is an Internet gateway required when using a VPC endpoint?

Answers

1. Answer: Interface endpoints connect to a vast array of AWS services powered by PrivateLink. Gateway endpoints connect to S3 or DynamoDB.

2. Answer: No, the private Amazon backbone network is used.

A VPC endpoint is a virtual interface that allows resources inside a VPC to communicate with other AWS resources outside the VPC without traversing the Internet. For example, you can connect to an S3 bucket over the AWS private backbone using a VPC endpoint.

Interface Endpoints

Interface endpoints connect to services powered by PrivateLink. This is compatible with a vast list of AWS resources, including CloudTrail, Elastic Load Balancing, Kinesis, Lambda, S3, DynamoDB, and much more. The interface endpoint is an ENI within an AWS VPC that has a private IP address within the VPC subnet of the resources that are consuming the service. This feeds traffic into a solution hosted in the service provider account. For example, a service provider has a data analysis tool running on EC2 instances in an AWS account. The service consumer can connect to those resources using an interface endpoint that is reachable inside a subnet in their own VPC. Figure 11.10 shows an interface endpoint being used by a service provider.

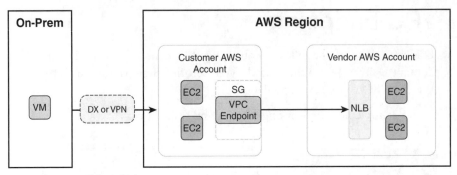

FIGURE 11.10   PrivateLink

Gateway Endpoints

A gateway endpoint connects to DynamoDB or S3. You configure the route table within your VPC to send traffic over a VPC endpoint instead of the Internet. A VPC can have multiple gateway endpoints to different services in a route table. This greatly enhances security. For example, for a private subnet in a VPC to access S3 without a gateway endpoint, you would need a public subnet with a NAT gateway, and the traffic would have to be routed over the public AWS network. With a gateway endpoint, the traffic never leaves the AWS private backbone, and there is no need for a public subnet or Internet gateway in this scenario. Figure 11.11 shows the initial configuration of a gateway endpoint for S3.

FIGURE 11.11   Configuring a gateway endpoint for S3

ExamAlert

Interface endpoints can be used to connect to services that use a vast array of AWS services. Gateway endpoints can connect only to S3 and DynamoDB.

Cram Quiz

Answer this question. The answer follows the question. If you cannot answer the question correctly, consider reading this section again until you can.

1. An S3 bucket contains sensitive data. You must restrict access to this bucket to a set of EC2 instances in a private subnet. What actions should you take to meet these requirements? (Choose three.)

   ○ **A.** Create an interface endpoint and a NAT gateway to connect to the bucket from the VPC.

   ○ **B.** Update the route table to point S3 traffic to a gateway VPC endpoint.

   ○ **C.** Configure a transit gateway to allow the VPC endpoint to communicate with S3.

   ○ **D.** Configure the bucket policy to allow access only to the VPC endpoint.

   ○ **E.** Create a gateway endpoint to connect to the bucket from the VPC.

Cram Quiz Answer

1. Answer: B, D, and E are correct. A gateway endpoint connects to DynamoDB or S3. NAT gateways or Internet gateways are not required. You can also configure the S3 bucket policy to limit access to only the traffic coming through the VPC endpoint.

VPC Peering

This section covers the following objective of Domain 5 (Networking and Content Delivery) from the official AWS Certified SysOps Administrator - Associate (SOA-C02) exam guide:

▶ 5.1 Implement networking features and connectivity

CramSaver

If you can correctly answer these questions before going through this section, save time by skimming the Exam Alerts in this section and then completing the Cram Quiz at the end of the section.

1. Can a VPC peering connection span multiple AWS regions and accounts?

2. An organization is connecting many VPCs using VPC peering connections. This solution has become overly complex and must be simplified. Which AWS networking product provides a solution to this issue?

Answers

1. Answer: Yes, VPC peering connections can be created with VPCs in different regions. A VPC peering connection can be established with a VPC in a different account, but the owner of the other account must accept your peering connection request.

2. Answer: The AWS Transit Gateway provides a highly available and scalable service that can be used to connect many VPCs. This eliminates the need for a complex full-mesh network of VPC peering connections and instead creates a simple hub-and-spoke topology.

About VPC Peering

A VPC peering connection is used to establish a connection between two VPCs over the global AWS backbone network without the requirement for a VPN. Peered VPCs can be in different regions and can even belong to different AWS accounts. The owner of one of the accounts sends a VPC peering request to the other account, which must be accepted for the peering connection to work. After the connection is created, you can update your route table to send specific traffic over the VPC peering connection. The CIDR ranges of peered VPCs must not overlap. In Figure 11.12, you can see an example of the route table configuration of two peered VPCs. Each VPC has a route to the other VPC that points to the peering connection (pcx-*nnnnn*).

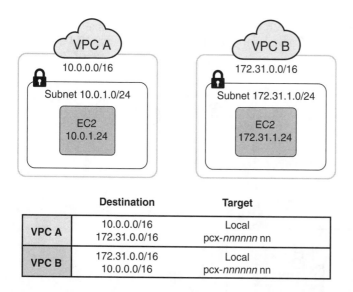

	Destination	Target
VPC A	10.0.0.0/16	Local
	172.31.0.0/16	pcx-*nnnnnn* nn
VPC B	172.31.0.0/16	Local
	10.0.0.0/16	pcx-*nnnnnn* nn

FIGURE 11.12 **VPC peering route table**

You can create multiple VPC peering connections; however, transitive peering is not supported. For example, in Figure 11.13, VPC 3 is configured with VPC peering connections to VPC 1 and VPC 2. This does not allow VPC 1 and VPC 2 to communicate through VPC 3.

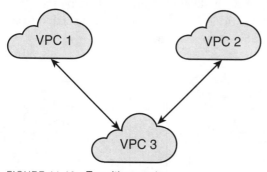

FIGURE 11.13 **Transitive peering**

Transit Gateway

As you add more VPCs, this architecture can become very complex. For example, Figure 11.14 shows many VPCs. Each has a Direct Connect VIF and VPN connections to a datacenter. (Note that the datacenter has only a single Direct Connect circuit but uses multiple VIFs to communicate with different VPCs.) There might also be VPC peering connections from each VPC to all the other

VPCs. For VPC A, that would mean managing five VPC peering connections, one VPN, and one Direct Connect circuit. Multiply that by many VPCs, and it becomes an administrative nightmare.

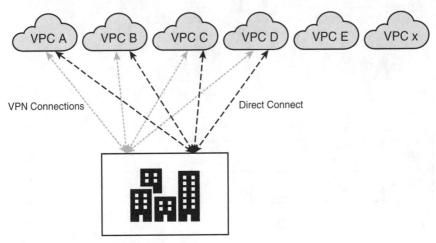

FIGURE 11.14 **Many VPCs**

The transit gateway can resolve this issue by allowing many VPCs to connect to it in a hub-and-spoke topology. You can also terminate VPNs or Direct Connect circuits on a transit gateway, allowing many VPCs to utilize these shared connections. Traffic that is sent via the transit gateway stays on the private AWS backbone and is automatically encrypted. A VPC connection to a transit gateway can use up to 50 Gbps of bandwidth.

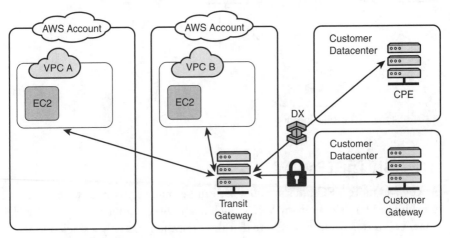

FIGURE 11.15 **Transit gateway**

ExamAlert

VPC Peering does not have an aggregate bandwidth limitation. Transit gateway connections to a VPC provide up to 50 Gbps of bandwidth. A VPN connection provides a maximum throughput of 1.25 Gbps.

Cram Quiz

Answer these questions. The answers follow the last question. If you cannot answer these questions correctly, consider reading this section again until you can.

1. Which types of connections are supported by a transit gateway? (Choose three.)

   ○ **A.** VPN to a physical datacenter

   ○ **B.** Direct Connect gateway

   ○ **C.** Internet gateway

   ○ **D.** Transitive connections between multiple VPCs

   ○ **E.** NAT gateway

2. You must create a VPC peering connection between your VPC and a customer's VPC. Your VPC has a CIDR range of 10.1.0.0/16. The customer VPC has a CIDR range of 10.2.0.0/16. What must be configured to allow EC2 instances in these VPCs to communicate? (Choose three.)

   ○ **A.** Configure a route in each VPC pointing to the CIDR range of the other VPC.

   ○ **B.** Configure a NAT gateway to present a public IP address for the instances that must communicate.

   ○ **C.** Configure an Internet gateway on each of the VPCs.

   ○ **D.** Configure the appropriate entries in NACLs and security groups.

   ○ **E.** A VPC peering connection request must be sent to the customer, and the customer AWS account must accept the request.

Cram Quiz Answers

1. Answer: A, B, and D are correct. A transit gateway allows the connected VPCs to communicate and allows attachments to an on-premises datacenter through either a VPC or Direct Connect.

2. Answer: A, D, and E are correct. A VPC peering connection must be established by sending a request to the customer account. After that request has been accepted, configure the necessary routes to send traffic over the VPC peering connection. Finally, open the necessary holes in the firewall to allow the desired traffic through.

VPC

This section covers the following objective of Domain 5 (Networking and Content Delivery) from the official AWS Certified SysOps Administrator - Associate (SOA-C02) exam guide:

▶ 5.1 Implement networking features and connectivity

CramSaver

If you can correctly answer these questions before going through this section, save time by skimming the Exam Alerts in this section and then completing the Cram Quiz at the end of the section.

1. What are some of the options to connect an on-premises datacenter to an AWS VPC?

2. Which VPN option requires the deployment of an EC2 instance?

Answers

1. Answer: AWS Managed VPN, AWS Direct Connect, AWS Direct Connect + VPN, and Software Site-to-Site VPN

2. Answer: Software Site-to-Site VPN

Hybrid cloud computing environments involve the use of physical datacenters and cloud computing services together. You might be using the cloud as a disaster recovery (DR) location. Or you might be using it to provide additional resources during periods of peak workloads (cloud bursting).

Regardless of the use case, it is vital to have a well-designed network that connects your datacenter to the AWS VPC. You may also need to connect VPCs in different regions or different AWS accounts to each other as well. The choices that you make can have a profound impact on how secure and performant these solutions are.

AWS-Managed VPN

An AWS-managed VPN is an IPsec VPN connection between your datacenter and an AWS VPC. The VPN terminates on a virtual private gateway in the AWS VPC. The virtual private gateway is a managed service and includes automated failover and the ability to support multiple connections. The maximum aggregate bandwidth supported by the VGW for VPN connections is 1.25 Gbps.

Figure 11.16 illustrates this concept. The customer-premises equipment (CPE) can be any hardware in your datacenter that supports an IPsec VPN. This component is referred to as the customer gateway (CGW) in the AWS Management Console and AWS documentation. Border Gateway Protocol (BGP) and static routes can be used to route traffic over the VPN. Encrypted traffic flows over the public Internet. You can configure a private Autonomous System Number (ASN) for BGP. If you do not specify an ASN, Amazon provides an ASN of 64512.

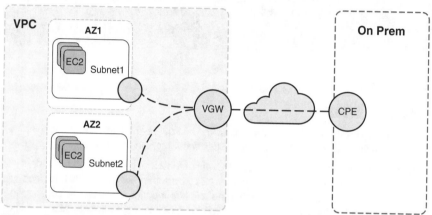

FIGURE 11.16   AWS-managed VPN

Each VPC has its own built-in DNS resolution. DHCP option sets can be used to forward certain DNS requests to an on-premises DNS instance. To assign your own domain name to your instances, you must create a custom DHCP option set. You then specify the domain name that exists on-premises, along with the addresses of the DNS servers to forward the requests to. This is important if you want to forward certain DNS requests to the on-premises DNS servers over the VPN.

Software Site-to-Site VPN

A software site-to-site VPN might be a requirement in regulatory environments that require full administrative control of both ends of the VPN connection. A software VPN appliance (such as OpenVPN) runs on an EC2 instance in the AWS VPC. There are many software VPN partner solutions in the AWS Marketplace. You must manage the configuration and availability of the VPN appliance because EC2 is not a managed service.

AWS services:

▶ **Managed VPN:** An IPsec VPN connection between a CGW in a physical datacenter and an AWS-managed virtual private gateway.

▶ **Software site-to-site VPN:** An IPsec VPN connection between a CGW in a physical datacenter and a customer-managed EC2 instance.

ExamAlert

You can configure multiple managed site-to-site VPN connections, but the maximum aggregate bandwidth of the virtual private gateway is 1.25 Gbps. To provide higher bandwidth over VPN, the transit gateway supports ECMP over multiple VPN connections.

Cram Quiz

Answer these questions. The answers follow the last question. If you cannot answer these questions correctly, consider reading this section again until you can.

1. An organization has configured a VPC with an Internet gateway and redundant private and public subnets in different AZs. A virtual private gateway has been deployed in the VPC, and a dual-tunnel VPN connection has been established to a router in the datacenter. NAT gateways have been created in both AZs. Identify each single point of failure in this design. (Choose all that apply.)

   ○ **A.** Virtual private gateway

   ○ **B.** Physical router

   ○ **C.** IGW

   ○ **D.** NAT gateway

2. Your VPC is connected to an on-premises datacenter using a managed site-to-site VPN. Application servers that run as VMs in the datacenter must be accessed by EC2 instances using their domain names. How can you accomplish this?

   ○ **A.** Create a Route 53 hosted zone for the on-premises domain name.

   ○ **B.** Create a Route 53 hosted zone for the VPC domain name.

   ○ **C.** Configure a DHCP option set in the VPC for the on-premises domain.

   ○ **D.** Configure a DHCP option set in the on-premises domain for the VPC.

Cram Quiz Answers

1. Answer: B is correct. The virtual private gateway and IGW are automatically redundant across AZs. NAT gateways are redundant within an AZ and have been created in both AZs. The only single point of failure is the router in the datacenter.

2. Answer: C is correct. DHCP option sets in the VPC can be used to forward certain DNS requests to an on-premises DNS instance. Configure the domain name that exists on-premises, along with the addresses of the DNS servers that the requests should be forwarded to.

Direct Connect

This section covers the following objective of Domain 5 (Networking and Content Delivery) from the official AWS Certified SysOps Administrator - Associate (SOA-C02) exam guide:

▶ 5.1 Implement networking features and connectivity

CramSaver

If you can correctly answer these questions before going through this section, save time by skimming the Exam Alerts in this section and then completing the Cram Quiz at the end of the section.

1. What speeds are available with a dedicated Direct Connect circuit?

2. What are the key differences between a dedicated versus hosted Direct Connect circuit?

Answers

1. Answer: 1 Gbps, 10 Gbps, 100 Gbps

2. Answer: A dedicated connection is a 1, 10, or 100 Gbps connection dedicated to a single customer. Hosted connections are sourced from an AWS Direct Connect Partner and can support lower bandwidth options for cost savings.

AWS Direct Connect

AWS Direct Connect provides private connectivity to your VPC over a dedicated physical connection. Direct Connect circuits can be either 1 Gbps, 10 Gbps, or 100 Gbps. You can request multiple Direct Connect circuits. Direct Connect can reduce network costs because transfer charges are often less expensive than Internet transfer charges.

Multiple virtual interfaces (VIFs) can be configured for a Direct Connect circuit. A Direct Connect public VIF is used to connect to public AWS resources such as S3. A Direct Connect private VIF is used to connect to resources within a VPC.

Your Direct Connect circuit can be terminated at a Direct Connect gateway. A Direct Connect gateway can be created in any region. An AWS Direct Connect gateway allows you to create connections from a single Direct Connect to multiple VPCs in different AWS regions.

AWS Direct Connect + VPN

A Direct Connect VIF can be used to establish a dedicated physical connection to a virtual private gateway. You can then use your CGW to establish an IPsec VPN connection to the virtual private gateway. This provides you with the low latency and dedicated throughput of Direct Connect while still allowing a secure end-to-end IPsec VPN connection.

Hosted and Dedicated Connections

A dedicated connection is dedicated to a single customer and supports speeds of 1, 10, or 100 Gbps. Hosted connections are sourced from an AWS Direct Connect partner. Hosted connections support many different speeds but support only a single VIF.

> **ExamAlert**
>
> Some questions on the exam require you to differentiate between public and private VIFs. Remember that public VIFs are only for public AWS resources like S3.

Cram Quiz

Answer these questions. The answers follow the last question. If you cannot answer these questions correctly, consider reading this section again until you can.

1. A company currently accesses sensitive data in an S3 bucket over the Internet. Which option would allow you to access this data over Direct Connect instead?

   ○ **A.** Configure an AWS private VIF and allow routes to AWS public resources to be learned via BGP.

   ○ **B.** Configure an AWS public VIF and allow routes to AWS public resources to be learned via BGP.

   ○ **C.** Configure an AWS private VIF and configure static summary routes to AWS public resources.

   ○ **D.** Configure an AWS public VIF and configure static summary routes to AWS public resources.

2. What is the primary benefit of Direct Connect versus a managed site-to-site VPN?

   ○ **A.** Increased redundancy and resiliency

   ○ **B.** Support of the BGP routing protocol

   ○ **C.** Additional support for DNS option sets

   ○ **D.** Higher bandwidth and more predictable throughput

Cram Quiz Answers

1. **Answer: B is correct.** A public virtual interface can access all AWS public services over Direct Connect. Routes to public prefixes are learned via BGP route advertisements.

2. **Answer: D is correct.** The maximum bandwidth of a VPN is 1.25 Gbps, and performance over the Internet is unpredictable. Direct Connect supports speeds up to 100 Gbps and traffic flows over the AWS backbone network.

AWS WAF

This section covers the following objective of Domain 5 (Networking and Content Delivery) from the official AWS Certified SysOps Administrator - Associate (SOA-C02) exam guide:

▶ 5.1 Implement networking features and connectivity

CramSaver

If you can correctly answer these questions before going through this section, save time by skimming the Exam Alerts in this section and then completing the Cram Quiz at the end of the section.

1. Which security solution can apply rate-based rules to stop DDoS or brute-force attacks?

2. On which services can the AWS WAF be deployed?

Answers

1. Answer: AWS WAF

2. Answer: CloudFront, Application Load Balancer, AppSync, and the API gateway

AWS WAF

The AWS Web Application Firewall (WAF) is a managed firewall service allowing you to configure rules that allow, block, or monitor (count) web requests based on conditions that you define. The AWS WAF can be deployed on Application Load Balancers (ALBs), the API gateway, AppSync, and CloudFront. It protects your resources and stops malicious traffic. Rules can be created based on conditions like HTTP headers, HTTP body, URI strings, SQL injection, and cross-site scripting. When used with CloudFront, AWS WAF can support custom origins outside of AWS such as on-premises web servers.

AWS WAF also supports rate-based rules that can help protect against DDoS and brute-force attacks. Rate-based rules are triggered when the number of requests from an IP address exceed a defined threshold. If an IP address exceeds the configured limit, additional requests are blocked.

AWS WAF managed rules provide preconfigured rules to protect against common threats. These rules are managed by AWS. Third-party provider rules from the AWS Marketplace can also be used. You can subscribe to these third-party rules, and they will be available for you to add to an AWS WAF web ACL. You can also create your own custom rules.

Cram Quiz

Answer these questions. The answers follow the last question. If you cannot answer
these questions correctly, consider reading this section again until you can.

1. VPC flow logs contain the following record:

```
2 123456789010 eni-1234a5aa123456789 17.14.10.2
172.16.10.12 49754 3389 6 20 4249 1418123456
1418123456 REJECT OK
```

   Which statements regarding this flow log are correct?

   ○ **A.** The traffic is being blocked by the AWS WAF at CloudFront.

   ○ **B.** The destination port is 3389, and 17.14.10.12 is the source IP address.

   ○ **C.** The source port is 3389, and 17.14.10.12 is the source IP address.

   ○ **D.** The traffic is being rejected by either a security group or a network ACL.

2. A DDoS attack from many different source IP addresses is reaching web servers running on EC2. You cannot create firewall rules for every source IP address
   because there are too many to manually track. How can you mitigate this attack?

   ○ **A.** Use a rate limit rule on the AWS WAF.

   ○ **B.** Use a dynamic rule in a security group that matches the attack pattern.

   ○ **C.** Create a dynamic NACL list based on the contents of VPC flow logs.

   ○ **D.** Block entire malicious subnets in the necessary security groups.

Cram Quiz Answers

1. Answer: B and D are correct. You can configure the AWS WAF to send logging
   information using Kinesis. AWS WAF logs do not show up in your flow logs. Flow
   logs contain traffic flows through the NACL and security groups.

2. Answer: A is correct. Rate-based rules track the number of requests from incoming IP addresses. When the configured limit is exceeded, the rule action is
   enforced on the offending IP addresses.

AWS Shield

This section covers the following objective of Domain 5 (Networking and Content Delivery) from the official AWS Certified SysOps Administrator - Associate (SOA-C02) exam guide:

▶ 5.1 Implement networking features and connectivity

CramSaver

If you can correctly answer these questions before going through this section, save time by skimming the Exam Alerts in this section and then completing the Cram Quiz at the end of the section.

1. What is the difference between AWS Shield Standard and AWS Shield Advanced?

2. What types of attacks does AWS Shield Standard protect against?

Answers

1. Answer: AWS Shield Standard is automatically enabled free of charge. AWS Shield Advanced is optional and provides additional protections against more sophisticated and larger attacks.

2. Answer: AWS Shield Standard protects against common infrastructure layer attacks like UDP floods and state exhaustion attacks like TCP SYN floods.

AWS Shield Standard

AWS Shield is a managed DDoS protection service. It is available in two different offerings: Standard and Advanced.

AWS Shield Standard is automatically enabled at no cost for all AWS customers. It does not protect as many services as AWS Shield Advanced. This basic protection level defends against frequently occurring network and transport layer DDoS attacks. Incoming traffic is inspected for malicious patterns in real time. For example, assume a DDoS attack is originating from many different IP addresses. AWS Shield checks for other anomalies and, if necessary, begins mitigating the traffic. Services that utilize CloudFront and Route 53 receive a higher level of comprehensive protection against all known infrastructure (Layer 3 and 4) attacks.

AWS Shield Advanced

AWS Shield Advanced is a paid service. It provides mitigations against large and sophisticated DDoS attacks and near real-time visibility into attacks. AWS Shield Advanced also provides integration with AWS Web Application Firewall. AWS Shield Advanced includes 24/7 access to the AWS DDoS Response Team (DRT). This includes live support from a team of AWS DDoS experts. Any scaling-related costs (ELBs, auto scaling groups, and so on) are credited if they are due to a DDoS attack. You can register up to 1000 AWS resources (load balancers, CloudFront distributions, Route 53 hosted zones, and so on) for protection with AWS Shield Advanced. Most attacks (99 percent) on CloudFront or Route 53 are mitigated within 1 second. If you wish to perform a DDoS test, you must request approval from AWS support. AWS Shield Advanced protects resources on EC2, Elastic Load Balancing, CloudFront, AWS Global Accelerator, and Route 53.

> **ExamAlert**
>
> AWS Shield Advanced enables protections for Amazon EC2, Elastic Load Balancing, Amazon CloudFront, AWS Global Accelerator, and Route 53 resources.

Cram Quiz

Answer this question. The answer follows the question. If you cannot answer the question correctly, consider reading this section again until you can.

1. What is a key difference between AWS Shield and the AWS WAF?

   ○ **A.** AWS Shield is included at no additional cost; the AWS WAF charges for each web ACL.

   ○ **B.** The AWS WAF cannot be configured on CloudFront.

   ○ **C.** The AWS WAF cannot be configured on a load balancer.

   ○ **D.** The AWS WAF does not offer managed rules.

Cram Quiz Answer

1. Answer: A is correct. The AWS WAF can be configured on CloudFront and on the Application Load Balancer. You are charged for each web ACL configured on AWS WAF.

What Next?

If you want more practice on this chapter's exam objectives before you move on, remember that you can access all of the Cram Quiz questions on the Pearson Test Prep software online. You can also create a custom exam by objective with the Online Practice Test. Note any objective you struggle with and go to that objective's material in this chapter.

CHAPTER 12

Domains, DNS, and Content Delivery

This chapter covers the following official AWS Certified SysOps Administrator - Associate (SOA-C02) exam domain:

▶ Domain 5: Networking and Content Delivery

(For more information on the official AWS Certified SysOps Administrator - Associate [SOA-C02] exam topics, see the Introduction.)

Domain Name Servers (DNS) are used to resolve domain names on the Internet and to direct traffic toward the appropriate resource. Complex DNS decisions must be made, and these choices can significantly impact the performance, cost, and availability of your web application.

Route 53

This section covers the following objective of Domain 5 (Networking and Content Delivery) from the official AWS Certified SysOps Administrator - Associate (SOA-C02) exam guide:

▶ 5.2 Configure domains, DNS services, and content delivery

CramSaver

If you can correctly answer these questions before going through this section, save time by skimming the Exam Alerts in this section and then completing the Cram Quiz at the end of the section.

1. What type of Route 53 record can be used to send requests to a CloudFront distribution?

2. What is the purpose of a Route 53 private hosted zone?

Answers

1. Answer: A Route 53 A record with an alias target can be used to send traffic to other AWS services like CloudFront.

2. Answer: A private hosted zone defines how Route 53 should respond to DNS queries for a domain and its subdomains within a VPC.

Route 53 is a hosted DNS service. It is one of the most popular services offered by AWS. It allows users to register domain names, apply routing policies, and perform infrastructure health checks on their web services. Route 53 works with web services running inside AWS (such as an EC2 web server) or private hosted applications such as web servers running in an on-premises datacenter.

Public and Private Zones

Figure 12.1 shows an EC2 instance that is a web server. All EC2 instances always have a private IP. This instance also has a public IP on a public subnet that is reachable from the Internet. If a user on the Internet wants to reach this website, Route 53 should resolve the user's request to the IP address of the web server. This example is considered a public hosted zone; however, you may have resources inside your VPC that also need to connect to this web server. You do not want that DNS query to be handled by the public hosted zone because that would force the traffic to traverse the Internet.

To avoid this situation, you can create a private hosted zone in Route 53 and associate it with the VPC. In Figure 12.1, users on the Internet and users in the VPC are resolving example.com. The result returned by the public hosted zone is a public IP. The private hosted zone resolves to a private IP address.

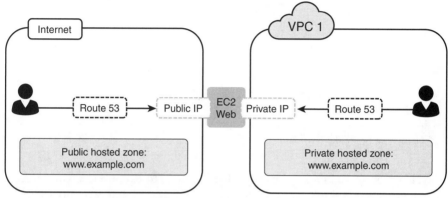

FIGURE 12.1   **Route 53 public and private zones**

Registering a Domain with Route 53

You can purchase domains within Route 53 or register domains that have been purchased elsewhere. In Figure 12.2, you can see a domain search being performed in the AWS Management Console.

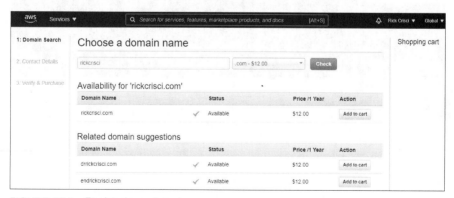

FIGURE 12.2   **Registering a domain**

After the domain is registered, you can configure DNS. In Figure 12.3, you can see the NS records for the purchased domain, as well as an alias record pointed to an Elastic Load Balancer (ELB). This means that when someone on the Internet resolves the address rickcrisci.link, the traffic is directed to the ELB.

FIGURE 12.3 **Public hosted zone**

An alias record is a DNS record type that is unique to Route 53. An alias record is used to forward traffic to an AWS service, such as a CloudFront distribution, an Elastic Load Balancer, or an S3 bucket. You can create an alias record at the zone apex. For example, if you register the domain rickcrisci.link, the zone apex is rickcrisci.link. There may also be subdomains (mobile.rickcrisci.link). Creating an alias record allows you to point the zone apex to another name instead of an IP address. You cannot create a CNAME record for the zone apex.

ExamAlert

An alias record can be used at the domain apex (such as example.com) or on subdomains. A CNAME record can be used on subdomains (such as mobile. example.com). An alias record can point to AWS services like CloudFront or an Elastic Load Balancer.

Cram Quiz

Answer these questions. The answers follow the last question. If you cannot answer these questions correctly, consider reading this section again until you can.

1. Your organization has multiple AWS accounts for different purposes. You use a dedicated account to manage all Route 53 configurations including domains and public hosted zones. There is also a different AWS account in which an auto scaling group of web servers runs behind an Internet-facing ELB. How can you configure Route 53 to send all traffic for example.com to the web servers?

   - ○ **A.** This configuration is possible only if you configure Route 53 and the ELB in the same AWS account.
   - ○ **B.** Configure an A record in Route 53 pointed to the IP address of the ELB in the other AWS account.
   - ○ **C.** Configure a CNAME record in Route 53 pointed to the ELB in the other AWS account.
   - ○ **D.** Configure an alias record in Route 53 pointed to the ELB in the other AWS account.

2. You have an RDS instance running in AWS account #1. A new application is being deployed in a new VPC within AWS account #2. A Route 53 private hosted zone exists in AWS account #1. What must be done to allow the VPC in AWS account #2 to be associated with the private hosted zone? (Choose two.)

   - ○ **A.** Create a VPC peering connection.
   - ○ **B.** Authorize the association between the private hosted zone in account #1 and the VPC in account #2.
   - ○ **C.** Run a command to create the association between the private hosted zone in account #1 and the VPC in account #2.
   - ○ **D.** Configure a public hosted zone that will be available to both VPCs.

Cram Quiz Answers

1. Answer: D is correct. A CNAME record cannot be used for the zone apex (example.com). The IP address of the ELB may change, so you should point to the DNS name of the ELB.

2. Answer: B and C are correct. You must first authorize the association of the VPC and the hosted zone. You do this with the **aws route53 create-vpc-association-authorization** command. Next, you establish the association with the **aws route53 associate-vpc-with-hosted-zone** command.

Route 53 Routing Policies

This section covers the following objective of Domain 5 (Networking and Content Delivery) from the official AWS Certified SysOps Administrator - Associate (SOA-C02) exam guide:

▶ 5.2 Configure domains, DNS services, and content delivery

CramSaver

If you can correctly answer these questions before going through this section, save time by skimming the Exam Alerts in this section and then completing the Cram Quiz at the end of the section.

1. Does geolocation-based routing consider latency as a factor for routing decisions?

2. Can failover routing be combined with other routing policies?

Answers

1. Answer: No. Geolocation routing is based only on the physical location of the DNS request.

2. Answer: Yes. Failover routing can be configured in a simple active/standby configuration, but it can also be used with other routing policies like weighted or geolocation routing.

Simple Routing Policy

The simple routing policy is the most basic option. Figure 12.4 shows traffic flow with a simple routing policy. The user generates a DNS query for example.com, and an A record is used to send all requests to a single destination. You can configure the time-to-live (TTL) for your DNS record. This determines how long the DNS entry remains cached in DNS resolvers. A longer TTL means that DNS resolvers query Route 53 less often, which reduces your charges. A shorter TTL means that you can update the DNS record across the Internet more quickly.

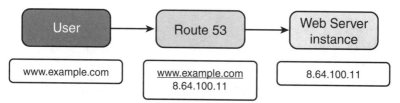

FIGURE 12.4 **Simple routing policy**

Weighted Routing Policy

Figure 12.5 shows an example of a weighted routing policy. Assume Web Server Instance 1 has been working properly for an extended period. Web Server Instance 2 is a new version of your website, and you want to trickle a small amount of traffic to it for testing purposes. The weighted routing policy here responds to DNS queries with the address of Web Server Instance 1 90 percent of the time, and Web Server Instance 2 10 percent of the time, effectively sending a small portion of the traffic to the new instance. You can also have failover routing enabled between these instances.

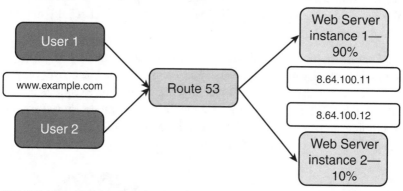

FIGURE 12.5 **Weighted routing policy**

Latency-Based Routing Policy

Figure 12.6 shows an example of a latency-based routing policy. User1 is in New York and gets lower latency by connecting to a web server in North Virginia. User2 is in California and is routed to the North California web server. Route 53 decides which record to provide based on latency data between the user and the different regions where the web server is hosted.

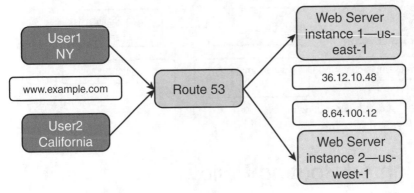

FIGURE 12.6 **Latency-based routing policy**

Failover Routing Policy

Route 53 health checks monitor the health and performance of your web resources. Health checks can monitor a specific resource (such as a web server or load balancer) or the status of an Amazon CloudWatch alarm. You can configure DNS failover based on the status of a health check. This is a great way to configure availability across regions or between an on-premises datacenter and AWS. You can configure a CloudWatch alarm for each health check if you want to be alerted about failures.

Figure 12.7 shows multiple resources that perform the same function. In this case, they are interchangeable web servers in different regions. The active web server instance has failed, and Route 53 will now resolve all future requests to the healthy resource. This is a simple active/standby failover model; however you can also combine failover routing with other routing policies (weighted, latency-based) to spread the workload across multiple resources during normal operation.

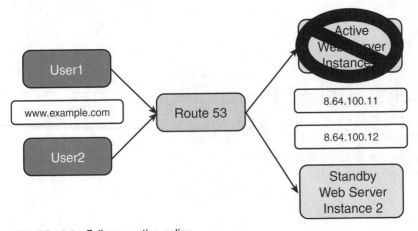

FIGURE 12.7 **Failover routing policy**

Geolocation Routing Policy

Geolocation routing lets you choose the resource record that will be returned based on the geographic location where DNS queries originate from. For example, you might want all requests that originate in the United States to resolve to a version of your website in the English language. Different geographic areas may resolve to different resources that provide your website in other languages. Geolocation routing does not consider latency. Geographic locations can include continents, by country, or by state in the United States. If Route 53 receives a DNS query and cannot identify the location, it provides a default record that you configure.

> **ExamAlert**
>
> Weighted routing is ideal for a blue/green deployment. The blue environment represents the established, reliable configuration. DNS can be used to switch traffic from the blue environment to the green or to roll back to the blue if necessary. Weighted routing allows you to begin this transition with a smaller percentage of traffic.

Cram Quiz

Answer these questions. The answers follow the last question. If you cannot answer these questions correctly, consider reading this section again until you can.

1. You have deployed an Auto Scaling Group (ASG) of EC2 instances behind an Application Load Balancer (ALB). Instances are distributed across three AZs. A Route 53 alias record is used for DNS and points to the load balancer. You must now gradually migrate this traffic to a new ALB and ASG. If an AZ fails, traffic must continue to flow to the surviving instances. What is the ideal way to accomplish this migration? (Choose two.)

   ○ **A.** Use a weighted routing policy to send a portion of traffic to the new ALB.

   ○ **B.** Use the ALB to detect and recover from an AZ failure.

   ○ **C.** Use Route 53 failover routing to detect and recover from an AZ failure.

   ○ **D.** Use a latency-based routing policy to send a portion of traffic to the new ALB.

2. A restaurant hosts a website in the us-west-1 region that highlights locations on the West Coast. Visitors from California should be directed to this website. They are preparing to open a new set of locations on the East Coast and want to host a different version of the website in us-east-1. All visitors from Florida should be directed to the website in us-east-1. Visitors from all other states should get the website that is hosted in us-west-1. Which routing policy should be used?

O **A.** Geoproximity routing

O **B.** Geolocation routing

O **C.** Latency-based routing

O **D.** Weighted routing

Cram Quiz Answers

1. Answer: A and B are correct. Weighted routing allows you to begin this transition with a smaller percentage of traffic and gradually move all traffic to the new ALB. The ALB handles availability *within* a region. Route 53 handles availability *across* regions.

2. Answer: B is correct. Geolocation routing lets you choose the resource record that will be returned based on the geographic location (state, nation, or continent) where DNS queries originate from.

S3 Static Website Hosting

This section covers the following objective of Domain 5 (Networking and Content Delivery) from the official AWS Certified SysOps Administrator - Associate (SOA-C02) exam guide:

▶ 5.2 Configure domains, DNS services, and content delivery

CramSaver

If you can correctly answer these questions before going through this section, save time by skimming the Exam Alerts in this section and then completing the Cram Quiz at the end of the section.

1. Should you use Route 53 when configuring a static website in S3?

2. Which security configurations must be made prior to using S3 to host a static website?

Answers

1. Answer: Route 53 can be used if you wish to use DNS to direct requests for your website to an S3 bucket endpoint.

2. Answer: You must configure the bucket permissions to allow public access and the bucket policy to allow public read access.

Configuring S3 Static Website Hosting

You can place static assets such as HTML files, scripts, and images in an S3 bucket. Doing so enables you to host a website with no web servers. After creating an S3 bucket, you can enable static website hosting on it under the properties screen, as seen in Figure 12.8. You must also allow public access to the bucket, as shown in Figure 12.9.

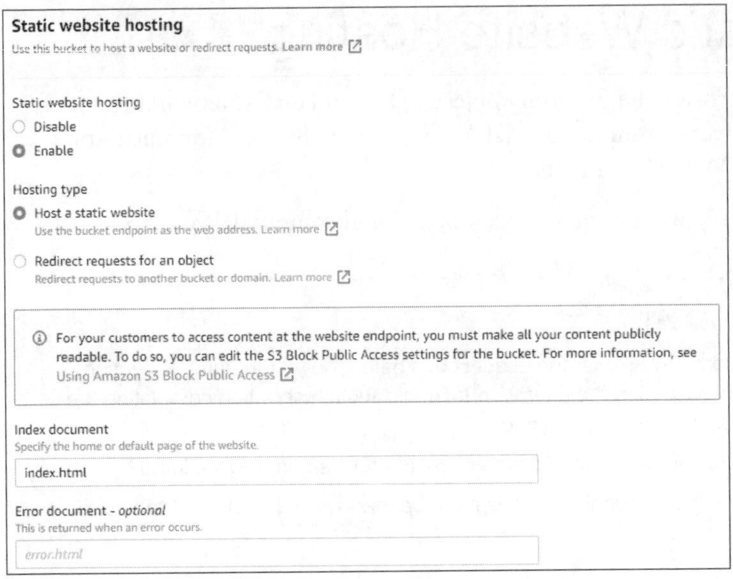

Static website hosting

Use this bucket to host a website or redirect requests. Learn more [↗]

Static website hosting

○ Disable

● Enable

Hosting type

● Host a static website
  Use the bucket endpoint as the web address. Learn more [↗]

○ Redirect requests for an object
  Redirect requests to another bucket or domain. Learn more [↗]

> ⓘ For your customers to access content at the website endpoint, you must make all your content publicly
> readable. To do so, you can edit the S3 Block Public Access settings for the bucket. For more information, see
> Using Amazon S3 Block Public Access [↗]

Index document
Specify the home or default page of the website.

    index.html

Error document - *optional*
This is returned when an error occurs.

    error.html

FIGURE 12.8   **Enabling static website hosting**

Block public access (bucket settings)

Public access is granted to buckets and objects through access control lists (ACLs), bucket policies, access point policies, or all. In order to ensure that public
access to all your S3 buckets and objects is blocked, turn on Block all public access. These settings apply only to this bucket and its access points. AWS
recommends that you turn on Block all public access, but before applying any of these settings, ensure that your applications will work correctly without
public access. If you require some level of public access to your buckets or objects within, you can customize the individual settings below to suit your
specific storage use cases. Learn more [↗]

    Edit

Block *all* public access
⚠ Off

  Block public access to buckets and objects granted through *new* access control lists (ACLs)
  ⚠ Off

  Block public access to buckets and objects granted through *any* access control lists (ACLs)
  ⚠ Off

  Block public access to buckets and objects granted through *new* public bucket or access point policies
  ⚠ Off

  Block public and cross-account access to buckets and objects through *any* public bucket or access point policies
  ⚠ Off

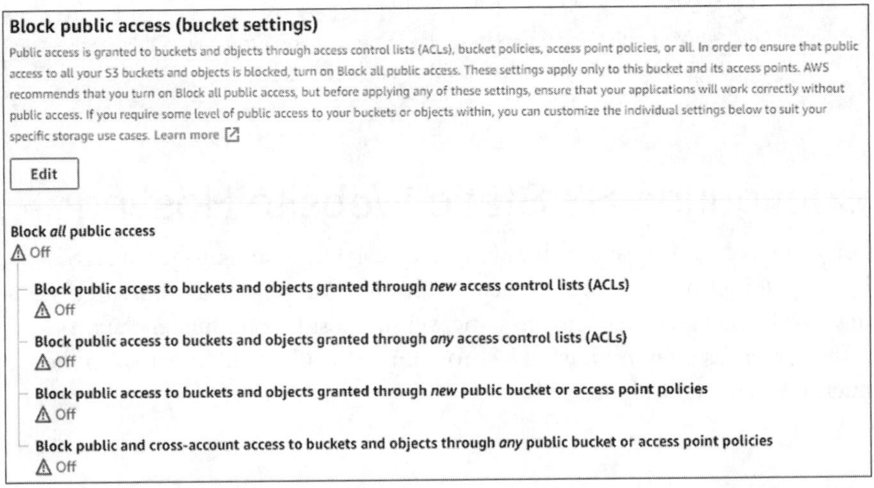

FIGURE 12.9   **S3 public access**

When the bucket is publicly available, the bucket policy must be updated to
grant public read access, as shown in Figure 12.10.

FIGURE 12.10 Bucket policy

You must now create or upload a landing page for the static website (typically called index.html). You can also upload an error page. When static website hosting was enabled, a bucket website endpoint was created, as shown in Figure 12.11. You can configure an alias record in Route 53 to point traffic for your website to this S3 bucket website endpoint.

Static website hosting   [Edit]
Use this bucket to host a website or redirect requests. Learn more [

Static website hosting
Enabled

Hosting type
Bucket hosting

Bucket website endpoint
When you configure your bucket as a static website, the website is available at the AWS Region-specific website endpoint of the bucket. Learn more [
http://rickcriscidemo.s3-website-us-east-1.amazonaws.com [

FIGURE 12.11 Bucket website endpoint

ExamAlert

An S3 static website does not require any servers and is a managed service. It can be used as a low-cost static backup for a primary website in the event of an outage by configuring failover routing in Route 53.

Cram Quiz

Answer these questions. The answers follow the last question. If you cannot answer these questions correctly, consider reading this section again until you can.

1. Which configurations must be completed to allow S3 static website hosting? (Choose three.)

   ○ **A.** Enable static website hosting on the bucket.

   ○ **B.** Manually create a bucket website endpoint.

   ○ **C.** Configure the bucket policy to allow public read access.

   ○ **D.** Configure the IAM policy to allow public read access.

   ○ **E.** Configure the bucket permissions to allow public access.

2. You must configure a Route 53 domain name (example.com) to route traffic to a static website hosted on EC2. If the EC2 instance is down, Route 53 should redirect requests to a static website in Amazon S3. Which configurations are required? (Choose two.)

   ○ **A.** Configure weighted routing in Route 53 with a health check being performed against the EC2 IP address and the S3 bucket.

   ○ **B.** Create an alias record for the S3 bucket as the secondary.

   ○ **C.** Create a CNAME record for the S3 bucket as the secondary.

   ○ **D.** Configure failover routing in Route 53 with a health check being performed against the EC2 IP address.

Cram Quiz Answers

1. Answer: A, C, and E are correct. To enable website hosting on S3, you must configure the bucket permissions to allow public access, enable static website hosting on the bucket, and configure the bucket policy to allow public read access.

2. Answer: B and D are correct. When a Route 53 health check against the EC2 instance returns unhealthy, the static website in S3 is what users see. When your health check returns healthy again, traffic is automatically routed back to the EC2 instance. There is no need for a health check on the S3 static website. An alias record must be used for the zone apex.

Amazon CloudFront

This section covers the following objective of Domain 5 (Networking and Content Delivery) from the official AWS Certified SysOps Administrator - Associate (SOA-C02) exam guide:

▶ 5.2 Configure domains, DNS services, and content delivery

CramSaver

If you can correctly answer these questions before going through this section, save time by skimming the Exam Alerts in this section and then completing the Cram Quiz at the end of the section.

1. How is traffic directed to the CloudFront Edge locations?

2. What are some options to remove outdated data from the CloudFront cache more quickly?

Answers

1. Answer: A Route 53 DNS record is used to redirect website traffic to a CloudFront distribution.

2. Answer: You can create an invalidation to remove objects from the cache. You can also create a new version of an object with a new name and update your website to reflect the new object.

Introduction to CloudFront

CloudFront is a content delivery network service that speeds up delivery of your static and dynamic web content. CloudFront spans a worldwide network of edge locations that are used to cache content. Route 53 is used to direct user requests to the CloudFront edge location that provides the lowest latency. If possible, the content is delivered to the user directly from the edge location. If a cache miss occurs, the content is delivered from the origin (an S3 bucket, EC2 instance, or a web server in an on-premises datacenter.)

Creating a CloudFront Distribution

CloudFront always begins with an origin. In this case, assume the origin is content in an S3 bucket. You can create a CloudFront distribution with the S3 bucket set as the origin. In Figure 12.12, the Origin Domain Name is configured to point to an S3 bucket. The Origin Path has not been configured but would allow you to specify a directory within the bucket. You can also set Restrict Bucket Access to an Origin Access Identity. That topic is covered in the next section.

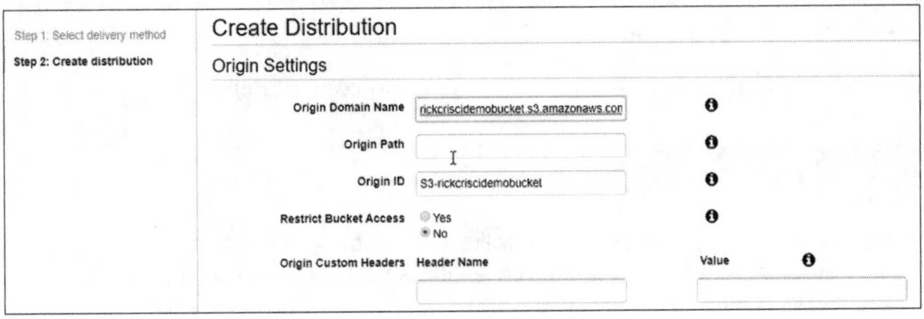

FIGURE 12.12   Creating a CloudFront distribution

Time-to-Live (TTL)

Data that is stored in the CloudFront Edge locations is considered current for a specific amount of time, as defined by the TTL. If data changes in the origin (for example, a video file is replaced in an S3 bucket), those changes are not visible to the end user until the TTL expires, and the cached version of the object is replaced. If you need to remove a file from CloudFront edge caches before it expires, you can perform an invalidation. You could also create a new version of an object, with a new name, and repoint the links on your website to that new version. But the easiest method of expiring the contents of the cache is with the TTL. In Figure 12.13, you can see the TTL configuration for a CloudFront distribution.

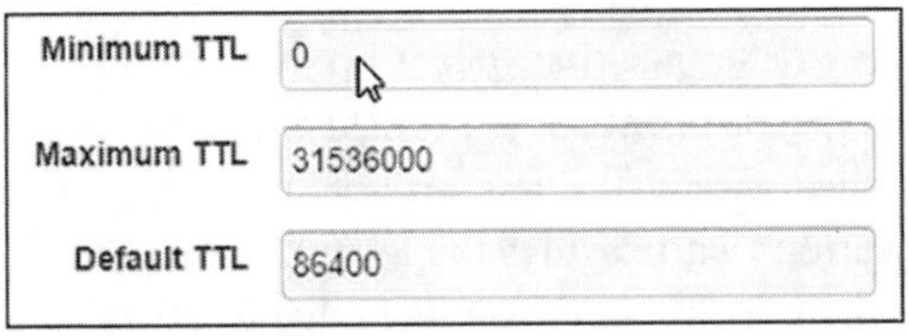

FIGURE 12.13   CloudFront TTL

Price Classes

The default price class for CloudFront includes all edge locations, which provides the best possible performance worldwide, but also is the most expensive option. Depending on the geographic location of your end users, you might be able to save money without a negative impact by choosing a different price class. In Figure 12.14, you can see the different price class options for a CloudFront distribution.

FIGURE 12.14 **Price class**

CloudFront and HTTPs

When you create a CloudFront distribution, you can configure different options for HTTPs. One option is to redirect HTTP to HTTPs. This allows users to connect to the content with HTTP, but the traffic is then redirected to secure HTTPs. You can also set the distribution to HTTPs only, and HTTP requests are not permitted.

You can also require HTTPs for communication between CloudFront and a custom origin. If you have already configured the HTTPS only option on the distribution, you can choose the Match Viewer origin protocol policy to enforce HTTPS between CloudFront and your custom origin as well. Or you can also set the option for HTTPS only for the origin protocol policy.

Final CloudFront Configuration Tasks

When the CloudFront distribution creation is complete, a domain name is automatically generated (see Figure 12.15). You can open this link in a browser directly, or you can configure a Route 53 alias record to point to it.

FIGURE 12.15 **CloudFront domain name**

> **ExamAlert**
>
> Waiting for the TTL is one way to expire undesired content from the cache at the edge locations, but you can speed up this process by using an invalidation. Invalidations can be expensive and are resource intensive.

Cram Quiz

Answer these questions. The answers follow the last question. If you cannot answer these questions correctly, consider reading this section again until you can.

1. Your website has a mix of static and dynamic content. A CloudFront distribution is being used to speed up the delivery of static assets such as images and videos. All static content is reachable through a subdomain called static.sample.com. Which Route 53 option should be used to configure this?

   ○ **A.** Create a CNAME record for sample.com that points to an alias record for the CloudFront distribution domain name.

   ○ **B.** Create a CNAME record for static.sample.com that points to an alias record for the CloudFront distribution domain name.

   ○ **C.** Create an A record for sample.com that points to an alias record for the CloudFront distribution domain name.

   ○ **D.** Create an A record for static.sample.com that points to an alias record for the CloudFront distribution domain name.

2. You have just decreased the TTL on a CloudFront distribution. Which of the following results may occur? (Choose two.)

   ○ **A.** Outdated content may persist for longer.

   ○ **B.** The cache hit ratio of the CloudFront distribution may drop.

   ○ **C.** CloudFront needs to retrieve less content from the origin.

   ○ **D.** Outdated content is purged from the cache more quickly.

Cram Quiz Answers

1. Answer: D is correct. Use Route 53 to create an alias record that points to the domain name of the CloudFront distribution. An alias record is similar to a CNAME record but can be created for subdomains or the zone apex. Route 53 responds to DNS queries that match and responds with the domain name that is associated with your distribution.

2. Answer: B and D are correct. Because the TTL is lower, the CloudFront distribution checks for outdated content more frequently. This results in more cache misses but also purges outdated content from the cache more quickly.

S3 Origin Access Identity

This section covers the following objective of Domain 5 (Networking and Content Delivery) from the official AWS Certified SysOps Administrator - Associate (SOA-C02) exam guide:

▶ 5.2 Configure domains, DNS services, and content delivery

CramSaver

If you can correctly answer these questions before going through this section, save time by skimming the Exam Alerts in this section and then completing the Cram Quiz at the end of the section.

1. What is the primary purpose of a CloudFront Origin Access Identity?

2. What security configuration must be performed on the S3 bucket to make the OAI effective?

Answers

1. Answer: An Origin Access Identity (OAI) is used to restrict access to an S3 bucket to a CloudFront distribution and to block direct access to the bucket domain name.

2. Answer: A bucket policy must be configured that limits access to the objects to the OAI user.

Configuring an Origin Access Identity

An Origin Access Identity (OAI) is used to restrict access to an S3 bucket. If a bucket is serving as the origin for a CloudFront distribution, there may be no legitimate reason to access the contents of the bucket directly using the S3 bucket domain. In Figure 12.16, Restrict Bucket Access has been selected, and the option to create a new OAI has been selected.

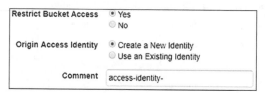

FIGURE 12.16 Origin Access Identity

The result of this configuration is a special user (OAI) that will be created for CloudFront. You must now configure the S3 bucket permissions so that only the OAI can access the restricted content. This is done by configuring an S3 bucket policy and identifying the OAI as a principal. Figure 12.17 shows a bucket policy that allows access to the OAI.

```
{
    "Version": "2008-10-17",
    "Id": "PolicyForCloudFrontPrivateContent",
    "Statement": [
        {
            "Sid": "1",
            "Effect": "Allow",
            "Principal": {
                "AWS": "arn:aws:iam::cloudfront:user/CloudFront Origin Access Identity E1KFVJ6NJOH5VC"
            },
            "Action": "s3:GetObject",
            "Resource": "arn:aws:s3:::cloudfrontrickcrisci/*"
        }
    ]
}
```

FIGURE 12.17   OAI bucket policy

ExamAlert

The OAI restricts bucket access so that only the CloudFront distribution has direct access to objects. Users can access these objects only through a web resource that is part of a CloudFront distribution.

Cram Quiz

Answer this question. The answer follows the question. If you cannot answer the question correctly, consider reading this section again until you can.

1. You have an S3 bucket that is the origin for a CloudFront distribution. Which actions must you take to ensure that users access objects in the bucket by using only CloudFront URLs? (Choose two).

   ○ **A.** Create an OAI that is associated with the CloudFront distribution.

   ○ **B.** Configure a IAM policy that identifies the OAI as a resource.

   ○ **C.** Create an OAI that is associated with the bucket.

   ○ **D.** Configure a bucket policy that identifies the OAI as a resource.

   ○ **E.** Configure a bucket policy that identifies the OAI as the principal and the bucket as the resource.

Cram Quiz Answer

1. Answer: A and E are correct. The OAI is a user that is associated with a Cloud-Front distribution. The bucket policy identifies this user as the principal and grants it access to a resource (the S3 bucket).

What Next?

If you want more practice on this chapter's exam objectives before you move on, remember that you can access all of the Cram Quiz questions on the Pearson Test Prep software online. You can also create a custom exam by objective with the Online Practice Test. Note any objective you struggle with and go to that objective's material in this chapter.

CHAPTER 13

Troubleshoot Network Connectivity

This chapter covers the following official AWS Certified SysOps Administrator - Associate (SOA-C02) exam domains:

▶ Domain 5: Networking and Content Delivery

(For more information on the official AWS Certified SysOps Administrator - Associate [SOA-C02] exam topics, see the Introduction.)

VPC Flow Logs

This section covers the following objective of Domain 5 (Networking and Content Delivery) from the official AWS Certified SysOps Administrator - Associate (SOA-C02) exam guide:

▶ 5.3 Troubleshoot network connectivity issues

CramSaver

If you can correctly answer these questions before going through this section, save time by skimming the Exam Alerts in this section and then completing the Cram Quiz at the end of the section.

1. What configuration tasks must be completed to enable flow logs on a VPC and view them in CloudWatch logs?

2. How frequently are flow logs aggregated by default?

Answers

1. Answer: Create an IAM policy and role, a CloudWatch log group, and a VPC flow log.

2. Answer: Flow logs aggregated once per 10 minutes by default.

VPC flow logs are used to capture information about the IP traffic flowing in or out of network interfaces in a VPC. Flow logs can be created for an entire VPC, a subnet, or an individual interface. You can capture all traffic, accepted traffic, or rejected traffic. It can be used to diagnose security group or Network ACL rules. VPC flow logs do not have a performance impact. The data captured can be published to CloudWatch logs or an S3 bucket. Flow logs do not provide the ability to view a real-time stream of traffic. Logs are published every 10 minutes by default but can be configured for faster delivery.

Configuring VPC Flow Logs

The first step required in configuring VPC flow logs is to create the appropriate IAM role. This role must have the permissions to publish VPC flow logs to CloudWatch logs. Figure 13.1 shows a sample IAM policy. There are prewritten policies that you can copy from the AWS documentation.

FIGURE 13.1   **Flow log IAM policy**

Now that the policy has been created, you must create an EC2 role that includes that policy, as shown in Figure 13.2. You must also give the new role a trust relationship with VPC flow logs.

FIGURE 13.2   **Flow log IAM role**

The next step is to create a CloudWatch log group. In Figure 13.3, you can see the configuration of a log group.

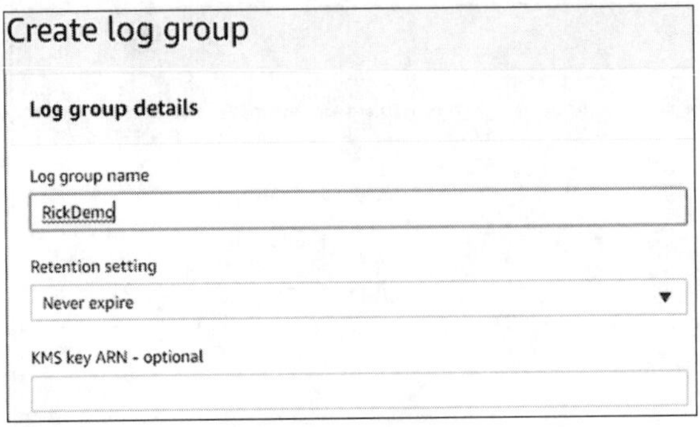

Create log group

Log group details

Log group name

RickDemo

Retention setting

Never expire ▼

KMS key ARN - optional

FIGURE 13.3   **Configuring a log group**

Now you are finally ready to enable flow logs. In Figure 13.4, a new flog log is created on a VPC. This flow log will capture all traffic information and send it to the CloudWatch log group shown in Figure 13.3. You could also send the records to an S3 bucket. The flow log has the necessary permissions to do this based on the flow log role shown in Figure 13.2. This flow log will track all interfaces in this VPC. To target a specific subnet or an interface, create the flow log on those objects.

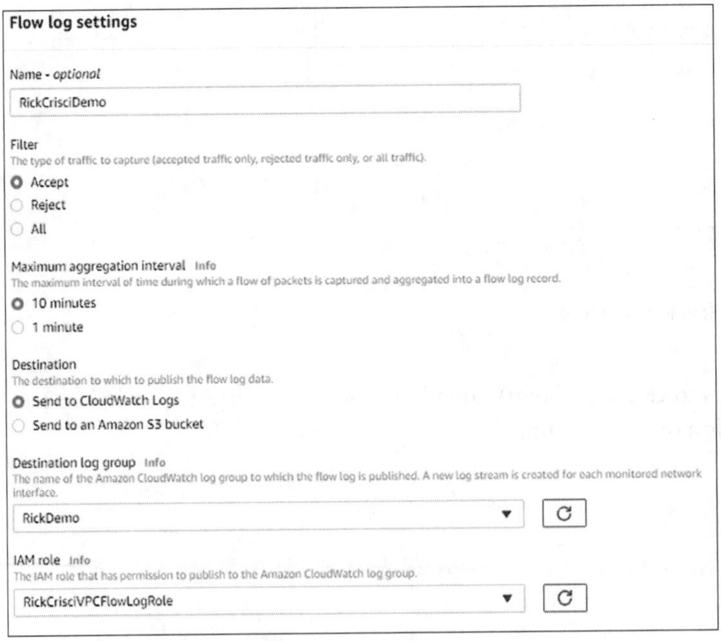

Flow log settings

Name - *optional*

RickCrisciDemo

Filter
The type of traffic to capture (accepted traffic only, rejected traffic only, or all traffic).

○ Accept
○ Reject
○ All

Maximum aggregation interval Info
The maximum interval of time during which a flow of packets is captured and aggregated into a flow log record.

○ 10 minutes
○ 1 minute

Destination
The destination to which to publish the flow log data.

○ Send to CloudWatch Logs
○ Send to an Amazon S3 bucket

Destination log group Info
The name of the Amazon CloudWatch log group to which the flow log is published. A new log stream is created for each monitored network interface.

RickDemo ▼ C

IAM role Info
The IAM role that has permission to publish to the Amazon CloudWatch log group.

RickCrisciVPCFlowLogRole ▼ C

FIGURE 13.4   **Creating a flow log on a VPC**

In Figure 13.5, you can see some of the captured flow logs. In this case, they are filtered based on a specific IP address (74.76.58.81) to reduce the amount of information displayed. Notice that the traffic has been accepted by the security group.

FIGURE 13.5   **Log event example**

Figure 13.6 shows traffic that has been blocked by the security group. In this case, 74.76.58.81 is the source IP, 10.1.101.112 is the destination IP, and port 22 is the source port.

FIGURE 13.6   **Rejected flow log**

> **ExamAlert**
>
> You must be capable of reading and interpreting flow logs and identifying source IP and destination IP addresses, ports, and whether the traffic was blocked or allowed. Also, you need to understand that traffic can be blocked by a network access control list, and that the NACL is enforced before the security group on incoming traffic.

Cram Quiz

Answer these questions. The answers follow the last question. If you cannot answer these questions correctly, consider reading this section again until you can.

1. You are using VPC flow logs to confirm the correct operation of a security group. You are unable to locate the correct log group in CloudWatch. What are potential causes for this issue? (Choose two.)

   ○ **A.** You need to wait longer for the logs to show up.

   ○ **B.** The CloudFront log group has been configured without the correct permissions.

   ○ **C.** The flow log has not captured any traffic.

   ○ **D.** The flow log is not configured with an S3 bucket.

2. Based on the figure shown, what is the most likely cause of the failed connection?

```
2021-04-15T13:11:49.000-04:00     2 702864269202 eni-09eca5230ee7380bf 74.76.58.81 10.1.101.112 56071 22 6 4 208 1618506709 ...
2 702864269202 eni-09eca5230ee7380bf 74.76.58.81 10.1.101.112 56071 22 6 4 208 1618506709 1618506725 REJECT OK
                                                                                                           [Copy]

2021-04-15T13:12:05.000-04:00     2 702864269202 eni-09eca5230ee7380bf 74.76.58.81 10.1.101.112 56071 22 6 1 52 1618506725 1...
2 702864269202 eni-09eca5230ee7380bf 74.76.58.81 10.1.101.112 56071 22 6 1 52 1618506725 1618506732 REJECT OK
                                                                                                           [Copy]
```

   ○ **A.** A security group is blocking incoming traffic from source IP 10.1.101.112.

   ○ **B.** A security group is blocking incoming traffic on port 22.

   ○ **C.** A security group is blocking outgoing traffic on port 22.

   ○ **D.** A security group is blocking outgoing traffic on port 6.

Cram Quiz Answers

1. Answer: A and C are correct. Flow logs are aggregated every 10 minutes by default. You may need to wait longer to see the traffic reflected in the flow logs. If there has not been any relevant traffic, there will not be flow log entries.

2. Answer: B is correct. Traffic is incoming from public IP 74.76.58.81, 10.1.101.112 is the destination IP, and port 22 is the source port.

ELB Access Logs

This section covers the following objective of Domain 5 (Networking and Content Delivery) from the official AWS Certified SysOps Administrator - Associate (SOA-C02) exam guide:

▶ 5.3 Troubleshoot network connectivity issues

CramSaver

If you can correctly answer these questions before going through this section, save time by skimming the Exam Alerts in this section and then completing the Cram Quiz at the end of the section.

1. What security configuration task must be completed for ELB access logs to function?

2. Are ELB access logs useful for troubleshooting issues such as spikes in request counts and Layer 7 access codes?

Answers

1. Answer: The logs are sent to an S3 bucket. The S3 bucket policy must be configured to grant ELB access logs write permissions.

2. Answer: Yes, ELB access logs capture request details and server responses.

ELB access logs are an optional feature that can be used to troubleshoot traffic patterns and issues with traffic as it hits the ELB. ELB access logs capture details of requests sent to your load balancer such as the time of the request, the client IP, latency, and server responses. Access logs are stored in an S3 bucket. Log files are published every five minutes, and multiple logs can be published for the same five-minute period.

The S3 bucket must be in the same region as the ELB. The bucket policy must be configured to allow access logs to write to the bucket. You can use tools such as Amazon Athena, Loggly, Splunk, or Sumo Logic to analyze the contents of ELB access logs.

ELB access logs also include HTTP response codes from the target. If a connection could not be established to the target, it is set to -. Figure 13.7 shows how to configure an S3 bucket as a destination for ELB access logs.

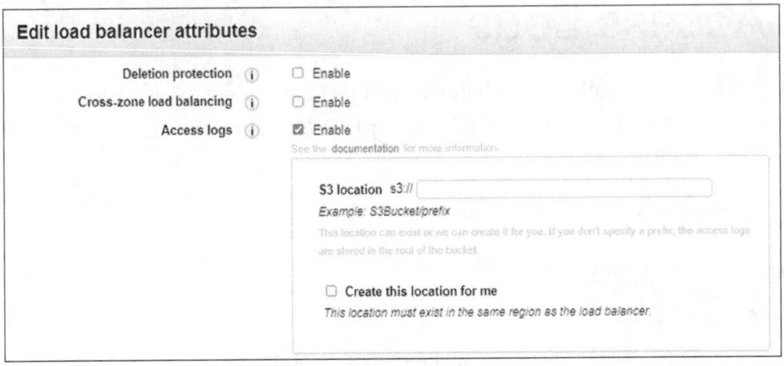

Edit load balancer attributes

Deletion protection ⓘ	☐ Enable	
Cross-zone load balancing ⓘ	☐ Enable	
Access logs ⓘ	☑ Enable	

See the documentation for more information.

S3 location s3:// [   ]

Example: S3Bucket/prefix

This location can exist or we can create it for you. If you don't specify a prefix, the access logs are stored in the root of the bucket.

☐ Create this location for me

This location must exist in the same region as the load balancer.

FIGURE 13.7   **Enabling ELB access logs**

ExamAlert

The S3 bucket that is used for ELB access logs must be in the same region as the bucket and must have a bucket policy that allows write permissions on the ELB access logs.

Cram Quiz

Answer these questions. The answers follow the last question. If you cannot answer these questions correctly, consider reading this section again until you can.

1. What are the minimum requirements for an S3 bucket that will be used to store ELB access logs? (Choose two.)

   ○ **A.** It must be in the same AZ as the ELB.

   ○ **B.** It must be in the same region as the ELB.

   ○ **C.** The bucket policy must be configured to grant write permissions to ELB logs.

   ○ **D.** Encryption must be manually enabled on the bucket.

2. Which information can be found in ELB access logs? (Choose three.)

   ○ **A.** The client's IP address

   ○ **B.** Latency

   ○ **C.** The ELB IP address

   ○ **D.** Server responses

   ○ **E.** S3 bucket name

Cram Quiz Answers

1. Answer: B and C are correct. The S3 bucket must be in the same region as the ELB. The bucket policy must be configured to allow ELB access logs to write to the bucket.

2. Answer: A, B, and D are correct. ELB access logs capture details of requests sent to your load balancer such as the time of the request, the client IP, latency, and server responses.

AWS WAF ACL Logs

This section covers the following objective of Domain 5 (Networking and Content Delivery) from the official AWS Certified SysOps Administrator - Associate (SOA-C02) exam guide:

▶ 5.3 Troubleshoot network connectivity issues

CramSaver

If you can correctly answer these questions before going through this section, save time by skimming the Exam Alerts in this section and then completing the Cram Quiz at the end of the section.

1. What three services must be configured to be able to perform comprehensive AWS WAF ACL logging?

2. What is the purpose on the Kinesis Data Firehose when configuring AWS WAF ACL logging?

Answers

1. Answer: The AWS WAF web ACL, Kinesis Data Firehose, and S3.

2. Answer: The logs are received by Kinesis Data Firehose, which can trim the logs and reduce the amount of data that gets stored in S3.

AWS WAF, Kinesis, and S3

The AWS Web Application Firewall (WAF) protects your resources and stops malicious traffic. Rules can be created based on conditions like HTTP headers, HTTP body, URI strings, SQL injection, and cross-site scripting. You can enable logging to get capture information such as the time and nature of requests and the web ACL rule that each request matched.

The logs are received by Kinesis Data Firehose, which can be used to trim the logs and reduce the amount of data that gets stored. The logs are commonly stored in S3 after being processed by Kinesis. The Kinesis delivery stream can easily be created using a CloudFormation template that is available on the AWS website.

To configure AWS WAF ACL comprehensive logging, the first step is to create the S3 bucket that the data will be stored in. You must configure an access policy to allow Kinesis Data Firehose to write to the S3 bucket. The next step is to create a Kinesis Data Firehose and give it the necessary IAM role to write to the S3 bucket. Finally, you must associate the AWS WAF with the Kinesis Data Firehose and enable logging.

These logs can be helpful when determining what types of rules should be created or modified. A web ACL can allow or deny traffic based on the source IP address, country of origin of the request, string match or regular expression (regex) match, or the detection of malicious SQL code or scripting. For example, a request could include a header with some identifying information, such as the name of the department. A string or regex match could be used to identify that traffic, and the logs could be used to determine the volume of matching requests.

> **ExamAlert**
>
> A web ACL can allow or deny traffic based on the source IP address, country of origin of the request, string match or regular expression (regex) match, or the detection of malicious SQL code or scripting. You can also use the logs that are generated to examine the number of requests, the nature of those requests, and where they originate from.

Cram Quiz

Answer these questions. The answers follow the last question. If you cannot answer these questions correctly, consider reading this section again until you can.

1. You want to identify and count requests that are hitting a web application from varying on-premises datacenters. All datacenters are in the same country but have different IP address ranges. There is no identifying information in the header to indicate which datacenter is the origin. What condition of the web ACL could be used to determine this?

   - ○ **A.** Destination IP match
   - ○ **B.** Source IP match
   - ○ **C.** Geo match
   - ○ **D.** String match

2. You need visibility into traffic that is reaching a set of EC2 web servers and must block SQL injection attacks before they can reach the instances. Where can you configure the AWS WAF with a SQL injection rule to accomplish this? (Choose all that apply.)

   - ○ **A.** CloudFront
   - ○ **B.** Classic Load Balancer
   - ○ **C.** Application Load Balancer
   - ○ **D.** Auto Scaling Group

Cram Quiz Answers

1. Answer: B is correct. The source IP address could be used to determine how many requests are coming from each datacenter.

2. Answer: A and C are correct. The AWS WAF can be configured on a CloudFront distribution, an Amazon API Gateway REST API, and an Application Load Balancer. It cannot be configured on a Classic Load Balancer.

CloudFront Logs

This section covers the following objective of Domain 5 (Networking and Content Delivery) from the official AWS Certified SysOps Administrator - Associate (SOA-C02) exam guide:

▶ 5.3 Troubleshoot network connectivity issues

CramSaver

If you can correctly answer these questions before going through this section, save time by skimming the Exam Alerts in this section and then completing the Cram Quiz at the end of the section.

1. You need to troubleshoot the success of connections using HTTP response codes. Which logs should you review?

2. When you enable logging on a CloudFront distribution, what configuration changes are required on the destination S3 bucket?

Answers

1. Answer: You should review the CloudFront and Application Load Balancer logs.

2. Answer: The destination bucket ACL is automatically updated to allow log delivery.

Using CloudFront Logs

CloudFront is a content delivery network service that speeds up delivery of your static and dynamic web content. You can enable standard logs on a Cloud-Front distribution and deliver them to an S3 bucket. Real-time logs are also possible and enable you to view request information within seconds of the requests occurring.

As incoming requests reach the CloudFront edge locations, data is captured about the request in a log file that is specific to a single distribution. These log files are saved to S3 periodically. If there are no requests for an hour, a log file is not generated. When you configure logging on a distribution, the destination bucket ACL is automatically updated to allow log delivery.

You should not choose a bucket that is an S3 origin to contain these logs. Also, buckets in the following regions are not currently supported as CloudFront access log destinations: af-south-1, ap-east-1, eu-south-1, and me-south-1.

Analyzing Standard Log Files

More than 30 fields are included in each log file. They contain the date and time of the request and also the edge location where they were received. Other fields shown include the source IP, protocol, and port.

Much like ALB access logs, the CloudFront logs also include the HTTP status code of the server's response. This is a critical tool for analyzing the success of requests.

You can also use Athena to perform overall analysis of CloudFront logs.

> **ExamAlert**
>
> You can use either CloudFront or ELB logs to analyze HTTP response codes and determine if requests were successfully served.

Cram Quiz

Answer this question. The answer follows the question. If you cannot answer the question correctly, consider reading this section again until you can.

1. Which data fields can be viewed in both CloudWatch and Application Load Balancer logs? (Choose three.)

   ○ **A.** The destination target group

   ○ **B.** IP and port of the requesting client

   ○ **C.** The distribution associated with the request

   ○ **D.** The HTTP response code

   ○ **E.** The date and time of the request

Cram Quiz Answer

1. Answer: B, D, and E are correct. CloudWatch logs do not display the target group of the ALB. ALB logs do not display the CloudFront distribution.

CloudFront Caching Issues

This section covers the following objective of Domain 5 (Networking and Content Delivery) from the official AWS Certified SysOps Administrator - Associate (SOA-C02) exam guide:

▶ 5.3 Troubleshoot network connectivity issues

CramSaver

If you can correctly answer these questions before going through this section, save time by skimming the Exam Alerts in this section and then completing the Cram Quiz at the end of the section.

1. Name one benefit and one drawback of increasing the TTL on objects in a CloudFront distribution.

2. What does the total error rate metric for a CloudFront distribution indicate?

Answers

1. Answer: Increasing the TTL means CloudFront will reach out to the origin for updated content less often, resulting in fewer cache misses. The drawback is that your users are more likely to get stale data from the cache.

2. Answer: The total error rate metric indicates the percentage of requests to the origin that result in a 400-type or 500-type response.

Improving Cache Hit Rate

The two major benefits of CloudFront are reducing latency experienced by requestors and reducing the hit count on your origin (S3, web server, and so on). As more objects are served from CloudFront, this reduces the workload that the origin must perform, and as a result, cost savings can be achieved.

The percentage of requests that are served by CloudFront (without pulling content from the origin) is called the cache hit ratio. You can observe the cache hit ratio in the CloudFront console. Increasing the TTL is one way to improve this ratio because CloudFront will reach out to the origin for updated content less often. Of course, this means that your users are more likely to get stale data from the cache.

CloudFront serves the cached version of a file from an edge location until the file expires. After a file expires, CloudFront forwards the request to the origin server. CloudFront may still have the latest version, in which case the origin returns the status code *304 Not Modified*. If a newer version exists in the origin, the origin returns the status code *200 OK* and the latest version of the file.

You can also improve caching based on cookie values. Instead of forwarding all cookies, configure specific cookies for CloudFront to forward to your origin. For example, assume that there are two cookies in a request, and each cookie has two possible values. In this case, CloudFront forwards four requests to the origin, and all four responses are cached in CloudFront, even if some of them are identical.

Similarly, you can configure CloudFront to cache based on only a limited set of specified headers instead of forwarding and caching based on all headers.

HTTP Status Codes from an Origin

When a cache miss occurs, the content must be retrieved from the origin. To the origin, this appears as a web request. The origin may return an HTTP error code (4xx or 5xx status codes). You can monitor, alarm, and receive notifications that include these HTTP response codes. CloudFront publishes six metrics with a one-minute granularity into Amazon CloudWatch:

▶ **Requests:** Total HTTP and HTTPS requests received.

▶ **Bytes Downloaded:** Total data downloaded by clients.

▶ **Bytes Uploaded:** Total data uploaded to your origin.

▶ **4xx Error Rate:** Percentage of requests that result in a 400-type response.

▶ **5xx Error Rate:** Percentage of requests that result in a 500-type response.

▶ **Total Error Rate:** Percentage of requests that result in a 400-type or 500-type response.

ExamAlert

You can monitor HTTP response codes that are returned from the origin using the 4xx Error Rate, 5xx Error Rate, and Total Error Rate metrics.

Cram Quiz

Answer these questions. The answers follow the last question. If you cannot answer these questions correctly, consider reading this section again until you can.

1. You need to monitor the total HTTP response codes from the origin that result in a 4xx or 5xx error. Which metric should you use?

   - ○ **A.** Cache hit rate
   - ○ **B.** Healthy host count
   - ○ **C.** Total error rate
   - ○ **D.** HTTP error rate

2. The TTL has expired on an object that is cached by a CloudFront distribution. However, the cached file still matches the most current version in the origin. How will CloudFront handle the next request for this file?

   - ○ **A.** CloudFront forwards the request to the origin server, which returns the status code *304 Not Modified*.
   - ○ **B.** CloudFront forwards the request to the origin server, which returns the status code *200 OK*.
   - ○ **C.** CloudFront forwards the request to the origin server, which returns the status code *304 Not Modified* and sends the latest version of the file to the CloudFront distribution.
   - ○ **D.** CloudFront forwards the request to the origin server, which returns the status code *200 OK* and sends the latest version of the file to the CloudFront distribution.

Cram Quiz Answers

1. Answer: C is correct. The percentage of requests to the origin that result in a 4xx or 5xx error is shown in the total error rate.

2. Answer: A is correct. When the TTL on a file expires, CloudFront forwards the next incoming request to the origin server. If CloudFront has the latest version, the origin returns the status code *304 Not Modified*.

Troubleshooting Hybrid and Private Links

This section covers the following objective of Domain 5 (Networking and Content Delivery) from the official AWS Certified SysOps Administrator - Associate (SOA-C02) exam guide:

▶ 5.3 Troubleshoot network connectivity issues

CramSaver

If you can correctly answer these questions before going through this section, save time by skimming the Exam Alerts in this section and then completing the Cram Quiz at the end of the section.

1. What task must be completed by the colocation provider for Direct Connect physical connectivity to be established?

2. A VPN connection establishment is failing during phase 1. What are some possible causes of this issue?

Answers

1. Answer: A cross-connect must be made between your device and the Direct Connect hardware.

2. Answer: IKE negotiation may fail due to a physical customer gateway that does not meet the AWS VPN requirements. Also a misconfigured preshared key prevents phase 1 from completing.

Troubleshooting Direct Connect

Direct Connect issues can be difficult to diagnose. The ideal approach is to use the OSI model to help isolate the potential issues and the underlying cause.

Layer 1 (physical) issues occur when you are having difficulty establishing physical connectivity to an AWS Direct Connect device. When a Direct Connect circuit is established, a cross-connect must be made between your port and the Direct Connect device. You can ask your colocation provider to validate that the cross-connect is properly established. You can also troubleshoot that all devices under your control are powered on and that the fiber-optic connection is properly connected.

Layer 2 (data link) issues occur when the physical connection is working properly, but the Direct Connect virtual interface (VIF) does not come up. These problems are typically the result of a misconfigured VLAN, improperly configured VLAN 802.1Q tagging, or ARP issues. Direct Connect is technically a Layer 2 offering. If Layer 2 is working properly, you can assume that any Layer 3 or Layer 4 issues are related to other configurations and not Direct Connect.

Layer 3 (network) and Layer 4 (transport) issues are routing related. Make sure that BGP is properly configured with the correct peer IPs and ASNs.

Troubleshooting AWS Managed VPNs

If you are establishing a new IPsec VPN, the first phase is Internet Key Exchange (IKE). If this phase fails, make sure that the customer gateway meets the AWS VPN requirements. IKEv1 and IKEv2 are supported, but other versions are not. Make sure that both ends of the VPN are configured with the correct preshared key.

Phase 2 is IPsec tunnel establishment. You can examine IPsec debug logs to isolate the exact cause of the phase 2 failure. You should verify that no firewalls are blocking Encapsulating Security Payload (ESP) protocol 50 or other IPsec traffic. Phase 2 should use the SHA-1 hashing algorithm and AES-128 as the encryption algorithm. If you are using policy-based routing (not BGP), make sure that you have properly identified the networks in both locations.

ExamAlert

Phase 1 of VPN establishment is IKE and relies on supported hardware and a correct preshared key. Phase 2 of VPN establishment is the IPsec tunnel and relies on the correct hashing and encryption algorithms.

Cram Quiz

Answer this question. The answer follows the question. If you cannot answer the question correctly, consider reading this section again until you can.

1. Physical connectivity for a Direct Connect circuit has been successfully established, but the VIF does not come up. What are some possible causes? (Choose two.)

   O **A.** 802.1Q misconfiguration

   O **B.** Improper cross-connect

   O **C.** VLAN misconfiguration

   O **D.** Improper routing configuration

Cram Quiz Answer

1. Answer: A and C are correct. Layer 2 issues are typically due to some sort of Layer 2 misconfiguration involving VLANs, 802.1Q trunks, or ARP.

What Next?

If you want more practice on this chapter's exam objectives before you move on, remember that you can access all of the Cram Quiz questions on the Pearson Test Prep software online. You can also create a custom exam by objective with the Online Practice Test. Note any objective you struggle with and go to that objective's material in this chapter.

CHAPTER 14

Cost Optimization Strategies

This chapter covers the following official AWS Certified SysOps Administrator - Associate (SOA-C02) exam domain:

▶ Domain 6: Cost and Performance Optimization

(For more information on the official AWS Certified SysOps Administrator - Associate [SOA-C02] exam topics, see the Introduction.)

In this chapter, you learn how to use AWS strategies and services to optimize your costs. AWS offers several services to optimize costs, including Trusted Advisor, AWS Compute Optimizer, and Cost Explorer.

You also learn how to use AWS Budgets to limit cost overruns on your AWS accounts. Additionally, you learn how to set up billing alarms, which can be used to notify you if you reach a threshold, such as a maximum amount you want to spend in a month.

Operational Optimization

This section covers the following objective of Domain 6 (Cost and Performance Optimization) from the official AWS Certified SysOps Administrator - Associate (SOA-C02) exam guide:

▶ 6.1 Implement cost optimization strategies

CramSaver

If you can correctly answer these questions before going through this section, save time by skimming the Exam Alerts in this section and then completing the Cram Quiz at the end of the section.

1. How many components does a cost allocation tag have?

2. What is an example of one of the EC2 checks that Trusted Advisor performs for cost optimization?

Answers

1. Answer: A tag has two components: a key and a value.

2. Answer: Low Utilization of Amazon EC2 Instances, Amazon EC2 Reserved Instance Lease Expiration, or Amazon EC2 Reserved Instance Optimization.

It might sound odd, but Amazon doesn't want you to spend too much money on AWS services. Yes, the company would be happy if you migrated your infrastructure to AWS and spent a lot of money on its platform, but Amazon doesn't want you spending more money than required to meet your business goals.

There is a very simple reason for this: customers who feel as if they are paying too much for a product or service are likely to look to an alternative vendor for a solution. Unfortunately, if you aren't using the tools that Amazon provides to optimize costs, you can easily end up paying more than you need to.

Cost Allocation Tags

In previous chapters, you learned how to apply tags to resources. Recall that a tag is metadata that can be used to group resources for a variety of different functions, including automation tasks, and to group resources by business unit.

A tag has two components: a key and a value. The key is a name that can be used on multiple resources. For example, a key named "department" could be applied to different resources, such as S3 buckets or EC2 instances. The value of the tag would be used to indicate which department is responsible for the resource.

In larger organizations, each department has its own budget for AWS resources. In situations like this, cost allocation tags are used to determine which department is responsible for the costs associated with a resource.

A cost allocation tag starts as a regular resource tag. Typically, these tags can be assigned when creating a resource or after the resource has already been created. For example, Figure 14.1 demonstrates tags being assigned to an EC2 resource as it is being created, whereas Figure 14.2 demonstrates tags being assigned to an existing EC2 resource.

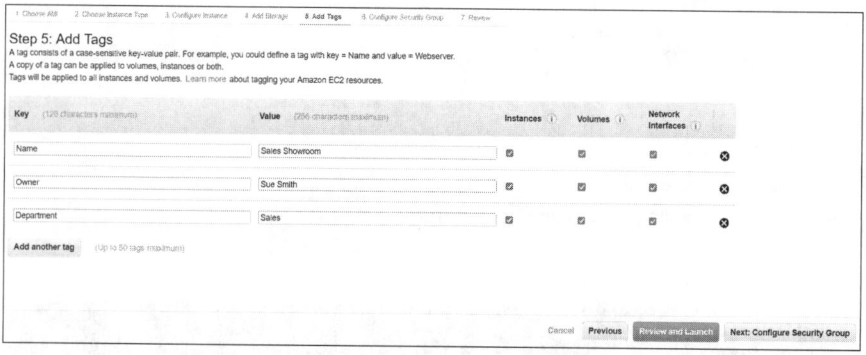

FIGURE 14.1   Applying tags while creating an EC2 resource

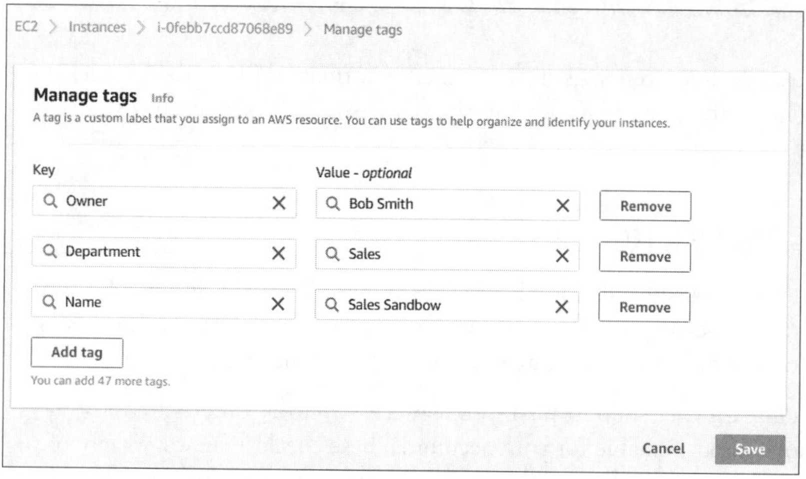

FIGURE 14.2   Applying tags to an existing EC2 instance

After you have applied tags to resources, you can generate cost allocation tags. This can be done in the Billing & Cost Management Dashboard by enabling the Detailed Billing Reports [Legacy] option located under the Billing Preferences section, as shown in Figure 14.3. Note that this feature requires an S3 bucket to save the cost allocation reports.

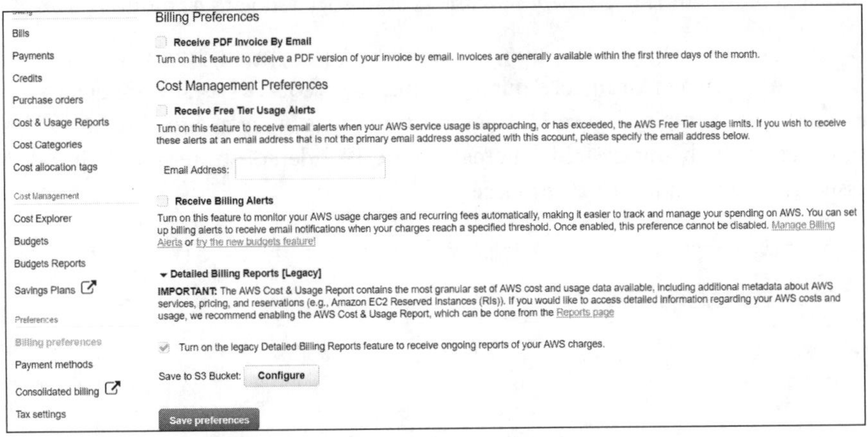

FIGURE 14.3 **Enabling cost allocation reports**

> **ExamAlert**
>
> Cost allocation tags require the collection of billing data. This operation is available if Cost Explorer is enabled, so one reason you might not see any cost allocation tags is that Cost Explorer hasn't been enabled.

The cost allocation report is stored in a CVS-formatted file in the S3 bucket that you specify. The report denotes the costs associated with each cost allocation tag.

Trusted Advisor

Chapter 9, "Security and Compliance," introduced Trusted Advisor. This tool performs checks on your AWS account for five categories. One of those categories is cost optimization (although this is not one of the free categories).

Depending on your support plan, you may have up to 17 different cost optimization checks available for your account. These checks review a variety of different resources, including AWS Lambda functions, database services (RDS,

Redshift, ElastiCache), and EC2 instances. For example, EC2 checks include the following:

▶ **Low Utilization of Amazon EC2 Instances:** This check looks at CPU utilization to determine which EC2 instances appear to be not operating in a cost-effective manner.

▶ **Amazon EC2 Reserved Instance Lease Expiration:** This check provides a report about EC2 Reserved Instances that have expired recently (within the last 30 days) or are expiring soon.

▶ **Amazon EC2 Reserved Instance Optimization:** This check is designed to provide information regarding your EC2 Reserved Instance versus your EC2 On-Demand instance.

For the exam, you should be familiar with the cost optimization checks that are available with Trusted Advisor. Table 14.1 provides a list beyond the EC2 checks.

TABLE 14.1 **Trusted Advisor Cost Optimization Checks**

Database	Performance	Miscellaneous
RDS Idle DB Instances	Idle Load Balancers	Underutilized EBS Volumes
Underutilized Redshift Clusters	OpenSearch Service Reserved Instance Optimization	Unassociated Elastic IP Addresses
ElasticCache Reserved Node Optimization	Lambda Functions and Excessive Timeouts	Route 53 Latency Resource Record Sets
Redshift Reserved Node Optimization	Lambda Functions with High Error Rates	Savings Plan
RDS Reserved Instance Optimization		Amazon Comprehend Underutilized Endpoints

AWS Compute Optimizer

Determining whether a compute resource is cost-effective can be difficult without metrics. The AWS Compute Optimizer performs metric checks on AWS compute resources and generates recommendations that are designed to help you reduce your AWS costs. Figure 14.4 shows the types of resources on which Compute Optimizer can perform metric analysis.

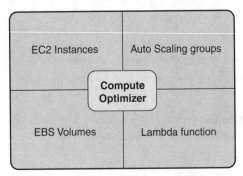

FIGURE 14.4 Compute Optimizer metrics

The metrics that are analyzed by Compute Optimizer depend on the resource. For example, the EBS volume metrics include the following:

▶ VolumeReadBytes

▶ VolumeWriteBytes

▶ VolumeReadOps

▶ VolumeWriteOps

The list of EC2 instance metrics that Compute Optimizer analyzes is larger and includes standard CloudWatch metrics like CPUutilization, NetworkIn, and NetworkOut. The analyzed metrics can also include memory utilization; however, recall that in order for CloudWatch to gather these metrics, a CloudWatch agent must be installed on the EC2 instance.

One of the biggest benefits of Compute Optimizer is that it provides recommendations. For example, the recommendations that Compute Optimizer creates for EC2 instances include a column called Finding, as shown in Figure 14.5.

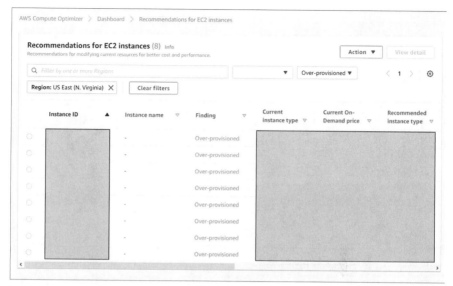

FIGURE 14.5   Recommendations for EC2 instances

The Finding value can be one of the following:

▶ **Under-provisioned:** If one or more metrics do not meet your performance requirements, the EC2 instance is labeled as Under-provisioned.

▶ **Over-provisioned:** If one or more metrics indicate that a component of the EC2 instance can be downsized and still meet performance requirements, it is labeled as Over-provisioned.

▶ **Optimized:** All metrics meet performance requirements.

> **ExamAlert**
>
> You can also see recommendations regarding rightsizing of your EC2 instances by going to the AWS Cost Management service and choosing Rightsizing Recommendations.

Cost Explorer

AWS Cost Explorer is a tool that allows you to view your AWS costs by service in an easy-to-see graphic. The display can show usage by Service, Instance Type, Region, and other breakdowns. See Figure 14.6 for an example.

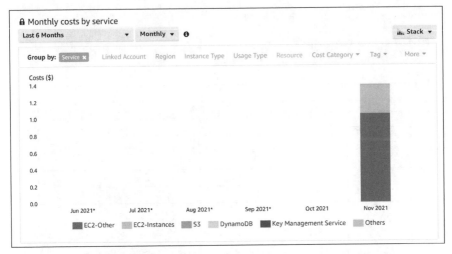

FIGURE 14.6   **AWS Cost Explorer**

ExamAlert

By default, the costs are displayed per month. You can change this view to display costs per hour to gain a higher granular view of your costs.

AWS Budgets and Billing Alarms

One of the concerns your organization may have is that an individual or group may use too many resources, resulting in a high bill. You can use AWS Budgets to prevent this from happening. This tool provides a wizard in which you can create a budget. The first step of this tool is to create a budget type (Cost Budget is the most commonly used type), as shown in Figure 14.7.

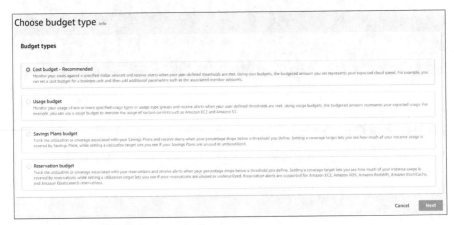

FIGURE 14.7   **AWS budget type selection**

The next step is to set up your budget. The exact questions depend on the budget type that you choose. For example, for Cost Budget, you would select period of the budget (monthly, quarterly, or yearly), if this is a recurring budget or it stops at a specific time, and the amount of the budget.

In the third step, you can set up alerts. These alerts can be used to notify you if you are getting close to your budget maximum. Alerts can be either mailed to individuals, sent via Amazon SNS (Simple Notification Service, which can be used as a text-messaging service), or via Chatbot (Amazon Chime or Slack).

A fourth option step is to attach an action to an alert. For example, you could create an action that would automatically stop a specific EC2 instance.

You also have the option of setting up a billing alarm, but for this to be active, you first need to enable Billing Alerts. This is done by going to the Billing service, selecting Billing Preferences, and marking the Receive Billing Alerts option, as shown in Figure 14.8.

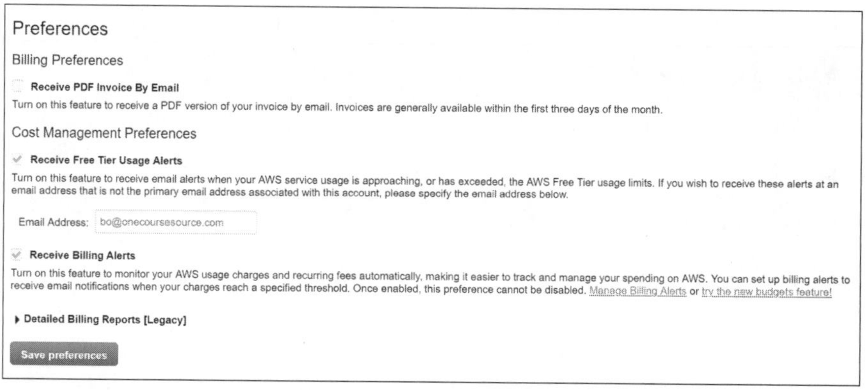

FIGURE 14.8 **Enabling billing alerts**

When this feature is enabled, you can create a billing alarm using CloudWatch. You can create an alarm for a specific metric, such as EC2 usage, but you can also create an alarm for Total Estimated Charge.

Managed Services

A managed service is any service that is partly or completely managed by AWS. AWS provides many managed services, including the following:

▶ **Amazon RDS:** This service is considered a managed service because Amazon sets up the database that you choose (Aurora, MySQL, MariaDB, Oracle, SQL Server, or PostgreSQL) and provides a way to automate management tasks, like performing backups of your database, patching the database software, and providing data replication.

▶ **AWS Fargate:** AWS Fargate is a serverless compute resource that utilizes containers. It is considered a managed service because Amazon takes care of the management of software patching, securing the container, and scaling.

▶ **EFS:** The Amazon Elastic File System is a storage location where you can place files. It is considered a managed service because it grows automatically in size as needed and you don't need to manage provisioning, patching, or maintaining EFS.

There are many advantages of managed services that you should consider when deploying resources in the cloud. You also might see several questions on the exam related to these advantages, so be ready for questions related to managed services. Advantages include

▶ Scalability

▶ Data compliance

▶ Minimized downtime

▶ Reliability

▶ Lower costs

▶ Higher security

Cram Quiz

Answer these questions. The answers follow the last question. If you cannot answer these questions correctly, consider reading this section again until you can.

1. You need to determine how much a department is spending on EC2 instances each month. Which tool will help you solve this problem?

   ○ **A.** Cost allocation tags

   ○ **B.** Trusted Advisor

   ○ **C.** AWS Compute Optimizer

   ○ **D.** AWS Budgets

2. Which of the following is not considered an advantage of managed services?

   ○ **A.** Scalability

   ○ **B.** Minimized downtime

   ○ **C.** Greater control over resources

   ○ **D.** Lower costs

Cram Quiz Answers

1. Answer: A is correct. With cost allocation tags, you can associate a tag for the department on all of its EC2 instances and then enable cost allocation reports to see the resulting costs each month.

2. Answer: C is correct. Because AWS manages parts of the resource, you don't gain greater control over the resource but rather have less control. The other answers are all advantages of managed services.

What Next?

If you want more practice on this chapter's exam objectives before you move on, remember that you can access all of the Cram Quiz questions on the Pearson Test Prep software online. You can also create a custom exam by objective with the Online Practice Test. Note any objective you struggle with and go to that objective's material in this chapter.

CHAPTER 15

Performance Optimization

This chapter covers the following official AWS Certified SysOps Administrator - Associate (SOA-C02) exam domain:

▶ Domain 6: Cost and Performance Optimization

(For more information on the official AWS Certified SysOps Administrator - Associate [SOA-C02] exam topics, see the Introduction.)

In the preceding chapter, you focused on strategies and tools to optimize the costs of your AWS resources. In this chapter, the focus shifts toward performance optimization. You learn about the six pillars of the AWS Well-Architected Framework and then explore the differences between Operational Excellence and Performance Efficiency. Then you learn about Amazon's five phases of the monitoring process so that you understand how to best use monitoring to pinpoint performance issues.

This chapter concludes with some suggestions on optimizing compute performance, datastore performance, and database performance in the AWS cloud infrastructure.

Optimizing for Performance

This section covers the following objective of Domain 6 (Cost and Performance Optimization) from the official AWS Certified SysOps Administrator - Associate (SOA-C02) exam guide:

▶ 6.2 Implement performance optimization strategies

CramSaver

If you can correctly answer these questions before going through this section, save time by skimming the Exam Alerts in this section and then completing the Cram Quiz at the end of the section.

1. True or False: Reliability and sustainability are two of the pillars of the AWS Well-Architected Framework.

2. What are the five phases of the monitoring process?

Answers

1. Answer: True.

2. Answer: Generation, aggregation, real-time processing and alarming, storage, and analytics.

Monitoring for Performance Efficiency

Amazon touts a concept called the AWS Well-Architected Framework. The goal of this framework is to help you build an efficient infrastructure in AWS that takes into consideration a variety of different components. These components are called pillars, as shown in Figure 15.1.

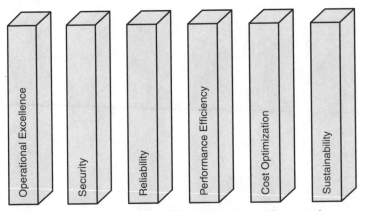

FIGURE 15.1   Six pillars of the AWS Well-Architected Framework

Many of these topics were covered in previous chapters. For example, Chapter 9, "Security and Compliance," and Chapter 10, "Data Protection at Rest and in Transit," address the Security pillar.

Two of the pillars may seem to be similar and can often cause confusion: the Operational Excellence pillar and the Performance Efficiency pillar. Although they may sound similar, these pillars address different AWS features and components. Amazon describes these pillars as follows:

> ▶ **Operational Excellence pillar:** "The operational excellence pillar focuses on running and monitoring systems, and continually improving processes and procedures. Key topics include automating changes, responding to events, and defining standards to manage daily operations."

> ▶ **Performance Efficiency pillar:** "The performance efficiency pillar focuses on structured and streamlined allocation of IT and computing resources. Key topics include selecting resource types and sizes optimized for workload requirements, monitoring performance, and maintaining efficiency as business needs evolve."

Although this chapter focuses on topics related to the Performance Efficiency pillar, it is important to compare this to the Operational Excellence pillar to understand better the difference between these two pillars. Besides the short definitions that Amazon uses to describe these pillars, you may find it easier to understand the difference by comparing the design principles that Amazon has developed for each pillar. Table 15.1 outlines these design principles.

TABLE 15.1 Amazon's Design Principles of Operational Excellence and Performance Efficiency

Operational Excellence	Performance Efficiency
Perform operations as code	Democratize advanced technologies
Make frequent, small, reversible changes	Go global in minutes
Refine operations procedures frequently	User serverless architectures
Anticipate failure	Experiment more often
Learn from all operational failures	Consider mechanical sympathy

ExamAlert

The AWS Well-Architected Framework is a big topic. Although you don't need to be an expert on this topic for the exam, having a basic understanding of the pillars and their purpose will help you with some difficult questions on the exam.

Both the Operational Excellence and Performance Efficiency pillars rely on monitoring resources, but the way in which the monitoring data is used is different. Performance Efficiency is the focus of this section, so the monitoring process described in this section centers around resource metrics related to ensuring the resources are running at the standards that your organization has defined.

Amazon has also defined five different phases of the monitoring process, which you should be aware of for the exam. See these five phases in Figure 15.2.

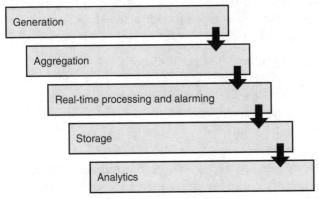

FIGURE 15.2   **Amazon's five phases of the monitoring process**

Generation

The focus of the Generation phase is to determine the scope of what you will monitor. Although just monitoring everything might sound like a good idea, this can lead to information overload, making analyzing the data difficult. Also, monitoring can increase costs, so you should carefully consider what you monitor.

During this phase, you also determine your thresholds. For Performance Efficiency, it is important to determine minimum and maximum thresholds that meet your business needs. For example, you may consider the CPU utilization of an EC2 instance of between 40 and 80 percent most optimal for performance of a particular system. In that case, you should plan on setting thresholds that match this range.

Aggregation

In the Aggregation phase, you determine which sources of monitoring data provide you with a more complete view of your AWS environment. For example, an EC2 instance that is used to run a web server uses data that is stored on an EBS volume. As a result, monitoring the EC2 instance performance and the performance of the EBS volume can provide the best overall view of the solution's performance efficiency.

Real-Time Processing and Alarming

As discussed in previous chapters, monitoring tools that are provided by AWS allow you to process events in real time and generate alarms. It is during this phase that you determine which effects to process and produce alarms.

Again, producing alarms for many events is tempting, but realize that creating too many alarms can have an adverse effect. For example, people who are receiving alarms may develop a habit of ignoring them if too many unimportant alarms are generated. Remember that alarms should be issued when immediate action is required, not just for informational purposes.

Storage

Monitoring data must be stored somewhere. This storage can cost money when housed in the cloud, so you want to develop a retention policy to determine how long to keep monitoring data. During the Storage phase, you should also consider where the data will be stored and who should have access to the data. In addition, you should develop policies for transporting the data securely.

Analytics

Monitoring data by itself is rarely useful. During the Analytics phase, you should develop procedures on how the data will be analyzed. Will you rely on a person reading data on a dashboard, or will you use an automated tool to provide reports and insights on the monitoring data?

Optimizing Compute Performance

Several enhanced EC2 capabilities can be used to improve compute performance. This section focuses on these capabilities.

Enhanced Networking

On some EC2 instance types, you can enable a feature called enhanced networking at no cost if the operating system that is running on the EC2 instance is Linux or Windows. This feature results in higher performance by making use of a technology called SR-IOV (Single Root—Input/Output Virtualization).

There are three primary benefits of using enhanced networking:

▶ Higher bandwidth

▶ Higher packets per second (PPS)

▶ Consistently lower inter-instance latencies

Configuration of enhanced networking takes place within the Linux system rather than through modification of an option via the AWS Management Console. This process requires logging in to the Linux system and executing a combination of Linux and AWS commands. The exact steps are beyond the scope of this chapter, but you should be aware of the two different enhanced networking methods, each of which has different steps to enabling, as outlined in Table 15.2.

TABLE 15.2 **Enhanced Networking Methods**

Elastic Network Adapter (ENA)	Intel 82599 Virtual Function (VF) Interface
Supports network speeds of up to 100 Gbps	Supports network speeds of up to 10 Gbps
For all instance types except T2, C3, C4, D2, I2, M4 (excluding m4.16xlarge), and R3	For the following instance types: C3, C4, D2, I2, M4 (excluding m4.16xlarge), and R3

> **ExamAlert**
>
> If you look carefully at Table 15.2, you will realize that neither method includes the T2 instance type. The reason is that enhanced networking is not supported at all for this instance type. This results in a potential exam question related to why enhanced networking is not working on a specific EC2 instance.

Instance Store

In terms of performance, having storage physically attached to the same system that your EC2 instance is running can have a dramatic impact. An instance store provides this type of block storage device for your EC2 instance. Instance stores are designed to be temporary storage devices, and you can't detach them from your EC2 instance.

The size of the instance store depends on the instance type, and not all instance types support instance stores. Also, the instance store is lost if the EC2 instance is stopped, hibernated, or terminated. Instance stores can be created while launching your EC2 instance, as shown in Figure 15.3, or added to an existing EC2 instance during installation.

Step 4: Add Storage

Your instance will be launched with the following storage device settings. You can attach additional EBS volumes and instance store volumes to your instance, or edit the settings of the root volume. You can also attach additional EBS volumes after launching an instance, but not instance store volumes. Learn more about storage options in Amazon EC2.

Type (i)	Device (i)	Snapshot (i)	Size (GiB) (i)	Volume Type (i)	IOPS (i)	Delete on Termination (i)	
Root	/dev/sda1	snap-a3256366	8	Standard ▾	N/A	☑	
Instance Store 0 ▾	/dev/sdb ▾	N/A	N/A	N/A	N/A	N/A	✖

Add New Volume

FIGURE 15.3   Adding an instance store when launching an EC2 instance

Placement Groups

By default, when you create a new EC2 instance in a region, AWS tries to place the new EC2 instance on different hardware from your existing EC2 instances. The reason is to limit the chances of a hardware failure impacting all of your EC2 instances.

You have some control over where your EC2 instances are placed by using placement groups. You associate a new EC2 instance with a placement group when launching the EC2 instance, as shown in Figure 15.4.

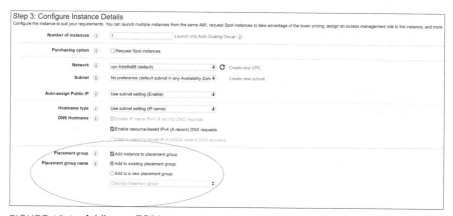

FIGURE 15.4   Adding an EC2 instance to a placement group

The three primary placement strategies that you can use when defining a placement group are as follows:

▶ **Cluster:** You use this method when you want your EC2 instances to be physically close to each other within an availability zone (AZ). This reduces latency issues when communicating between the instances via the network.

▶ **Partition:** This strategy creates logical partitions so a group of instances within one partition does not share hardware with a group of instances in another partition.

▶ **Spread:** This strategy ensures that a small group of instances is spread across different hardware. It is similar to the default behavior of how AWS places EC2 instances, but when you have a lot of EC2 instances, the default behavior can result in some instances sharing underlying hardware; however, this method is designed to make sure that the group of instances does not share hardware.

Optimizing Datastore Performance

One feature of an EC2 instance that can have an impact on the performance of the instance is the EBS storage device. You can monitor the EBS metrics by using CloudWatch. This includes the following metrics:

▶ Read bandwidth

▶ Write bandwidth

▶ Read throughput

▶ Write throughput

▶ Average queue length

▶ Time spent idle

▶ Average read size

▶ Average queue length

▶ Average read latency

▶ Average write latency

▶ Burst balance

When viewed over time, these metrics can be used to determine if you need to modify the volume. You can change the following components of an EBS volume: type and size.

Changing the size can have an impact on how fast the volume can perform read/write operations. You should be aware of the following volume types and the impact they have on EBS performance:

▶ **General-Purpose SSD:** Cost-effective storage devices that provide decent speed. These are also often referred to as gp2 and gp3; the main difference is that gp3 has a better maximum throughput per volume.

▶ **Provisioned IOPS SSD:** Higher cost but faster storage devices. These are also often referred to as io1 and io2; the main difference is that io2 has slightly better durability.

▶ **Magnetic:** The slowest volume types, which should be used only when data is not accessed frequently.

Besides offering more storage space, the size of the volume also has an impact on the maximum input/output per second (IOPS) of the volume. For gp2, this value is not dependent on volume size, being fixed at 100 IOPS and burstable to 3,000 IOPS (burstable meaning it can "jump up" to this value for short periods of time). However, the size of the volume can have an impact on IOPS for other volume types, as shown in Figure 15.5.

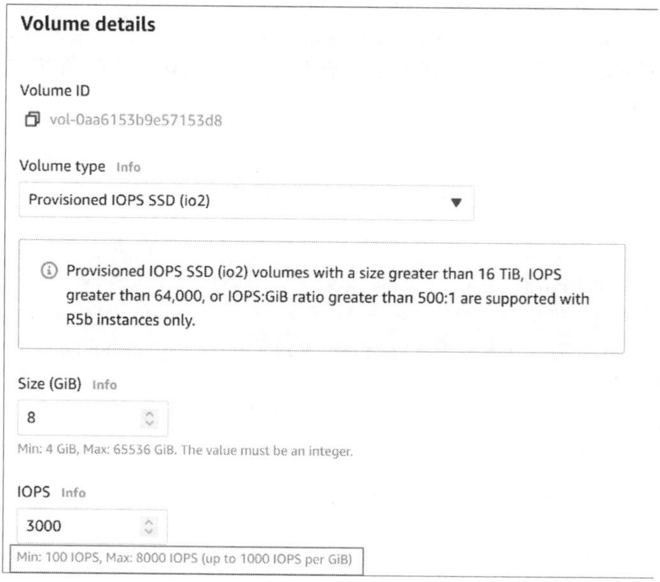

FIGURE 15.5 **IOPS impacted by volume size**

Besides EBS, you should also be aware of features of S3 buckets that can impact the performance of the bucket:

▶ **S3 transfer acceleration:** Uses Amazon CloudFront to enable access to bucket contents from edge locations in different geographic locations in the world. Note that this feature is not supported in all regions.

▶ **S3 multipart uploads:** Allows for larger objects to be uploaded in separate parts, which improves performance as the parts are uploaded in parallel.

Optimizing Database Performance

Each database has specific configuration settings that can be used to optimize the performance of the database. For the exam, you don't need to know these specific settings, but you should be aware of RDS features that can be used to optimize the performance of any of the databases managed by RDS:

▶ **RDS Performance Insights:** This optional feature enables you to identify where bottlenecks are impacting database performance.

▶ **RDS Proxy:** This service makes use of a collection of connections to the database that are maintained to provide multiple paths to communicate to the RDS database instance. This improves application performance by reducing the increase in CPU and memory utilization when new connections to a database instance are created.

Cram Quiz

Answer these questions. The answers follow the last question. If you cannot answer these questions correctly, consider reading this section again until you can.

1. Which pillar of the AWS Well-Architected Framework has the design principle of "Experiment more often"?

   ○ **A.** Reliability

   ○ **B.** Operational Excellence

   ○ **C.** Performance Efficiency

   ○ **D.** Cost Optimization

2. Which of the following is not considered an advantage of enhanced networking?

   ○ **A.** Larger packet sizes

   ○ **B.** Higher bandwidth

   ○ **C.** Higher PPS

   ○ **D.** Consistently lower inter-instance latencies

3. Which of the following is not an EBS metric?

   ○ **A.** Read bandwidth

   ○ **B.** Read throughput

   ○ **C.** Average queue length

   ○ **D.** Average transport time

Cram Quiz Answers

1. Answer: C is correct. "Experiment more often" is one of the five design principles of the Performance Efficiency pillar. Other design principles for Performance Efficiency include democratize advanced technologies, go global in minutes, use serverless architectures, and consider mechanical sympathy.

2. Answer: A is correct. Enhanced networking does not allow for larger packet sizes, but the rest of the answers are advantages of enhanced networking.

3. Answer: D is correct. Average transport time is not an EBS metric. The rest of the answers are all valid EBS metrics.

What Next?

If you want more practice on this chapter's exam objectives before you move on, remember that you can access all of the Cram Quiz questions on the Pearson Test Prep software online. You can also create a custom exam by objective with the Online Practice Test. Note any objective you struggle with and go to that objective's material in this chapter.

Glossary

ACM (AWS Certificate Manager) A service provided by AWS that allows you to manage certificates.

Active-passive upgrade A process in which an upgrade is deployed to the active environment and the passive environment is not changed.

Alias record A DNS record type that is used to forward traffic to an AWS service like CloudFront or an ELB.

Amazon Athena A serverless interactive query service that enables you to query static data on S3 via SQL.

Amazon Cloud Hardware Security Module (CloudHSM) A cloud-enabled hardware security device.

Amazon CloudTrail An API call logging service that enables you to maintain a complete record of actions against the AWS infrastructure.

Amazon CloudWatch An AWS cloud monitoring service that allows you to store metrics and logs from any device running on AWS or on-premises.

Amazon DocumentDB A fully managed, instance-based nonrelational document database service in AWS.

Amazon DynamoDB A fully managed, cloud-native, serverless nonrelational key-value and document database service in AWS.

Amazon Elastic Block Storage (EBS) A block-accessible, network-attached, persistent storage for volumes that connect to EC2 instances and ECS containers.

Amazon Elastic Cloud Computing (EC2) A service that deploys and operates virtual machines running Linux and Windows in the AWS cloud.

Amazon Elastic Container Service (ECS) A service that enables you to deploy, orchestrate, and operate containers in the AWS cloud.

Amazon Elastic File System (EFS) A service that provides a network-attached file system that supports the NFS protocol and allows you to share files among EC2 instances, ECS containers, and other services.

Amazon Elastic Kubernetes Services (EKS) A service that enables you to deploy, orchestrate, and operate Kubernetes clusters in the AWS cloud.

Amazon Elastic Load Balancing (ELB) A service that allows load balancing of traffic across multiple EC2 instances, ECS containers, or other IP addressable targets.

Amazon Elastic Map Reduce (EMR) A service that enables you to run open-source big data workloads in the AWS cloud.

Amazon Elastic Transcoder A service that provides cost-effective and scalable fully managed media transcoding.

Amazon ElastiCache A fully managed instance-based caching service for deployment of Redis or Memcached in-memory data stores in AWS.

Amazon Glacier An archive storage solution that can be automatically integrated with S3.

Amazon GuardDuty A tool that performs threat detection functions in your AWS infrastructure.

Amazon Identity and Access Management (IAM) A service that enables you to control access to AWS as well as access to your applications in one place.

Amazon Inspector A service that provides an assessment of services running in AWS with a prioritized, actionable list for remediation.

Amazon Key Management Service (KMS) A service that enables you to define a unified way to manage encryption keys for AWS services and applications.

Amazon Keyspaces A fully managed, serverless Cassandra nonrelational database service in AWS.

Amazon Kinesis A fully managed set of services that enables you to capture, process, and store streaming data at any scale.

Amazon Lambda A service that enables you to process simple functions in the AWS cloud.

Amazon Neptune A fully managed, instance-based graphing database service in AWS.

Amazon QLDB A fully managed, serverless ledger database service in AWS.

Amazon RedShift A fully managed instance-based data warehousing service for deployment of petabyte-scale data clusters at very low cost.

Amazon Relational Database Service (RDS) A fully managed instance-based relational database service for deployment and management of Amazon Aurora, PostgreSQL, MySQL, MariaDB, Oracle, and Microsoft SQL Server databases in AWS.

Amazon Simple Storage Service (S3) A service designed to store unlimited amounts of data. S3 is the ultimate object storage system. All objects in S3 are accessible via standard HTTP requests.

Amazon WorkDocs A document editor and collaboration service that has its own extensible SDK against which you can develop applications for your workforce or your clients.

Amazon WorkMail An enterprise email and calendar service that seamlessly integrates with almost any email client.

Amazon WorkSpaces A managed virtual desktop infrastructure (VDI) service where you can create Windows desktops, manage their domain membership, their application configuration, and the distribution of the desktops to the individuals within your organization.

Application Load Balancer (ALB) The next-generation layer 7 load-balancing solution that can handle HTTP and HTTPS traffic.

Asymmetric encryption A method in which you use a different key to encrypt and decrypt data. One key is referred to as the public key, and the other is called the private key.

Autoscaling A service that can automatically scale the number of instances to meet traffic demands.

Availability zones (AZs) Fault isolation environments within AWS regions.

AWS Aurora A service that stores all the data on a cluster volume that is replicated to six copies across (at least) three availability zones.

AWS Autoscaling A service that automates the scale-in and scale-out operations of instances based on performance metrics.

AWS CLI (command-line interface) A tool that allows you to perform actions within AWS using text-based commands.

AWS CloudFormation A standard way to implement Infrastructure as Code (IaC) when deploying resources in AWS.

AWS Cognito A centralized authentication service for mobile and web users that can easily be federated with external directories through OpenID Connect, OAuth 2.0, and SAML 2.0.

AWS Compute Optimizer A tool to perform metric checks on AWS compute resources and generate recommendations that are designed to help you reduce your AWS costs.

AWS Config   A configuration state recording service that can detect state changes, perform alerting based on rules, and provide resource inventory and relationship mapping.

AWS Cost Explorer   A tool that allows you to view your AWS costs by service in an easy-to-see graphic.

AWS DataSync   A service that synchronizes file systems in the production location with other file systems in the backup location or with S3.

AWS Device Farm   A tool for testing an application on mobile devices in the Amazon cloud at scale before deploying them to production.

AWS Direct Connect   A private optical fiber connection service that connects on-premises sites with AWS.

AWS Elastic Beanstalk   A service that allows you to automatically deploy infrastructure needed for an application.

AWS ElastiCache   A service that provides a shared, network-attached, in-memory datastore that fulfills the needs of caching content in memory.

AWS EventBridge   A new service built on the same API structure as CloudWatch and that is slated to replace it.

AWS Fargate   A service that provides a serverless compute resource that utilizes containers.

AWS Glue   A serverless ETL and catalog service that enables you to manage data at scale and execute data transformation at very low cost.

AWS Inspector   A tool that helps you determine security vulnerabilities on applications for which you deploy on an EC2 instance within AWS.

AWS Internet of Things (IoT) Services   A set of services designed to provide everything required to run IoT, including the FreeRTOS operating system and components that help manage and work with IoT devices at any scale.

AWS Managed VPN   An IPsec VPN connection between your datacenter and an AWS VPC.

AWS OpsWorks   A managed service for running Chef-, Puppet-, and Stacks-compatible configuration management services in the AWS cloud.

AWS Pinpoint   A service that allows developers to easily engage users on their devices with targeted, segmented (ML) marketing using email, SMS, and mobile push.

AWS Resource Access Manager (RAM)   A service that allows you to share resources across multiple AWS accounts.

AWS SageMaker   A set of developer tools that allows you to design, build, and train machine learning models very quickly.

AWS SDK (software developer kit)   A toolkit that provides software developers the tools needed to communicate with AWS.

AWS Security Hub   A tool that allows you to execute security checks across your AWS environment automatically.

AWS Shield   A managed distributed denial-of-service (DDoS) protection service.

AWS Shield Advanced   A service that enables protections for Amazon EC2, Elastic Load Balancing (ELB), Amazon CloudFront, AWS Global Accelerator, and Route 53 resources.

AWS VPN Gateway (VGW)   A component of the VPC that provides the capability for establishing VPN connection with on-premises sites.

AWS Snow Family   Data transfer devices that allow for physically moving data from on-premises to the cloud at any scale.

AWS Storage Gateway   A hybrid storage solution that exposes AWS as storage services to on-premises servers.

AWS Systems Manager   A collection of tools that provides a single pane of glass that allows for full visibility of the resources within an organization's infrastructure.

AWS Web Application Firewall (WAF)   A managed firewall service allowing you to configure rules that allow, block, or monitor (count) web requests based on conditions that you define.

AWS Well-Architected Framework   A framework that helps you build an efficient infrastructure in AWS while taking into consideration a variety of different components: operational excellence, security, reliability, performance efficiency, cost optimization, and sustainability.

CA (certificate authority)   An entity that validates, signs, and issues digital certificates.

Cache hit ratio   The percentage of requests that are served by CloudFront (without pulling content from the origin).

Canary release   An upgrade technique in which new features are released to a specific set of beta testers to determine whether the features have a negative impact on the software.

CloudWatch Logs Insights   An interface in which SQL-like queries can be run to search and filter through the log content, run transformations, and visualize data.

Community cloud environments   A hybrid deployment where members of a community share resources to all members of the community.

CRL (certificate revocation list)   A list that defines the certificates that the CA no longer considers valid.

CSR (certificate signing request)   A request to a CA to generate a digital certificate.

Development environment   An environment where you develop new software or modify existing software that your organization is developing.

Digital certificate   A unique value that contains a collection of data that is used to identify an entity.

Disaster recovery (DR) environment   An identical copy of the production environment that is used to quickly restore a compromised environment.

Disaster recovery plan   A plan to recover the primary operating environment from remotely stored backups.

Edge caching   A caching strategy to frequently deliver content to multiple customers, typically through a content delivery network (CDN).

Edge locations   Globally distributed locations that provide additional latency reduction when delivering applications from AWS.

Elastic IP   A persistent static IP assigned to an instance.

Elastic IP Address (EIP)   A dedicated IP address that is not released, even if the associated instance is stopped or terminated, as long as the ENI remains.

Elastic Load Balancer (ELB)   A service that enables you to distribute traffic across multiple instances of an application for high availability.

Elastic Network Interface (ENI)   A virtual network interface in a VPC.

ELB Classic   The previous-generation load balancer that forwards traffic to one or more availability zones within a region.

Encryption   The process of transforming data from its original form to a form that, when viewed, does not reveal the original data.

Failover routing   A routing technique that provides responses based on the health of two or more DNS targets.

Gateway endpoint   An ENI within an AWS VPC that connects only to DynamoDB or S3.

Gateway Load Balancer (GLB)   A load balancer designed to distribute traffic across third-party virtual appliances.

Geolocation routing   A routing technique that forces users from certain regions or countries into specific AWS regions.

Geoproximity routing   A routing technique that routes users from locations nearby to the closest region.

Hybrid cloud environments   Connected cloud deployments across a private and public solution.

Infrastructure as a Service (IaaS)   A service delivery model that delivers raw compute, storage, and network capacity to the cloud customer.

Inline caching   A database caching approach that utilizes a service that manages reads and writes to and from the database.

Interface endpoint   An ENI within an AWS VPC that has a private IP address within the VPC subnet of the resources that are consuming the service.

KMS (Key Management Service)   A service that allows you to create encryption keys and control their access. Both symmetric and asymmetric keys can be created.

Latency-based routing   A routing technique that measures the latency from the client to the DNS target and delivers the response with the lowest latency target.

Lazy loading   A type of side-loaded caching that caches every read request from the database until it expires.

LTS (long-term support) build
A stable build that should be supported for a longer than average period of time.

Managed VPN An IPsec VPN connection between a customer gateway in a physical datacenter and an AWS-managed VGW.

Memcached A high-performance, distributed key, in-memory key-value store supported by ElastiCache.

Multifactor authentication (MFA)
A method of authenticating a user that requires more than one way of verifying the identity of that user.

Multivalue answer routing A routing technique that returns up to eight responses for each request.

NAT gateway An AWS managed service that allows instances in private subnets to connect to the Internet but prevents the Internet from initiating connections to these instances.

Network access control list (NACL)
A stateless firewall that is applied to a subnet.

Network Load Balancer (NLB)
The next-generation layer 4 load-balancing solution that can handle TCP, UDP, and SSL/TLS traffic.

OpenID Connect An identity provider standard used to establish a trust connection to your AWS account.

Platform as a Service (PaaS) A delivery service model that delivers more refined and specific services like databases, application front and back ends, and message queues.

Private cloud environments Cloud environments deployed within an organization available only on the private network.

Private key A unique cryptographic key that is never shared.

Production environment An environment where the live solution is deployed.

Public cloud An environment that delivers cloud services in several locations that are independent of each other geographically and distributed globally.

Public key A unique cryptographic key that is publicly shared.

Public key infrastructure (PKI) A standard that defines how digital certificates are created, revoked, managed, stored, used, and distributed.

Quality assurance (QA) environment
An environment where testing is performed before migrating changes to a production environment. It should mirror the current production environment.

Recovery-point objective (RPO)
The defined point on how much data can be lost during an event that requires you to restore data.

Recovery-time objective (RTO)
The defined time allowed to recover the data and bring it fully online.

Redis A full-fledged in-memory database supported by ElastiCache.

Roadmap A timeline for the implementation of the product from start to finish; it provides an easy way to visualize the lifecycle management of a project.

Rolling upgrade The process of frequently providing updates to software.

SAML (Security Assertion Markup Language) An identity provider standard used to establish a trust connection to your AWS account.

Security group A stateful firewall that is applied to individual interfaces on various network-based resources including EC2 and RDS instances running in a VPC.

Server-side caching A caching strategy used when content stored within a web service is requested frequently. The server caches the response in memory.

Service-layer agreement (SLA) An agreement that defines the uptime that your application will theoretically be able to deliver.

Sharding A database partitioning technique that distributes the dataset across multiple primary database engines.

Side-loading caching A database caching approach that is performed by an application that is aware of the cache and database as two distinct entities.

Simple routing A routing technique that provides one response of each DNS request.

Software as a Service (SaaS) A delivery service model that delivers fully functional applications that are relatively easy for any user to consume.

Stable release A release that is ready for a production environment.

Staging environment An environment that replicates the production environment to determine potential problems there and acts as a replacement when the production environment fails.

Symmetric encryption A method where you use the same key (a unique value of some sort) to both encrypt and decrypt the data.

Transit gateway A network transit hub that VPCs connect to in a hub-and-spoke topology, enabling communication across VPCs.

Virtual Private Cloud (VPC) A service in which applications are deployed and maintained and that enables you to define both public and private network environments with complete control over routing and granular security.

Virtual Private Gateway (VGW) A managed service that includes automated failover and the ability to support multiple connections.

VPC Peering A connection used to establish a communication between two VPCs over the global AWS backbone network without the requirement for a VPN.

Weighted routing A routing technique that provides responses based on the weight of the values for each record.

Writethrough A type of side-loaded caching where data is written to both the database and cache.

Index

Numbers

A

264. DHCP option sets can be used to forward certain DNS requests to an on-premises DNS instance. This is necessary if you want to forward certain DNS requests to the on-premises DNS servers over the VPN.

265. Managed VPN is an IPsec VPN connection between a CGW in a physical datacenter and an AWS-managed VGW.

266. Software site-to-site VPN is an IPsec VPN connection between a CGW in a physical datacenter and a customer-managed EC2 instance.

267. You can configure multiple managed site-to-site VPN connections, but the maximum aggregate bandwidth of the VGW is 1.25 Gbps.

268. To provider higher bandwidth over VPN, the transit gateway supports ECMP over multiple VPN connections.

269. AWS Direct Connect provides private connectivity to your VPC over a dedicated physical connection.

270. A Direct Connect VIF can be used to establish a dedicated physical connection to a VGW. You can then use your CGW to establish an IPsec VPN connection to the VGW.

271. Public VIFs are only for public AWS resources like S3.

272. AWS Web Application Firewall is a managed firewall service allowing you to configure rules that allow, block, or monitor (count) web requests based on conditions that you define.

273. AWS Shield is a managed DDoS protection service.

274. AWS Shield Advanced enables protections for Amazon EC2, Elastic Load Balancing (ELB), Amazon CloudFront, AWS Global Accelerator, and Route 53 resources.

275. Route 53 is a hosted DNS service that allows users to register domain names, apply routing policies, and perform infrastructure health checks on their web services.

276. An alias record is a DNS record type that is used to forward traffic to an AWS service like CloudFront or an ELB.

277. An alias record can be used at the domain apex (e.g., example.com) or on subdomains.

278. A CNAME record can be used on subdomains (e.g., mobile.example.com).

279. Weighted routing is ideal for a blue/green deployment. The blue environment represents the established, reliable configuration. DNS can be used to switch traffic from the blue environment to the green, or to roll back to the green if necessary.

280. Weighted routing allows you to begin this transition with a smaller percentage of traffic.

281. An S3 static website does not require any servers and is a managed service. It can be used as a low-cost static backup for a primary website in the event of an outage by configuring failover routing in Route 53.

282. CloudFront is a content delivery network service that speeds up delivery of your static and dynamic web content.

283. Data that is stored in the CloudFront Edge locations is considered current for a specific amount of time, as defined by the time-to-live.

284. Waiting for the TTL is one way to expire undesired content from the cache at the edge locations, but you can speed this up using an invalidation. Invalidations can be expensive and are resource intensive.

285. The OAI restricts bucket access so that only the CloudFront distribution has direct access to objects. Users can access these objects only through a web resource that is part of a CloudFront distribution.

286. VPC flow logs are used to capture information about the IP traffic flowing into or out of network interfaces in a VPC.

287. In the exam, you must be capable of reading and interpreting flow logs and identifying source IP and destination IP addresses, ports, and if the traffic was blocked or allowed.

288. Traffic can be blocked by a network access control list (NACL), and the NACL is enforced before the security group on incoming traffic.

289. ELB access logs capture details of requests sent to your load balancer, such as the time of the request, the client IP, latency, and server responses.

290. The S3 bucket that is used for ELB access logs must be in the same region as the bucket and must have a bucket policy that allows the ELB access logs write permissions.

291. AWS Web Application Firewall protects your resources and stops malicious traffic.

292. A Web ACL can allow or deny traffic based on the source IP address, country of origin of the request, string match or regular expression (regex) match, or the detection of malicious SQL code or scripting.

293. You can use either CloudFront or ELB logs to analyze HTTP response codes and determine whether requests were successfully served.

294. The cache hit ratio is the percentage of requests that are served by CloudFront (without pulling content from the origin).

295. You can monitor HTTP response codes that are returned from the origin by using the 4xx Error Rate, 5xx Error Rate, and Total Error Rate metrics.

296. Phase 1 of VPN establishment is IKE and relies on supported hardware and a correct preshared key.

297. Phase 2 of VPN establishment is the IPsec tunnel and relies on the correct hashing and encryption algorithms.

298. Cost allocation tags require the collection of billing data. This operation is available if Cost Explorer is enabled, so one reason why you might not see any cost allocation tags is that Cost Explorer hasn't been enabled.

299. AWS Compute Optimizer performs metric checks on AWS compute resources and generates recommendations that are designed to help you reduce your AWS costs.

300. Compute Optimizer is available at no additional charge; however, it does run on compute resources that can result in a charge, and it requires Amazon CloudWatch monitoring, which may also result in a charge. As a result, Compute Optimizer is not enabled by default.

301. You can also see recommendations regarding rightsizing of your EC2 instances by going to the AWS Cost Management service and choosing Rightsizing Recommendations.

302. AWS Cost Explorer is a tool that allows you to view your AWS costs by service in an easy-to-see graphic.

303. By default, the costs are displayed per month. You can change this setting to display costs per hour to gain a higher granular view of your costs.

304. AWS Fargate is a serverless compute resource that utilizes containers.

305. AWS Well-Architected Framework helps you build an efficient infrastructure in AWS that takes into consideration a variety of different components: operational excellence, security, reliability, performance efficiency, cost optimization, and sustainability.

306. The operational excellence pillar focuses on running and monitoring systems, and continually improving processes and procedures.

307. The performance efficiency pillar focuses on structured and streamlined allocation of IT and computing resources. Key topics include selecting resource types and sizes optimized for workload requirements, monitoring performance, and maintaining efficiency as business needs evolve.

308. Amazon's five phases of the monitoring process are generation, aggregation, real-time processing and alarming, storage, and analytics.

309. The enhanced networking feature enables higher performance only in some EC2 instances by making use of a technology called Single Root—Input/Output Virtualization (SR-IOV).

310. Instance stores are designed to be temporary storage devices, and you can't detach them from your EC2 instance.

311. Placement group strategies include cluster, partition, and spread.

312. The cluster method should be used when you want your EC2 instances to be physically close to each other within an availability zone.

313. The partition method creates logical partitions, so a group of instances within one partition does not share hardware with a group of instances in another partition.

314. The spread method ensures that a small group of instances is spread across different hardware.

315. General-purpose SSDs are cost-effective storage devices that provide decent speed. They are also often referred to as gp2 and gp3.

316. Provisioned IOPS SSDs are higher cost but faster storage devices. They are also often referred to as io1 and io2.

317. Magnetic volumes are the slowest volume types that should be used only when data is not accessed frequently.

318. RDS Performance Insights is an optional feature that enables you to identify where bottlenecks are impacting database performance.

319. RDS Proxy is a service that makes use of a collection of connections to the database that are maintained in order to provide multiple paths to communicate to the RDS database instance.